SHEKHAR KAPUR'S

SNAKE WOMAN™

CREATED BY
SHEKHAR KAPUR

SCRIPT
ZEB WELLS

ART
MICHAEL GAYDOS

COVER ART
MUKESH SINGH &
SURESH SEETHARAMAN

ADDITIONAL COVER ART
MUKESH SINGH
MICHAEL GAYDOS
SURESH SEETHARAMAN &
K. SAMPATH KUMAR

COLORS
SAMPATH KUMAR & I. JEYABALAN

LETTERS
B. S. RAVI KIRAN
NILESH S. MAHADIK
& SUDHIR PISAL

PROJECT MANAGER
REUBEN THOMAS

ASSISTANT EDITORS
MAHESH KAMATH
CHARLIE BECKERMAN
& SANA AMANAT

EDITOR
MACKENZIE CADENHEAD

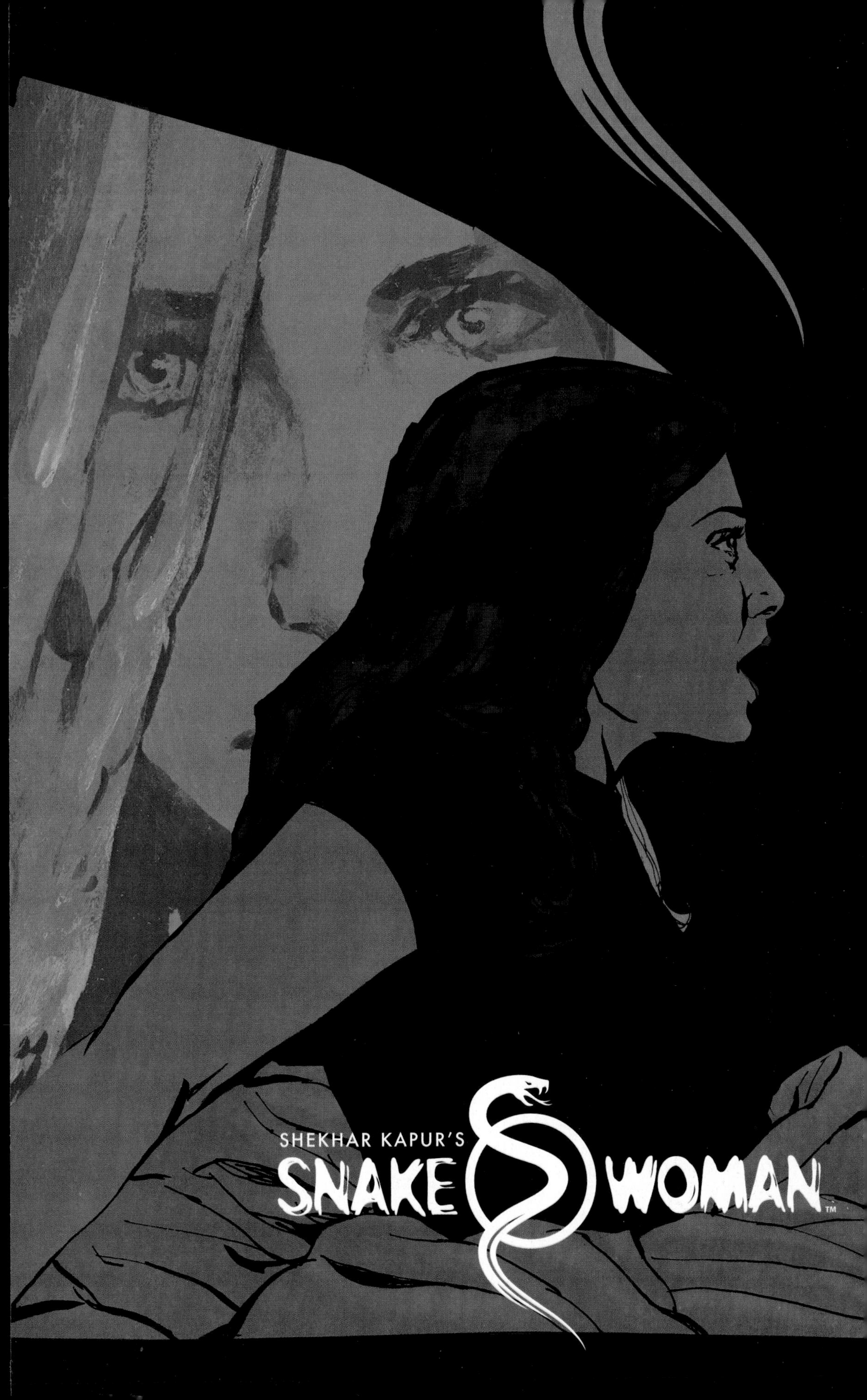
SHEKHAR KAPUR'S
SNAKE WOMAN™

VIRGIN COMICS

Chief Executive Officer and Publisher
SHARAD DEVARAJAN

Chief Creative Officer
and Editor-in-Chief
GOTHAM CHOPRA

President & Studio Chief
SURESH SEETHARAMAN

Chief Marketing Officer
LARRY LIEBERMAN

SRVP – Studio
JEEVAN KANG

Chief Visionaries
**DEEPAK CHOPRA,
SHEKHAR KAPUR,
SIR RICHARD BRANSON**

Head Of Operations
ALAGAPPAN KANNAN

Director of Development
MACKENZIE CADENHEAD

Special Thanks to:
**FRANCES FARROW, DAN PORTER,
CHRISTOPHER LINEN, PETER FELDMAN,
RAJU PUTHUKARAI AND MALLIKA CHOPRA**

SNAKE WOMAN Vol. 1, June 2007 published by VIRGIN COMICS L.L.C. OFFICE OF PUBLICATION: 594 Broadway, New York, NY 10012.
For advertising, licensing and sales info please contact:
info@virgincomics.com or (212) 584-4040. www.virgincomics.com

India is a
battlefield.

Not quite in a literal sense, but most definitely in a literary sense.
Its history rages with ancient allegorical battles; tales of the universal
struggle that faces all life, a struggle that cannot be reduced to
unsophisticated delineations like "good versus evil." Black and white
are mere guide-posts of the extreme, and we play in the world of
gray, the world that has no one correct course of action, because we
don't care who the winner is, we just care how the battle unfolds.
Our Snake Woman emerges in this admittedly bizarre, but
appropriately realistic version of the universe. She is an incarnation
of some of the many cosmic battles: temptation versus restraint,
the carnal versus the humane, vengeance versus forgiveness.
The adversaries are inconsequential—the conflict is what's alluring.
And it can be found everywhere in India from the epics of the Gods,
to the gritty snake fights in the streets.

I was about ten years old the first time my grandfather took me to
one of the cobra and mongoose fights. While not as prevalent today
as they once were, these duels still exist, especially in the crowded
alleyways of the old parts of cities all over India (for me, it was
Delhi) where small throngs congregate and throw down a few
rupees to bet on which of the two creatures will survive the battle.

I remember my initial excitement watching the sleek cobra and lean
mongoose both released from their respective cages a few feet apart,
facing one another. After first reconciling their strange surroundings
amidst so much hysteria, they quickly focused and faced-off. The
crowd hooted and hollered and pushed forward, the various men
crudely encouraging their respective fighters. And so the duel played
out: the mongoose danced frenetically around the serpent, swatting
with its paws at the graceful hooded cobra, which, in turn, dodged
the mongoose's reckless assaults, hissing with each move and
occasionally spitting back with a singular and precise snap

the other. There was something very primitive about the whole experience, watching the two hapless beings resort to a game of death because they were forced into it by a bunch of humans seeking some entertainment during their lunch breaks. After almost half an hour, the mongoose's energy waned until it finally, sadly flopped onto its side and took its last breath. For while it had been swatting energetically at the snake, somewhere along the line the cobra had landed a hit, buried its fangs into the mongoose and injected its deadly venom. It had happened so fast that no one really knew when exactly the fatal blow had occurred. After successfully poisoning its opponent, the cobra's singular objective was to wait out the inevitability of the mongoose's death while surviving the last bold assaults of the dying animal.

The battle between the cobra and the mongoose is not just a struggle for survival between two of God's creatures; it is the eternal cosmic dance between the past and the future, between ancient wisdoms and modern technologies. The cobra, in its wisdom, with patience and presence, waits for the precise moment to strike, knowing that only one bite from its venomous fangs will do the trick. Meanwhile, the mongoose dances, relentlessly stalking the serpent, hoping that all its blows will add up and wear the snake down, guaranteeing victory. It is wisdom versus persistence, and the right balance between the two ensures a clash that can last for hours, even, legend says, the whole day. But if one side falters, destruction is imminent.

Those of us who have spent considerable time in India affectionately describe it as being "a lot of everything" or "an assault on all the senses." It is a hard country to reconcile because it is full of contradictions, chock-full of the sacred and the profane, the divine and diabolical, all in excess all at the same time. Like the cobra and the mongoose, the tale of the Snake Woman is no different; it's both crude and cosmic, inhumane and existential all at the same time. But the lesson to take away from it is eternal: "Do what you must to ensure the duel never ends. For when it does, so does everything else."

And so, the battle begins.

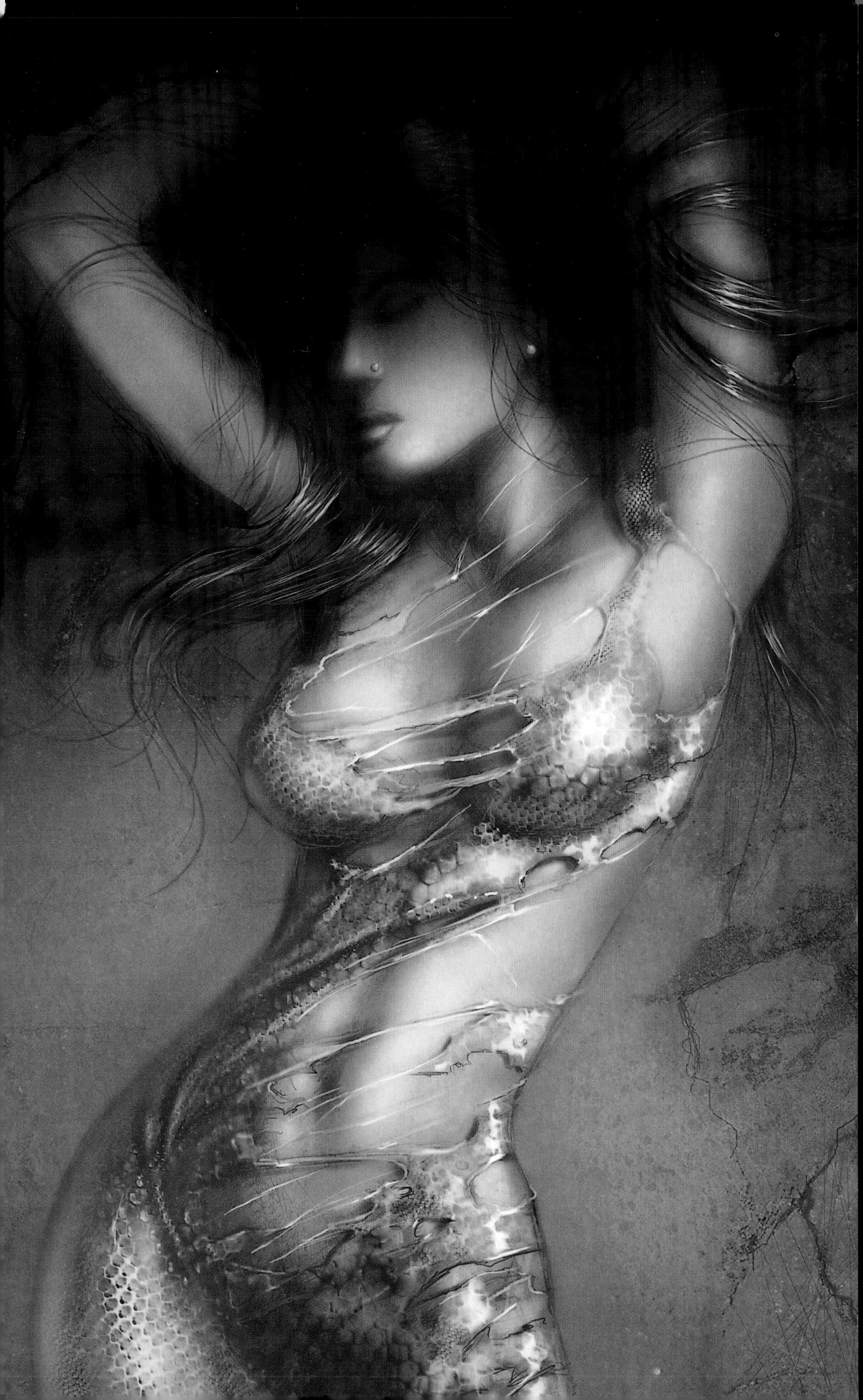

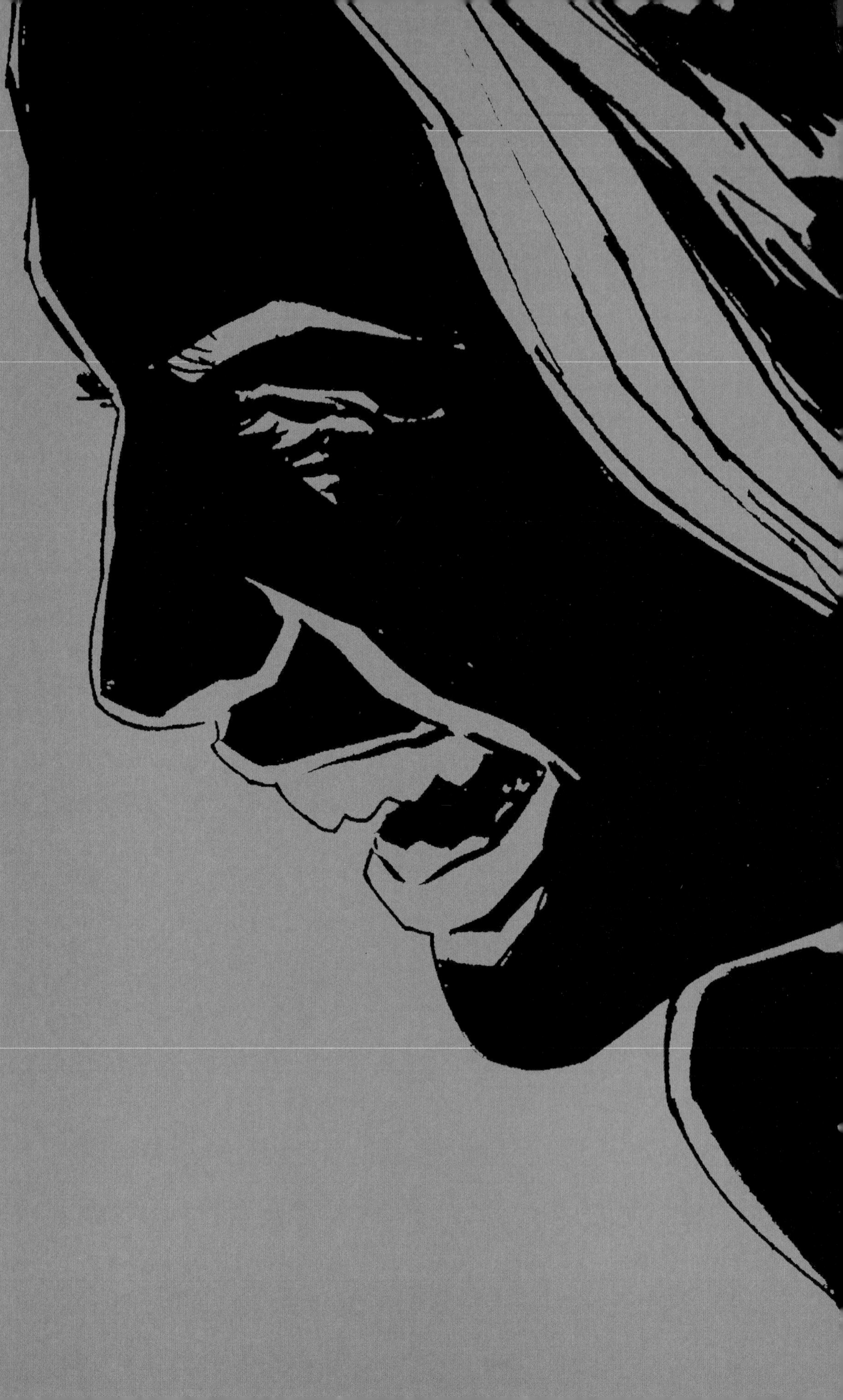

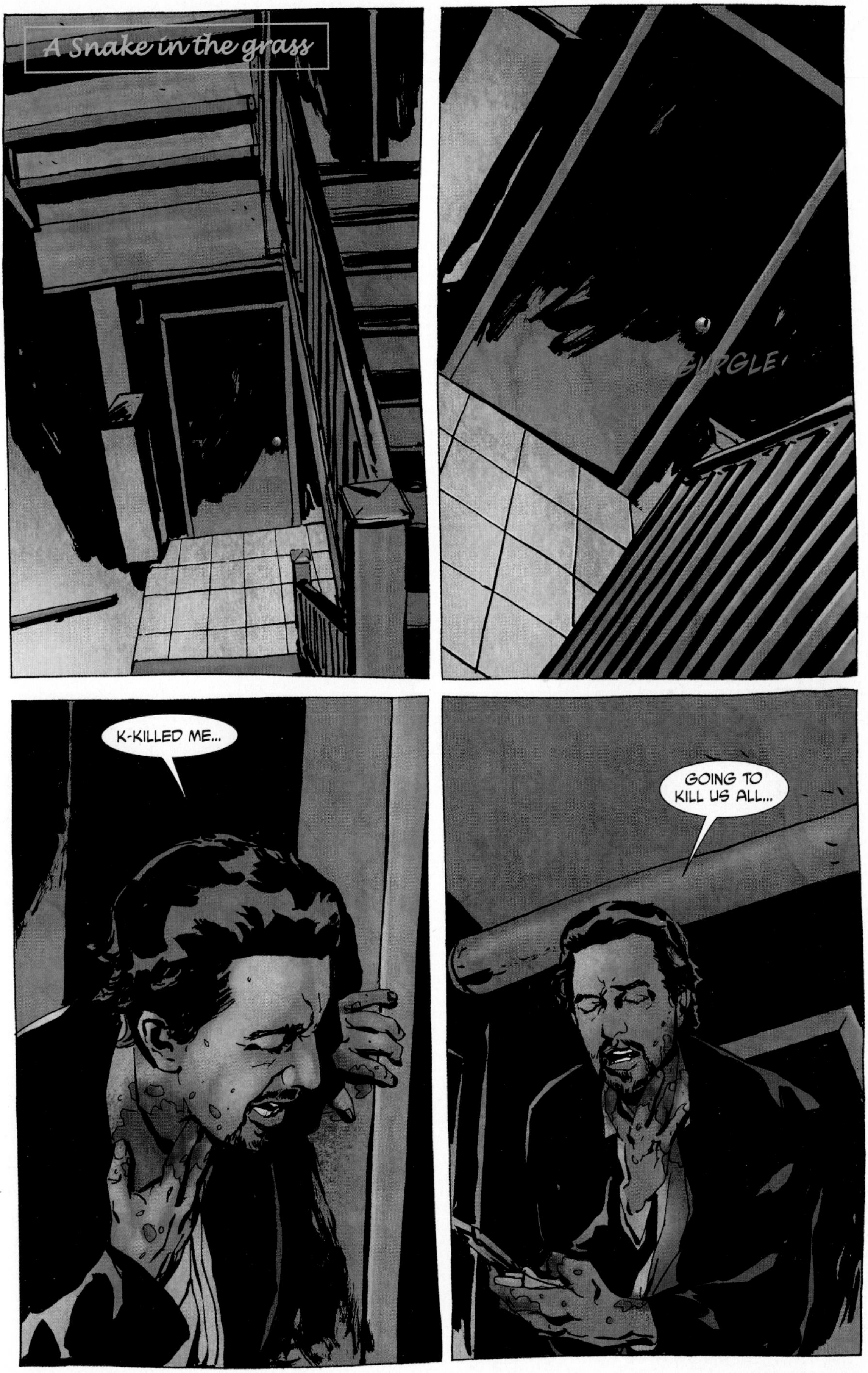
A Snake in the grass
GURGLE
K-KILLED ME...
GOING TO KILL US ALL...

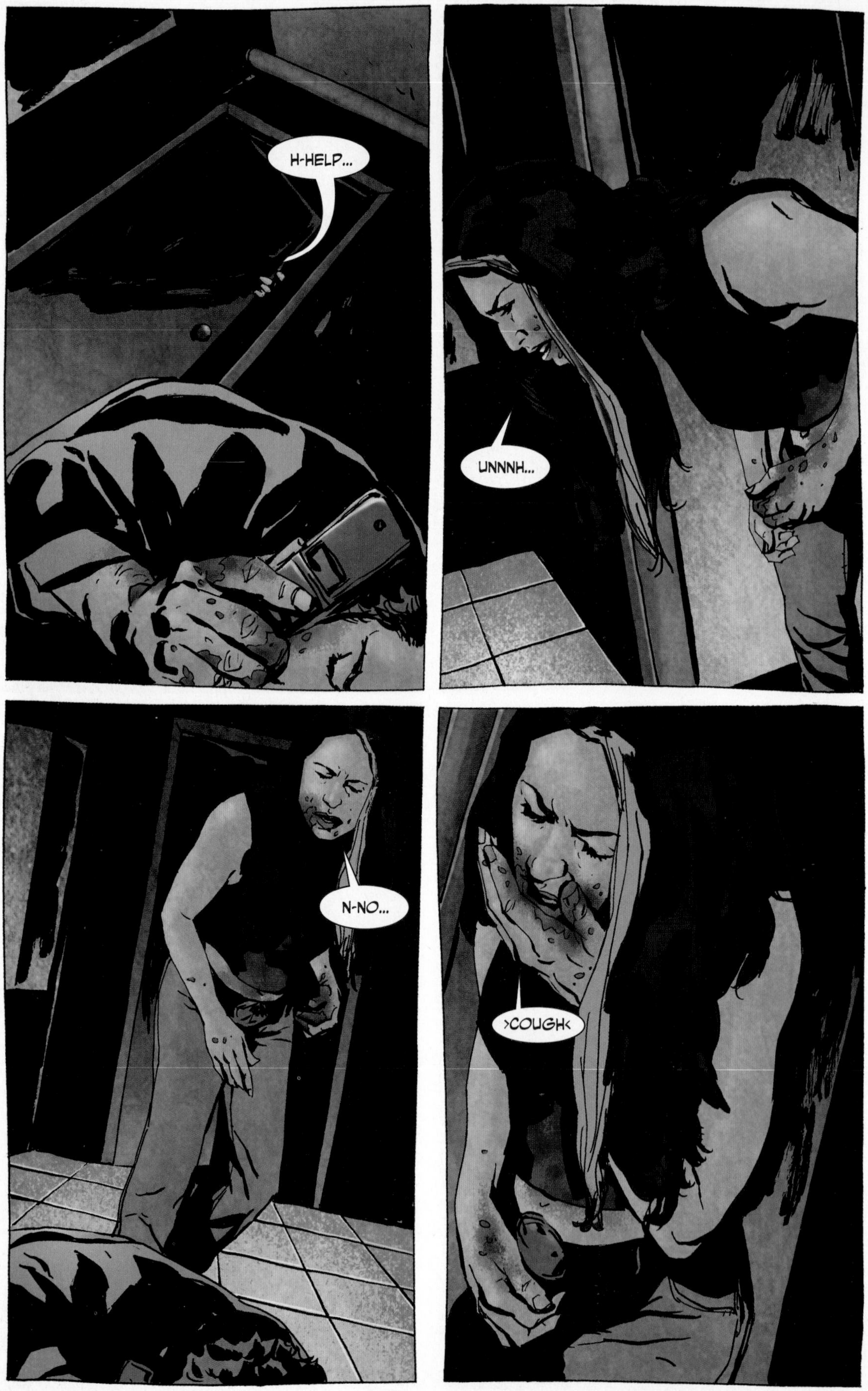
H-HELP...
UNNNH...
N-NO...
>COUGH<

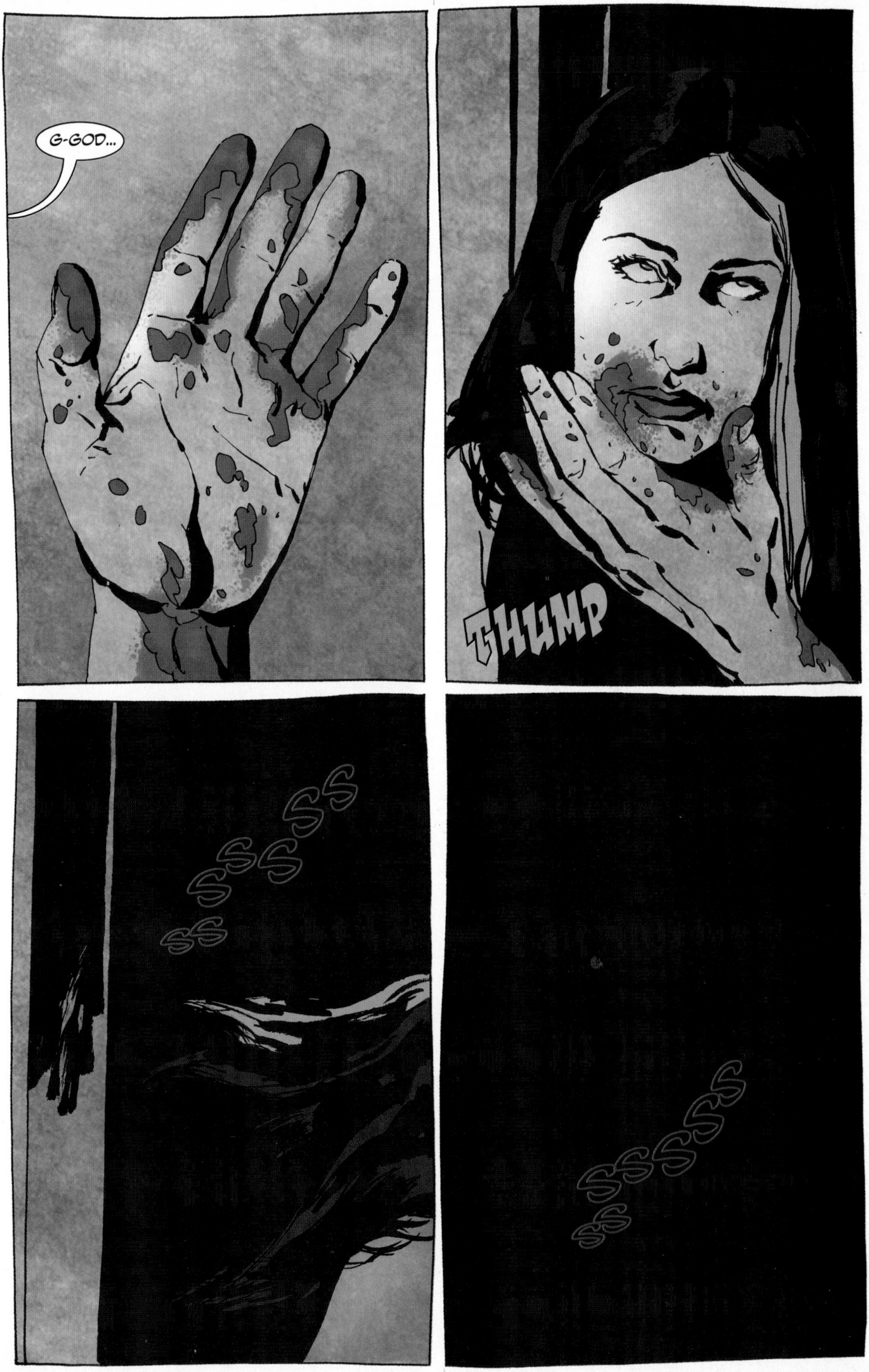
G-GOD...
THUMP
SSSSSSS
SSSSSSSS

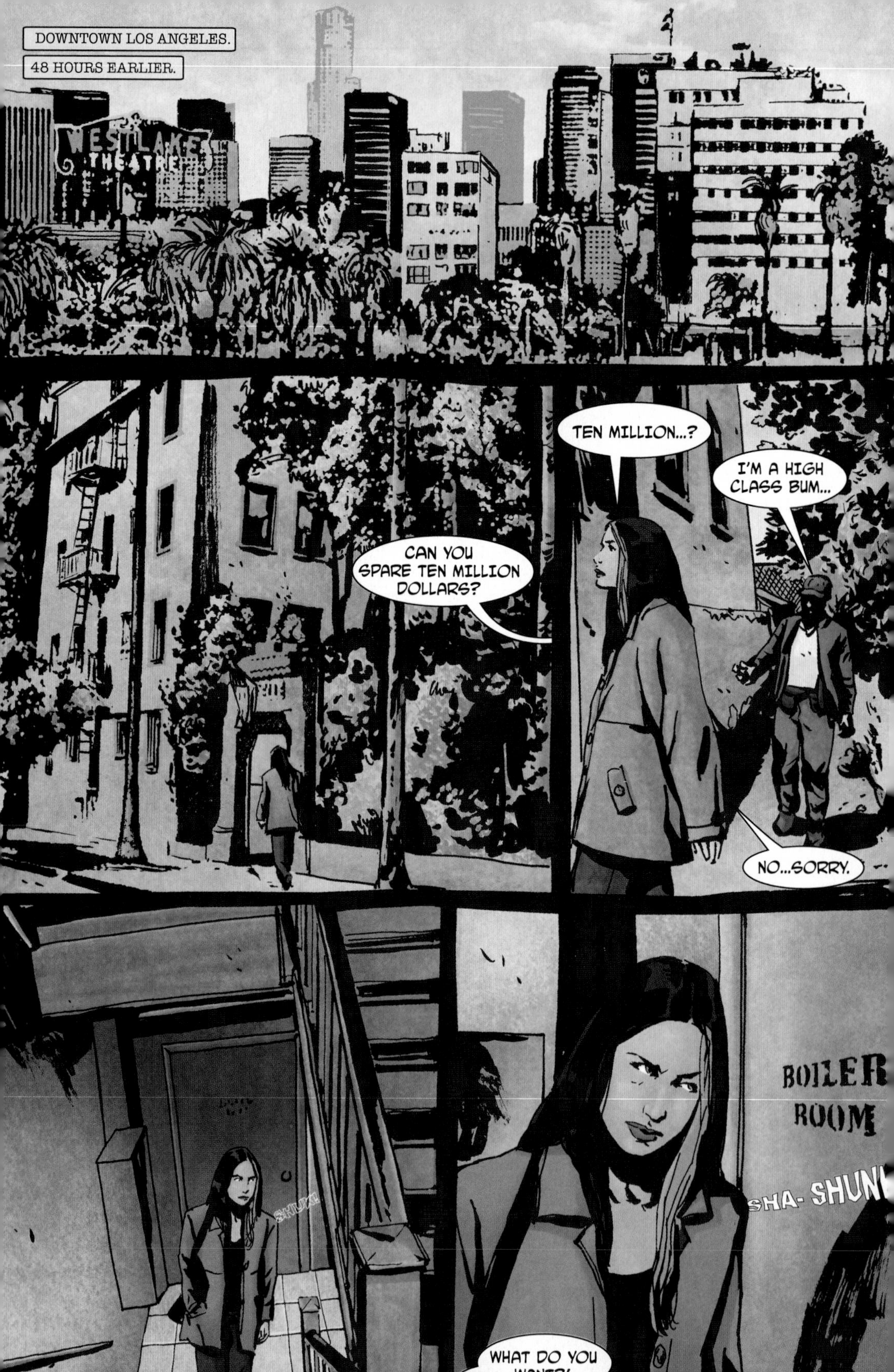
DOWNTOWN LOS ANGELES.
48 HOURS EARLIER.
WESTLAKE THEATRE
CAN YOU SPARE TEN MILLION DOLLARS?
TEN MILLION...?
I'M A HIGH CLASS BUM...
NO...SORRY.
BOILER ROOM
SHA- SHUN
WHAT DO YOU WANT?!

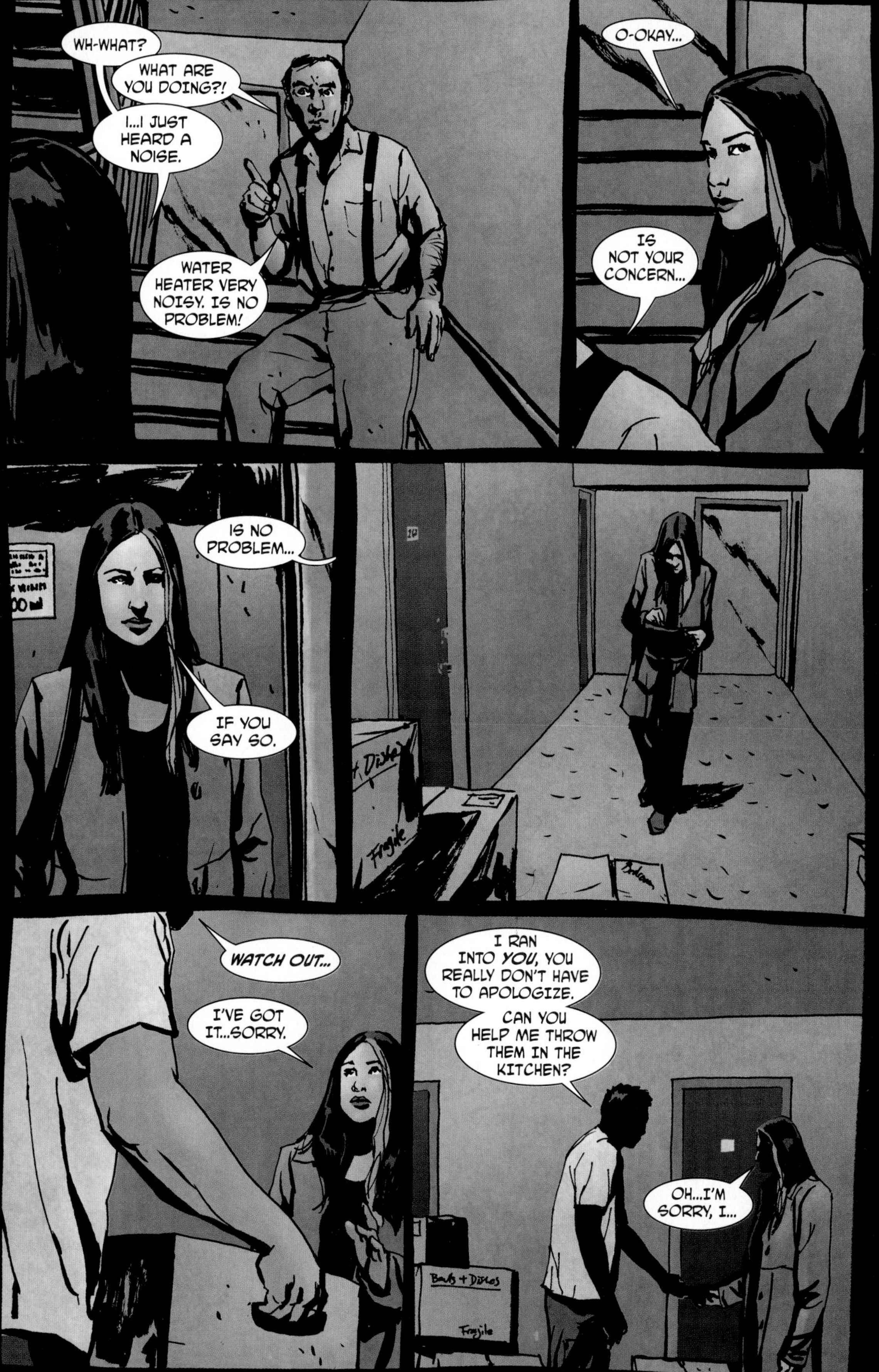
WH-WHAT?
WHAT ARE YOU DOING?!
I...I JUST HEARD A NOISE.
WATER HEATER VERY NOISY. IS NO PROBLEM!
O-OKAY...
IS NOT YOUR CONCERN...
IS NO PROBLEM...
IF YOU SAY SO.
WATCH OUT...
I'VE GOT IT...SORRY.
I RAN INTO YOU, YOU REALLY DON'T HAVE TO APOLOGIZE.
CAN YOU HELP ME THROW THEM IN THE KITCHEN?
OH...I'M SORRY, I...
Bowls + Dishes
Fragile

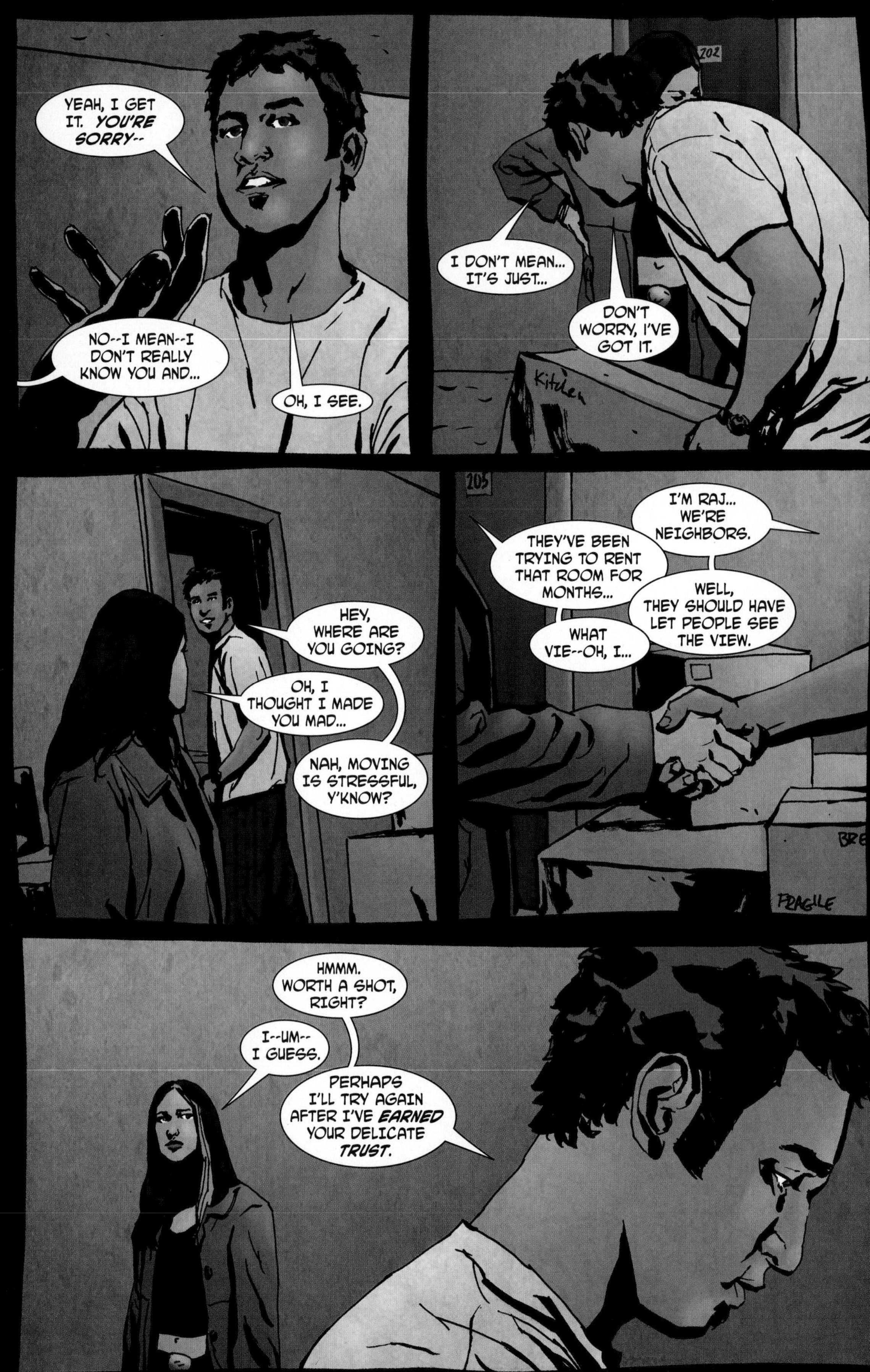
YEAH, I GET IT. *YOU'RE SORRY--*
NO--I MEAN--I DON'T REALLY KNOW YOU AND...
OH, I SEE.
202
I DON'T MEAN... IT'S JUST...
DON'T WORRY, I'VE GOT IT.
Kitchen
HEY, WHERE ARE YOU GOING?
OH, I THOUGHT I MADE YOU MAD...
NAH, MOVING IS STRESSFUL, Y'KNOW?
203
THEY'VE BEEN TRYING TO RENT THAT ROOM FOR MONTHS...
I'M RAJ... WE'RE NEIGHBORS.
WELL, THEY SHOULD HAVE LET PEOPLE SEE THE VIEW.
WHAT VIE--OH, I...
FRAGILE
HMMM. WORTH A SHOT, RIGHT?
I--UM-- I GUESS.
PERHAPS I'LL TRY AGAIN AFTER I'VE *EARNED* YOUR DELICATE *TRUST*.

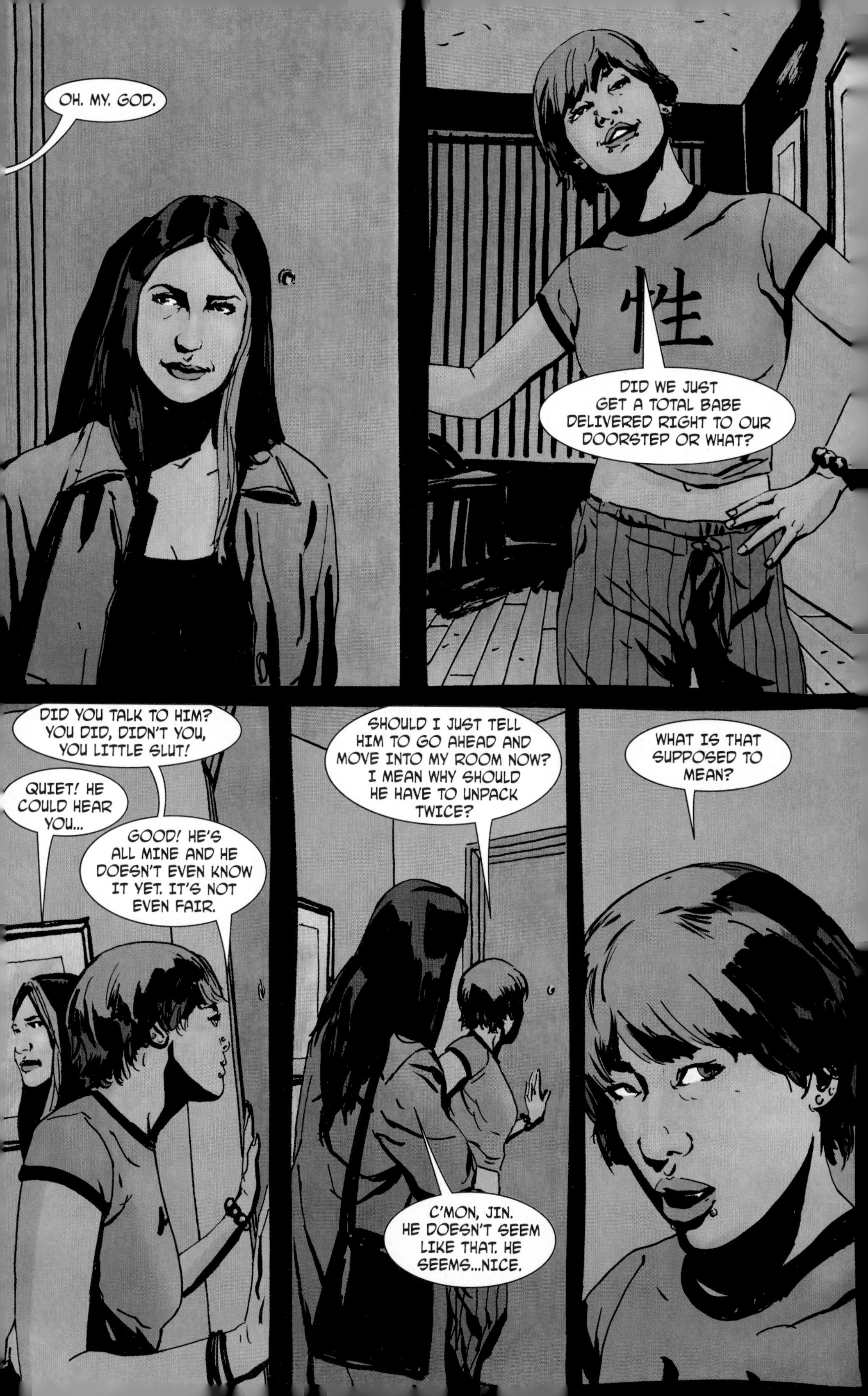
OH. MY. GOD.
DID WE JUST GET A TOTAL BABE DELIVERED RIGHT TO OUR DOORSTEP OR WHAT?
DID YOU TALK TO HIM? YOU DID, DIDN'T YOU, YOU LITTLE SLUT!
QUIET! HE COULD HEAR YOU...
GOOD! HE'S ALL MINE AND HE DOESN'T EVEN KNOW IT YET. IT'S NOT EVEN FAIR.
SHOULD I JUST TELL HIM TO GO AHEAD AND MOVE INTO MY ROOM NOW? I MEAN WHY SHOULD HE HAVE TO UNPACK TWICE?
C'MON, JIN. HE DOESN'T SEEM LIKE THAT. HE SEEMS...NICE.
WHAT IS THAT SUPPOSED TO MEAN?

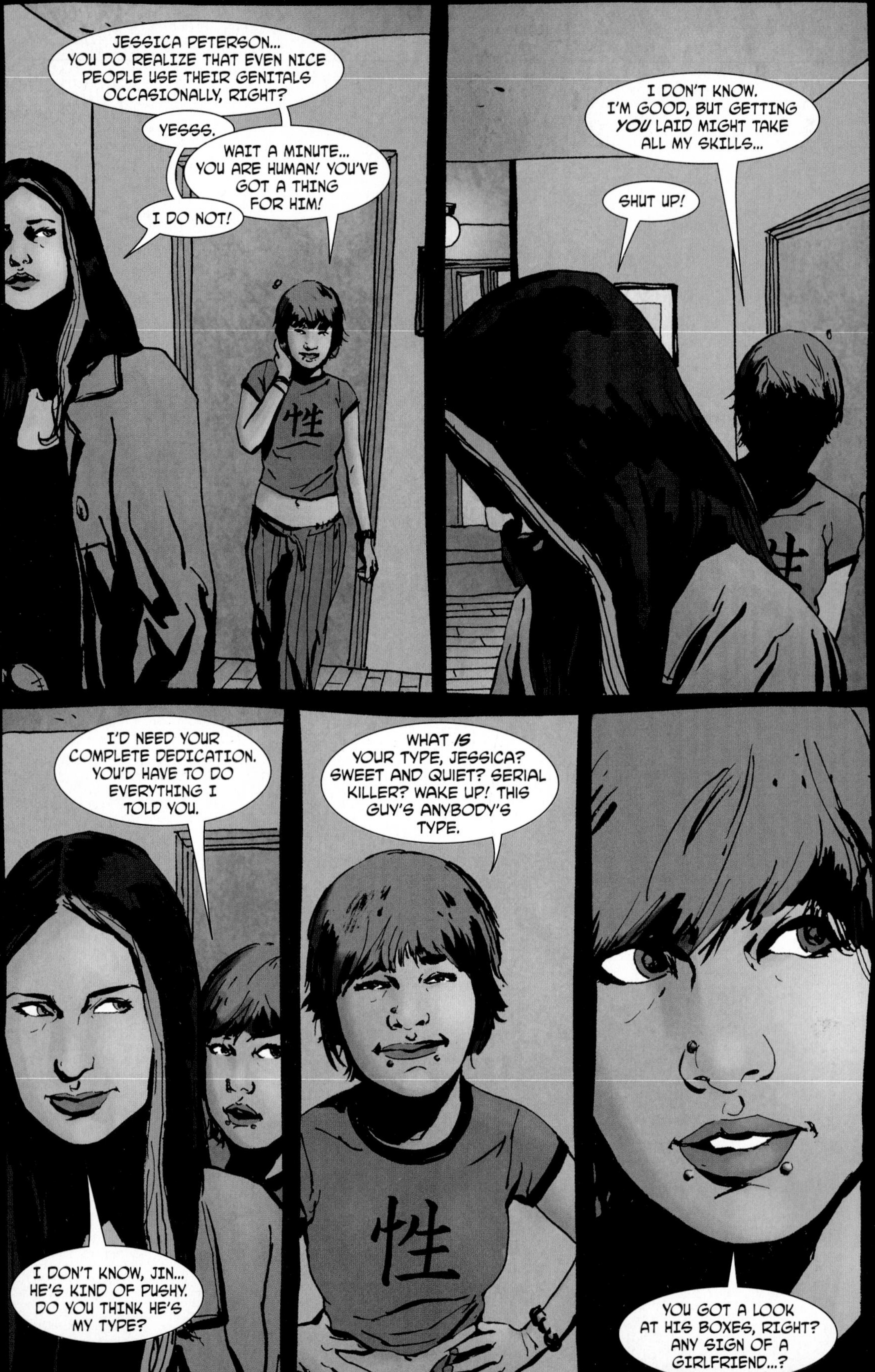
JESSICA PETERSON... YOU DO REALIZE THAT EVEN NICE PEOPLE USE THEIR GENITALS OCCASIONALLY, RIGHT?
YESSS.
WAIT A MINUTE... YOU ARE HUMAN! YOU'VE GOT A THING FOR HIM!
I DO NOT!
I DON'T KNOW. I'M GOOD, BUT GETTING *YOU* LAID MIGHT TAKE ALL MY SKILLS...
SHUT UP!
I'D NEED YOUR COMPLETE DEDICATION. YOU'D HAVE TO DO EVERYTHING I TOLD YOU.
I DON'T KNOW, JIN... HE'S KIND OF PUSHY. DO YOU THINK HE'S MY TYPE?
WHAT *IS* YOUR TYPE, JESSICA? SWEET AND QUIET? SERIAL KILLER? WAKE UP! THIS GUY'S ANYBODY'S TYPE.
YOU GOT A LOOK AT HIS BOXES, RIGHT? ANY SIGN OF A GIRLFRIEND...?

BAD KARMA

SHE EMERGES, FROM HER CITY'S LAIR, A MAIDEN SMALL, BUT KIND AND FAIR...

LOOK AT THEE, THE APPROACHING LASS...

LOOK AT THEE, THE APPROACHING LASS... HNNNN LOOKATTHEE, THEAPPROACHING LASS LOOKATTHEE, THEAPPROACHING LASS--

IT'S ALRIGHT BRINKLEY. RELAX...

I'M WORKING ON YOUR TIP...

HE BEHAVING HIMSELF...

BRINKLEY? HE DOESN'T BOTHER ME. KIND OF REMINDS ME OF MY DAD. AND COME ON, HE WRITES ME POEMS.

YEAH, WELL CHARLES MANSON WROTE POEMS TOO. JUST BE CAREFUL...

I'VE NEVER SEEN HIM IN HERE EXCEPT WHEN YOU'RE WORKING, YOU KNOW.

HE LIKES ME... HE JUST KNOWS MY SCHEDULE.

YEAH, BUT ISN'T JIN SUPPOSED TO BE WORKING TONIGHT?

SOMETHING TELLS ME HE WOULDN'T BE HERE IF JIN HAD SHOWED UP...

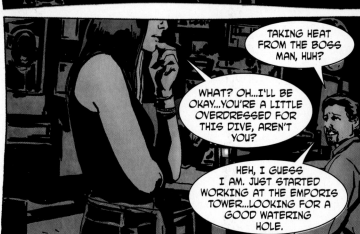

TAKING HEAT FROM THE BOSS MAN, HUH?

WHAT? OH...I'LL BE OKAY...YOU'RE A LITTLE OVERDRESSED FOR THIS DIVE, AREN'T YOU?

HEH, I GUESS I AM. JUST STARTED WORKING AT THE EMPORIS TOWER...LOOKING FOR A GOOD WATERING HOLE.

I'M RYAN, BY THE WAY...

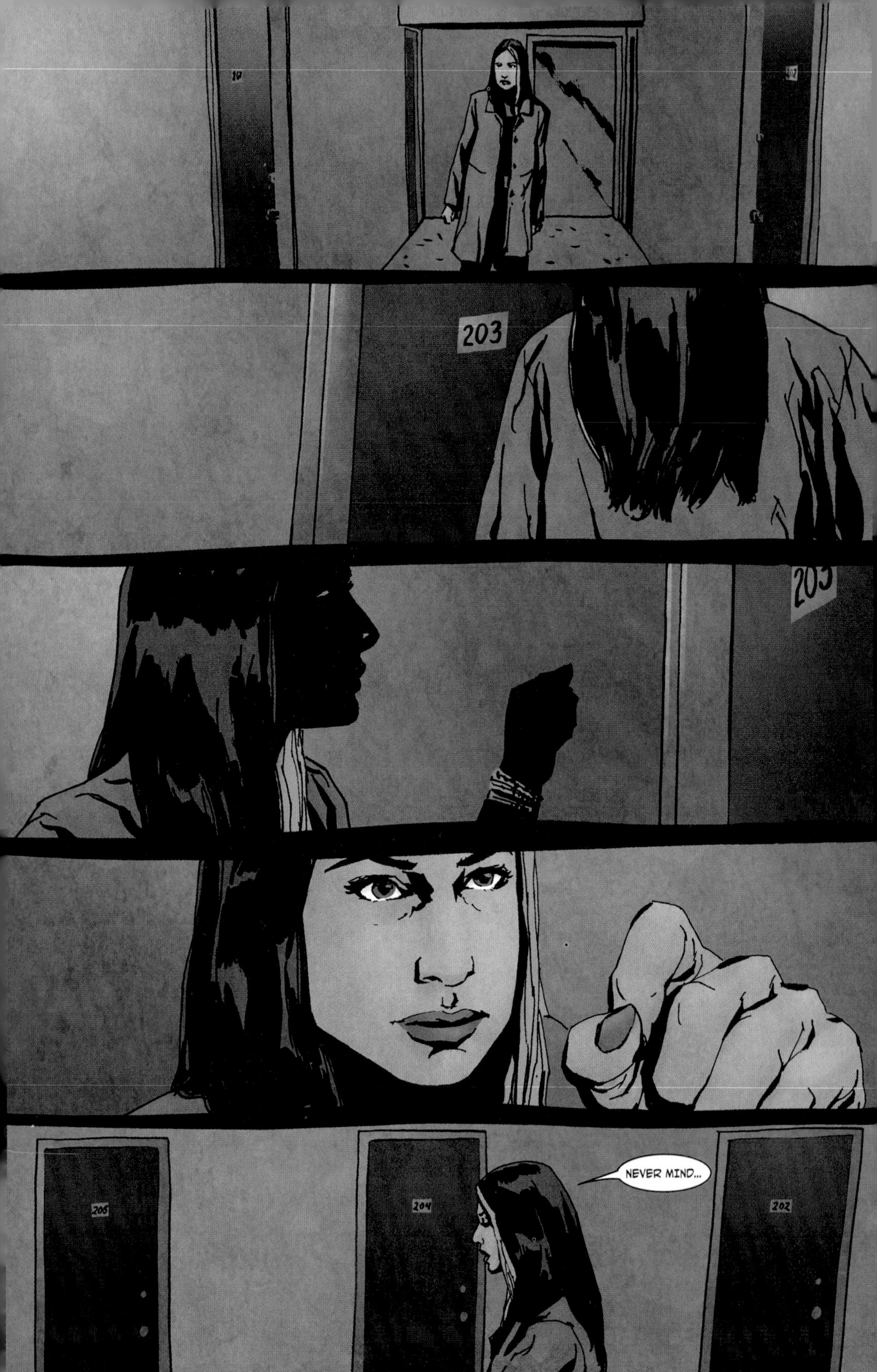
203
NEVER MIND...

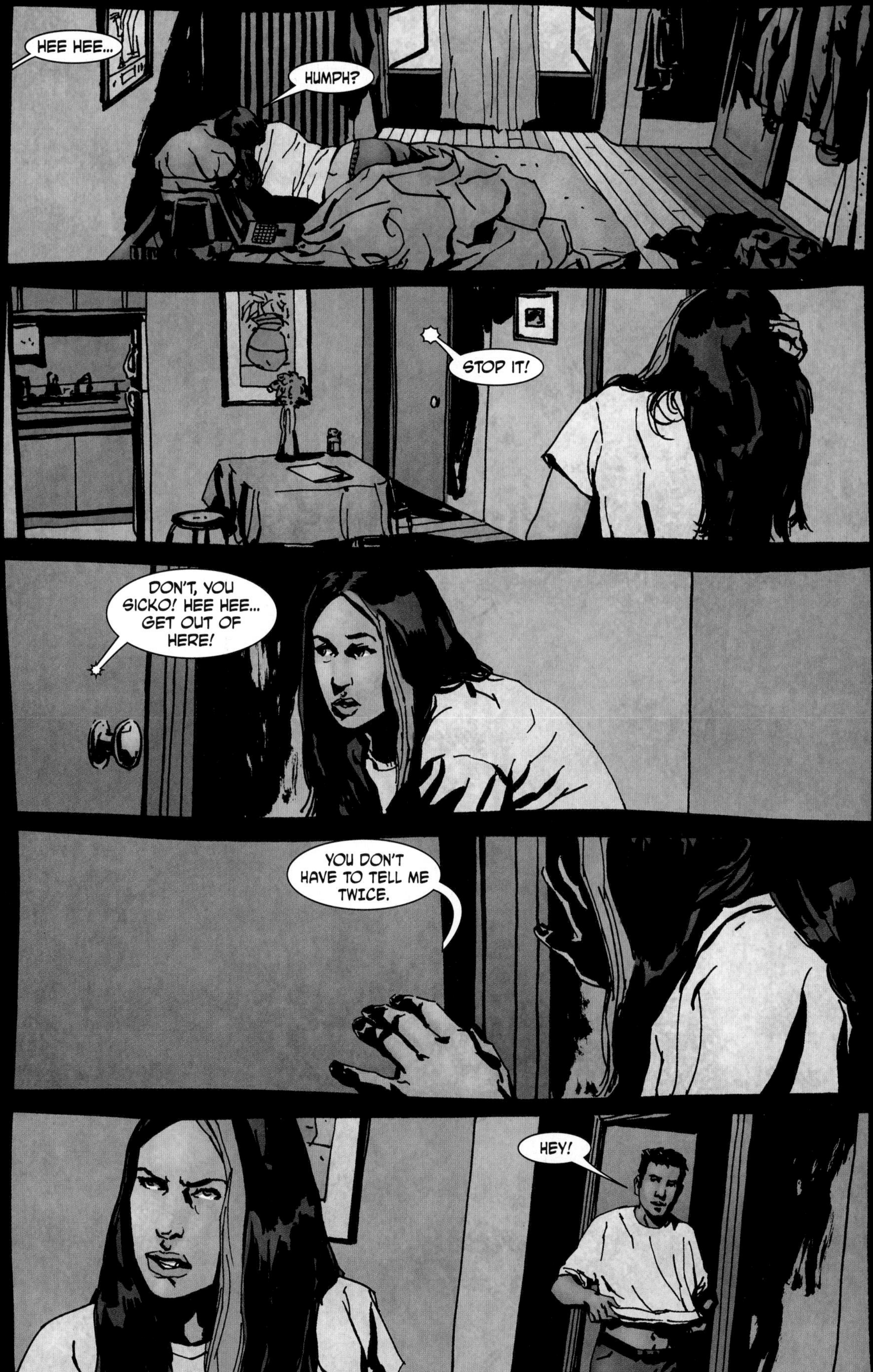
HEE HEE...
HUMPH?
STOP IT!
DON'T, YOU SICKO! HEE HEE... GET OUT OF HERE!
YOU DON'T HAVE TO TELL ME TWICE.
HEY!

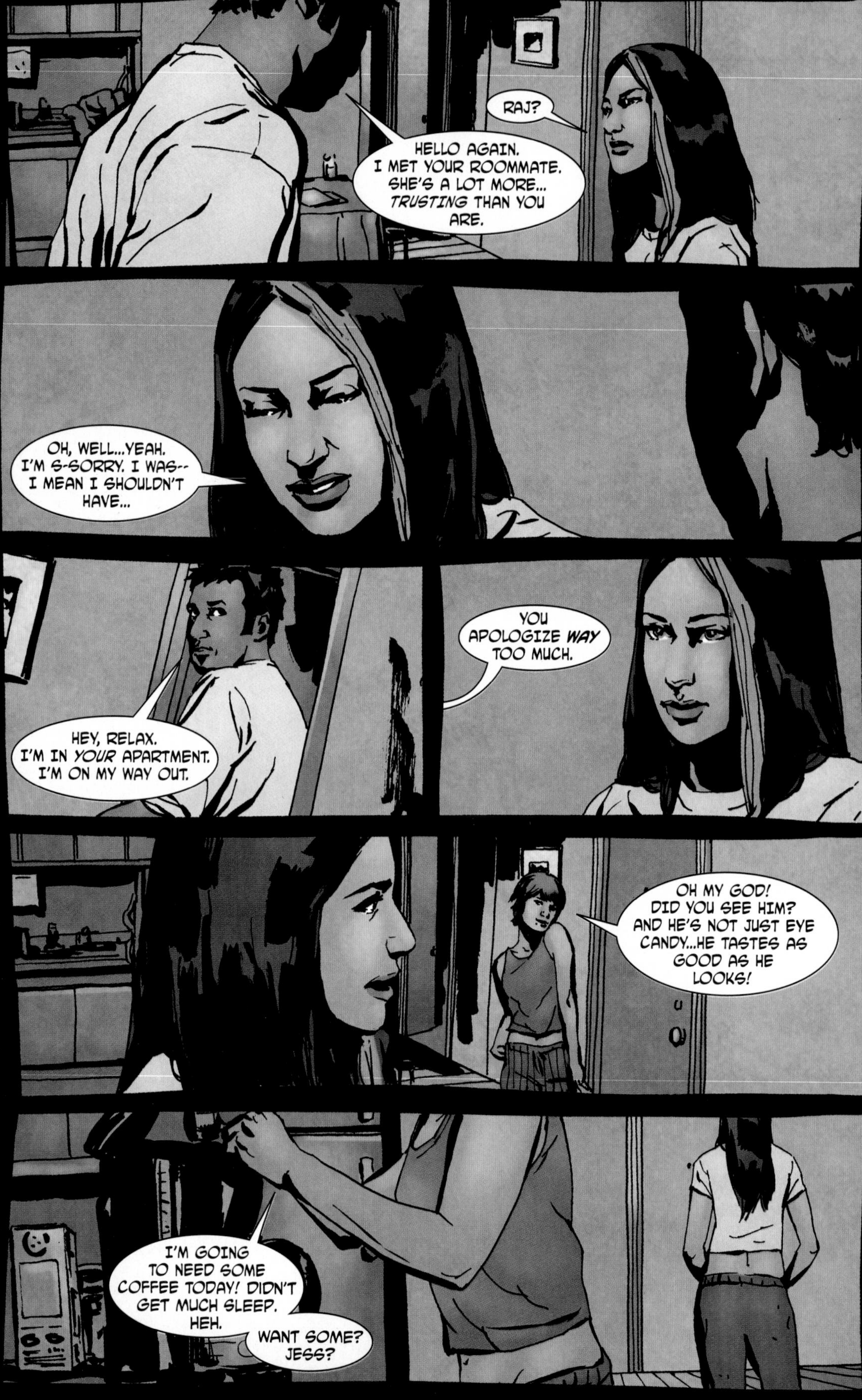
RAJ?
HELLO AGAIN. I MET YOUR ROOMMATE. SHE'S A LOT MORE... *TRUSTING* THAN YOU ARE.
OH, WELL...YEAH. I'M S-SORRY. I WAS-- I MEAN I SHOULDN'T HAVE...
HEY, RELAX. I'M IN *YOUR* APARTMENT. I'M ON MY WAY OUT.
YOU APOLOGIZE *WAY* TOO MUCH.
OH MY GOD! DID YOU SEE HIM? AND HE'S NOT JUST EYE CANDY...HE TASTES AS GOOD AS HE LOOKS!
I'M GOING TO NEED SOME COFFEE TODAY! DIDN'T GET MUCH SLEEP. HEH.
WANT SOME? JESS?

LATER...

FOR THE LAST TIME, JIN. I DON'T KNOW WHAT HE'S EXPECTING FROM YOU.

MAYBE I SHOULD PLAY IT COOL. I TOLD HIM TO COME BY THE BAR, TONIGHT. I HOPE I DIDN'T FREAK HIM OUT.

OH, JESS...LOOKS LIKE YOUR SECRET ADMIRER IS HERE. I'LL TAKE THE CUTE YUPPIE...

...MIGHT NEED HIM LATER TO MAKE RAJ JEALOUS.

YOU KNOW WHAT, JIN? I'VE GOT THIS ONE.

WHAT ABOUT...

JESSICA? I THINK I FINISHED YOUR POEM...

HEY, RYAN, RIGHT? YOU'RE BECOMING A REGULAR. WHAT CAN I GET FOR YOU?

YOUR FRIEND IS TRYING TO GET YOUR ATTENTION.

WHO? THE OLDER GUY? IT'S FINE. HE CAN BE A LITTLE NEEDY IS ALL.

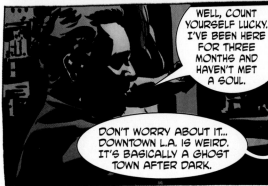

WELL, COUNT YOURSELF LUCKY. I'VE BEEN HERE FOR THREE MONTHS AND HAVEN'T MET A SOUL.

DON'T WORRY ABOUT IT... DOWNTOWN L.A. IS WEIRD. IT'S BASICALLY A GHOST TOWN AFTER DARK.

REGARDLESS, I'VE GOT AN '03 JAGUAR I'D TRADE YOU FOR YOUR FRIEND OVER THERE, IF YOU'RE WILLING TO PART WITH HIM.

HEE...SORRY, HE'S NOT FOR SALE. HE WRITES ME POEMS.

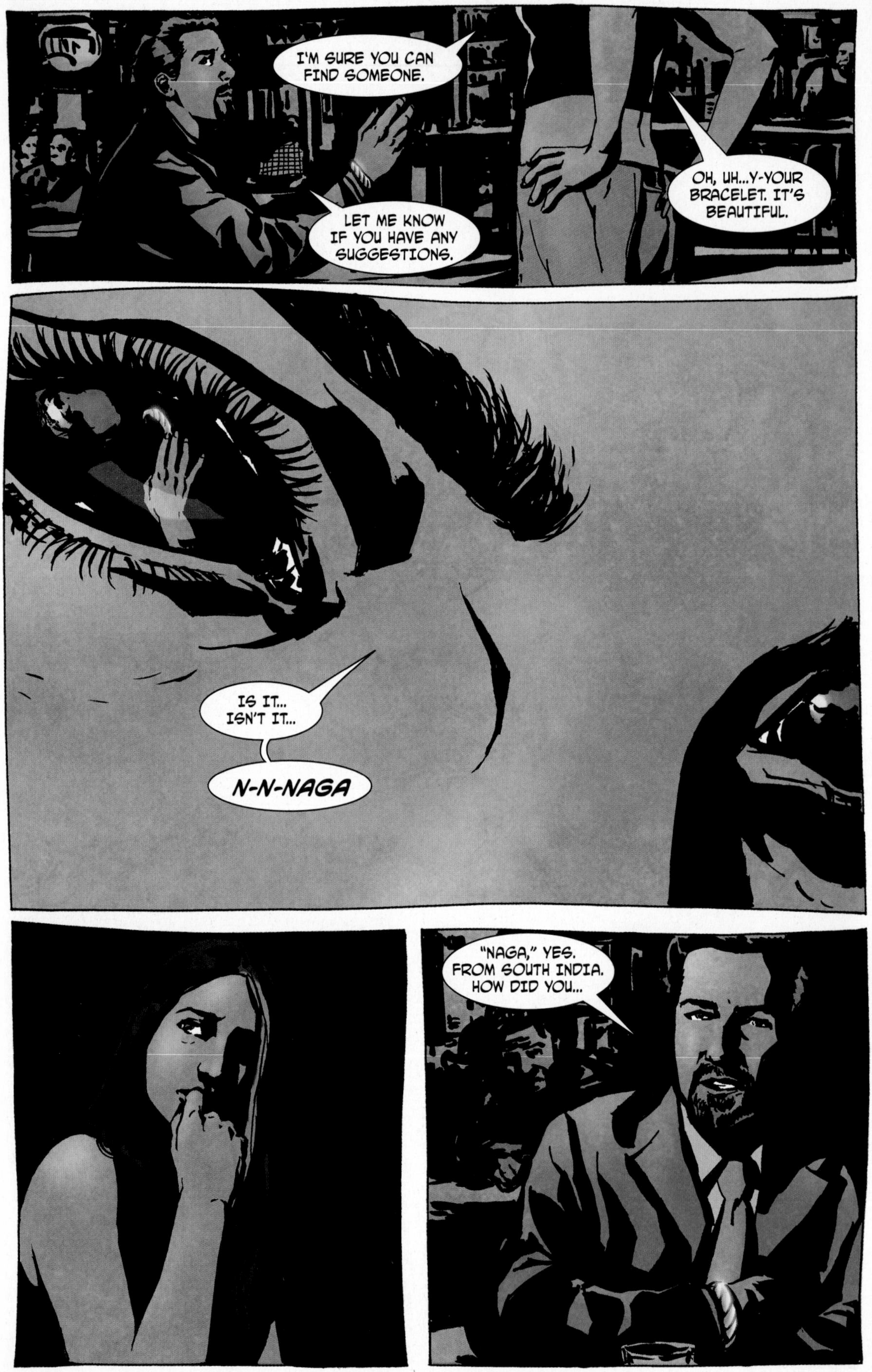
I'M SURE YOU CAN FIND SOMEONE.
LET ME KNOW IF YOU HAVE ANY SUGGESTIONS.
OH, UH...Y-YOUR BRACELET. IT'S BEAUTIFUL.
IS IT... ISN'T IT...
N-N-NAGA
"NAGA," YES. FROM SOUTH INDIA. HOW DID YOU...

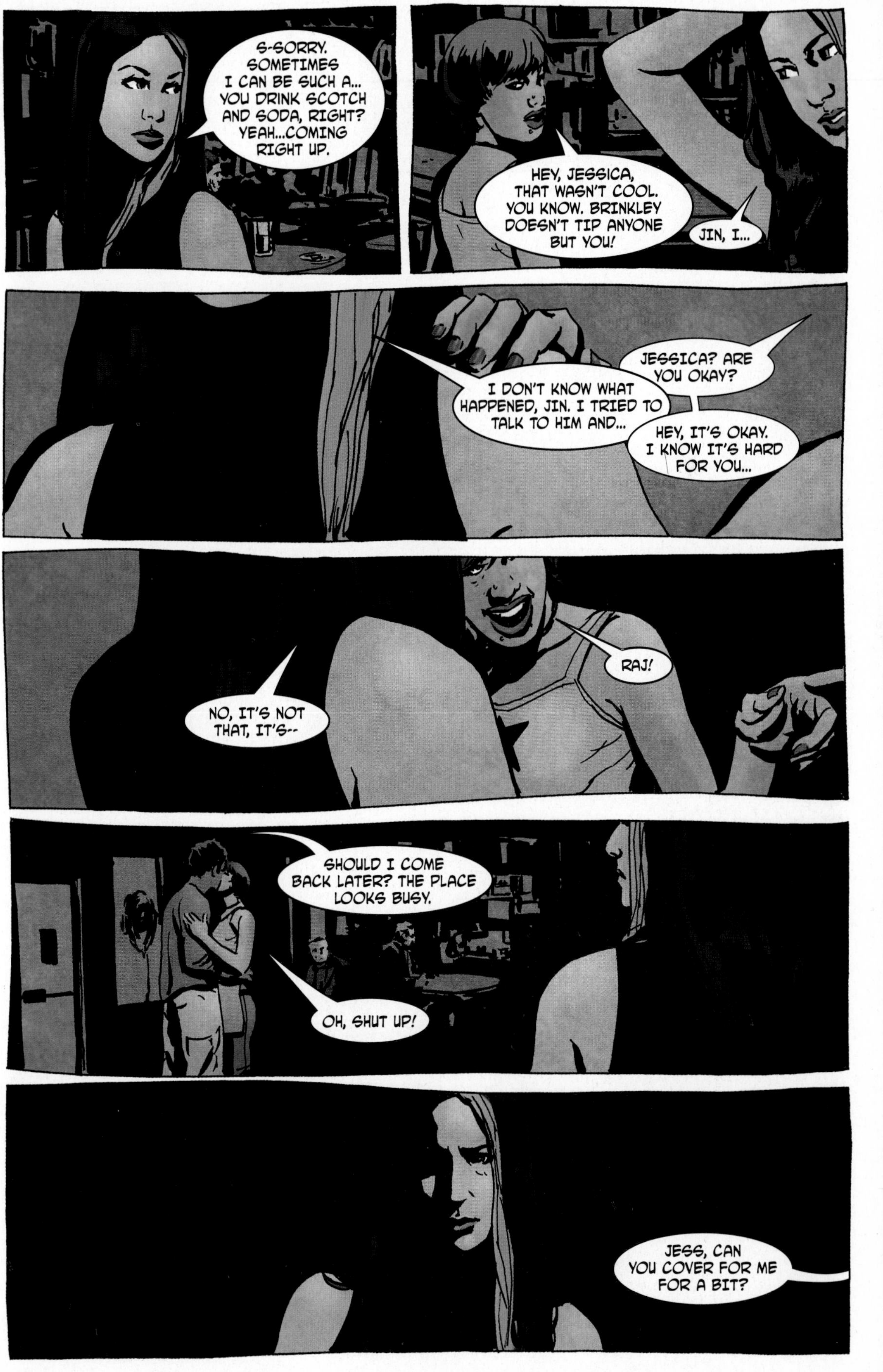
S-SORRY. SOMETIMES I CAN BE SUCH A... YOU DRINK SCOTCH AND SODA, RIGHT? YEAH...COMING RIGHT UP.
HEY, JESSICA, THAT WASN'T COOL. YOU KNOW. BRINKLEY DOESN'T TIP ANYONE BUT YOU!
JIN, I...
JESSICA? ARE YOU OKAY?
I DON'T KNOW WHAT HAPPENED, JIN. I TRIED TO TALK TO HIM AND...
HEY, IT'S OKAY. I KNOW IT'S HARD FOR YOU...
NO, IT'S NOT THAT, IT'S--
RAJ!
SHOULD I COME BACK LATER? THE PLACE LOOKS BUSY.
OH, SHUT UP!
JESS, CAN YOU COVER FOR ME FOR A BIT?

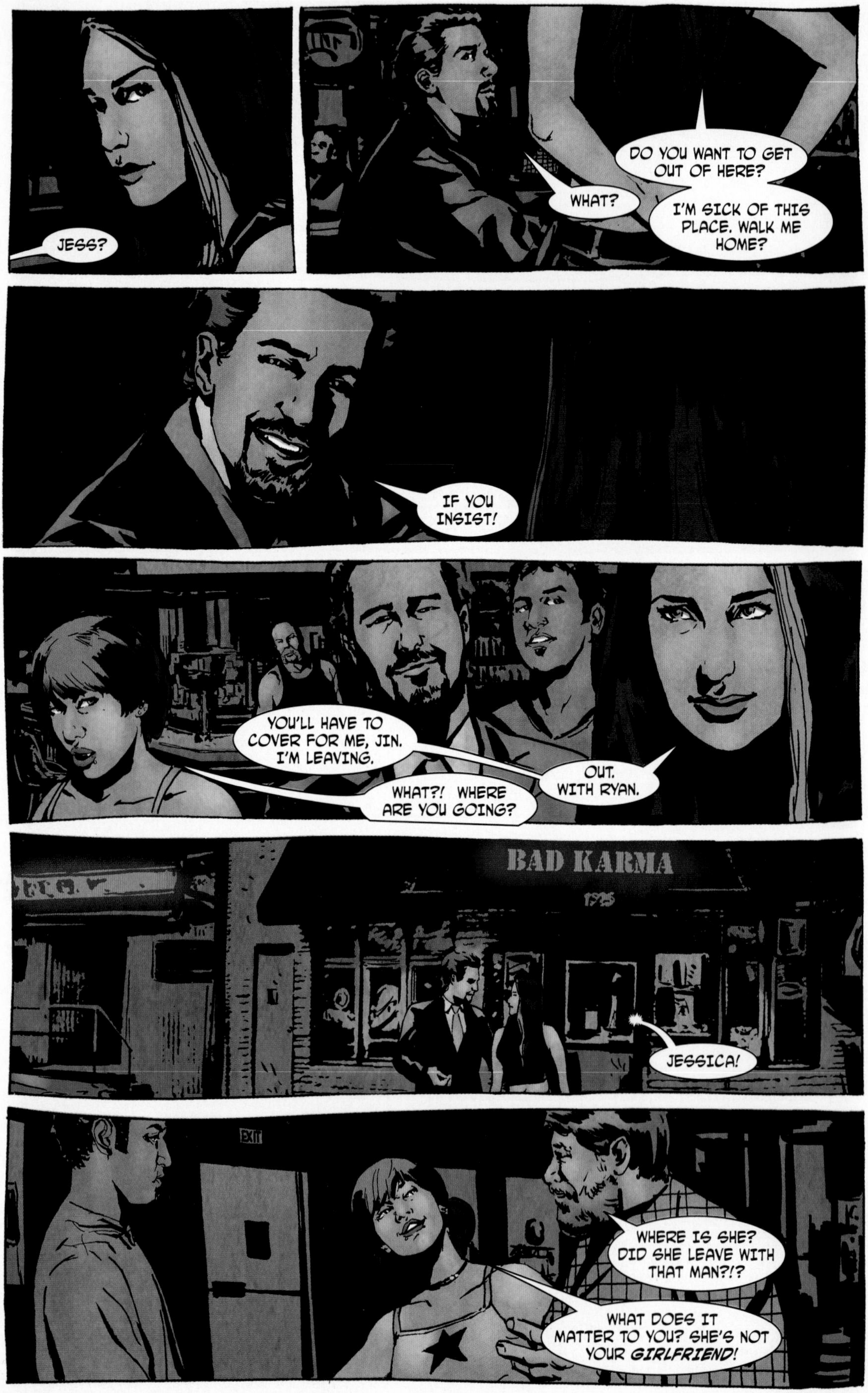
JESS?
DO YOU WANT TO GET OUT OF HERE?
WHAT?
I'M SICK OF THIS PLACE. WALK ME HOME?
IF YOU INSIST!
YOU'LL HAVE TO COVER FOR ME, JIN. I'M LEAVING.
WHAT?! WHERE ARE YOU GOING?
OUT. WITH RYAN.
BAD KARMA
1925
JESSICA!
EXIT
WHERE IS SHE? DID SHE LEAVE WITH THAT MAN?!?
WHAT DOES IT MATTER TO YOU? SHE'S NOT YOUR GIRLFRIEND!

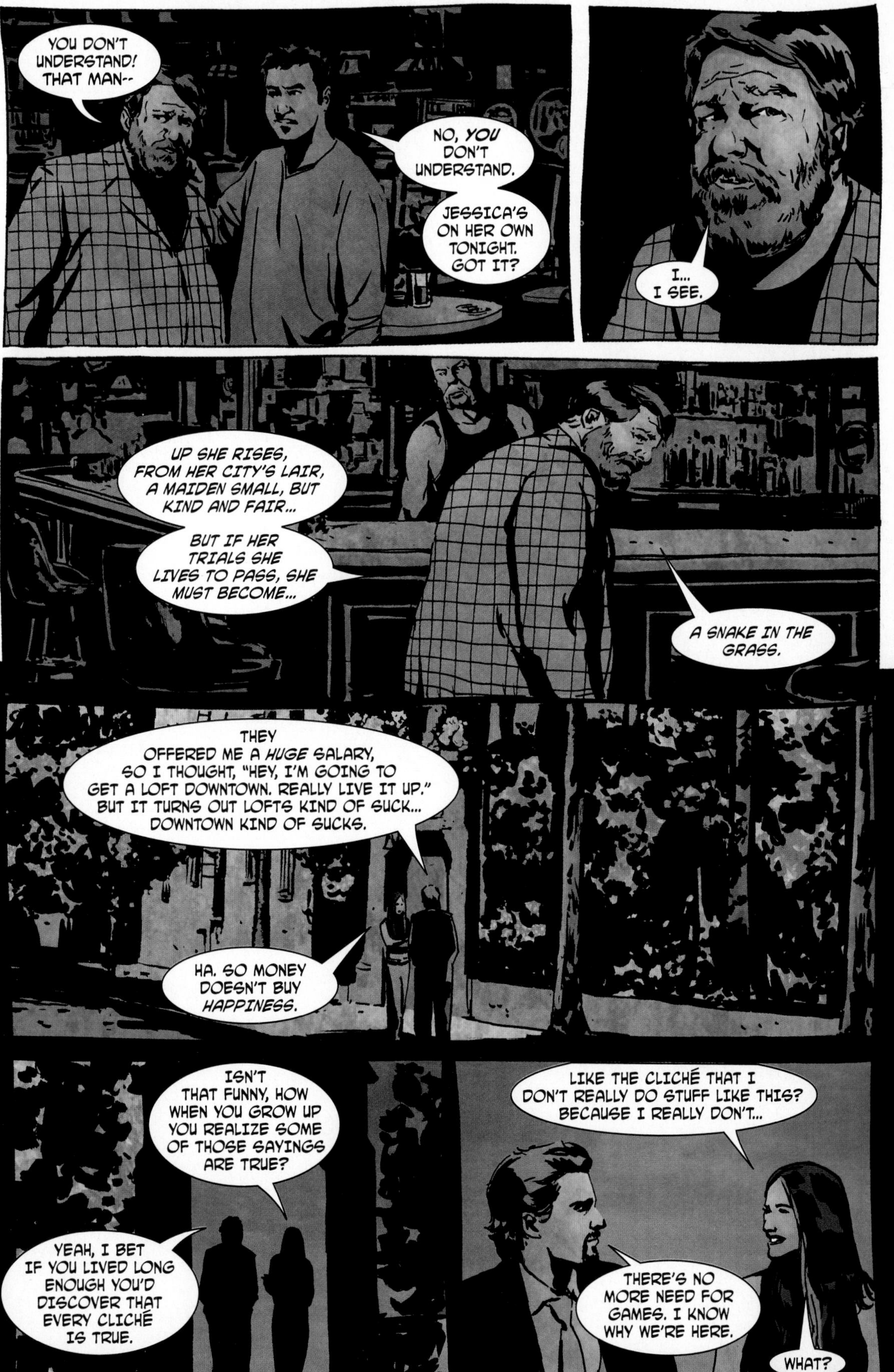

YOU DON'T UNDERSTAND! THAT MAN--
NO, *YOU* DON'T UNDERSTAND.
JESSICA'S ON HER OWN TONIGHT. GOT IT?
I... I SEE.
UP SHE RISES, FROM HER CITY'S LAIR, A MAIDEN SMALL, BUT KIND AND FAIR...
BUT IF HER TRIALS SHE LIVES TO PASS, SHE MUST BECOME...
A SNAKE IN THE GRASS.
THEY OFFERED ME A *HUGE* SALARY, SO I THOUGHT, "HEY, I'M GOING TO GET A LOFT DOWNTOWN. REALLY LIVE IT UP." BUT IT TURNS OUT LOFTS KIND OF SUCK... DOWNTOWN KIND OF SUCKS.
HA. SO MONEY DOESN'T BUY *HAPPINESS*.
ISN'T THAT FUNNY, HOW WHEN YOU GROW UP YOU REALIZE SOME OF THOSE SAYINGS ARE TRUE?
YEAH, I BET IF YOU LIVED LONG ENOUGH YOU'D DISCOVER THAT EVERY CLICHÉ IS TRUE.
LIKE THE CLICHÉ THAT I DON'T REALLY DO STUFF LIKE THIS? BECAUSE I REALLY DON'T...
THERE'S NO MORE NEED FOR GAMES. I KNOW WHY WE'RE HERE.
WHAT?

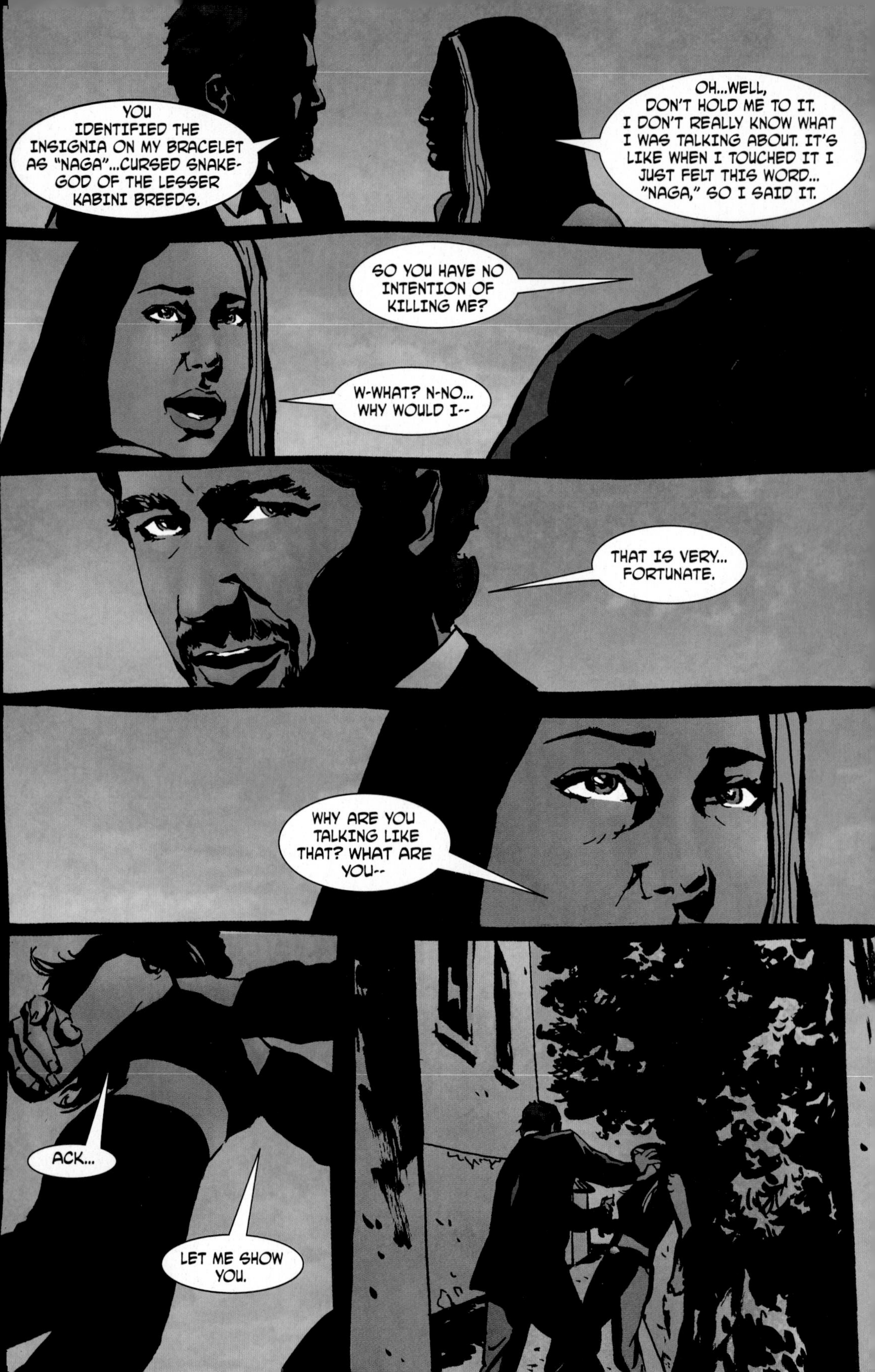
YOU IDENTIFIED THE INSIGNIA ON MY BRACELET AS "NAGA"...CURSED SNAKE-GOD OF THE LESSER KABINI BREEDS.
OH...WELL, DON'T HOLD ME TO IT. I DON'T REALLY KNOW WHAT I WAS TALKING ABOUT. IT'S LIKE WHEN I TOUCHED IT I JUST FELT THIS WORD... "NAGA," SO I SAID IT.
SO YOU HAVE NO INTENTION OF KILLING ME?
W-WHAT? N-NO... WHY WOULD I--
THAT IS VERY... FORTUNATE.
WHY ARE YOU TALKING LIKE THAT? WHAT ARE YOU--
ACK...
LET ME SHOW YOU.

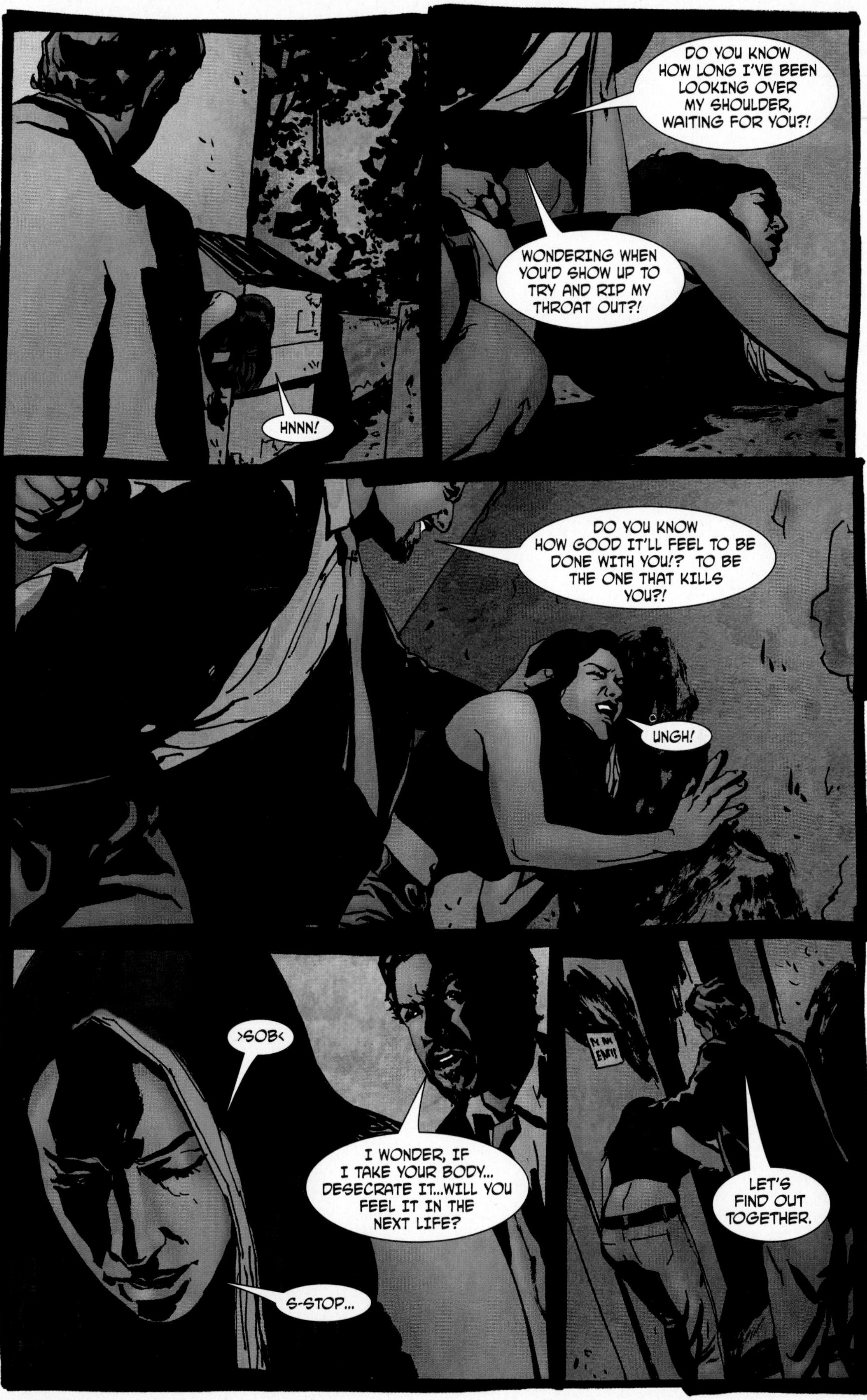
HNNN!
DO YOU KNOW HOW LONG I'VE BEEN LOOKING OVER MY SHOULDER, WAITING FOR YOU?!
WONDERING WHEN YOU'D SHOW UP TO TRY AND RIP MY THROAT OUT?!
DO YOU KNOW HOW GOOD IT'LL FEEL TO BE DONE WITH YOU!? TO BE THE ONE THAT KILLS YOU?!
UNGH!
>SOB<
S-STOP...
I WONDER, IF I TAKE YOUR BODY... DESECRATE IT...WILL YOU FEEL IT IN THE NEXT LIFE?
LET'S FIND OUT TOGETHER.

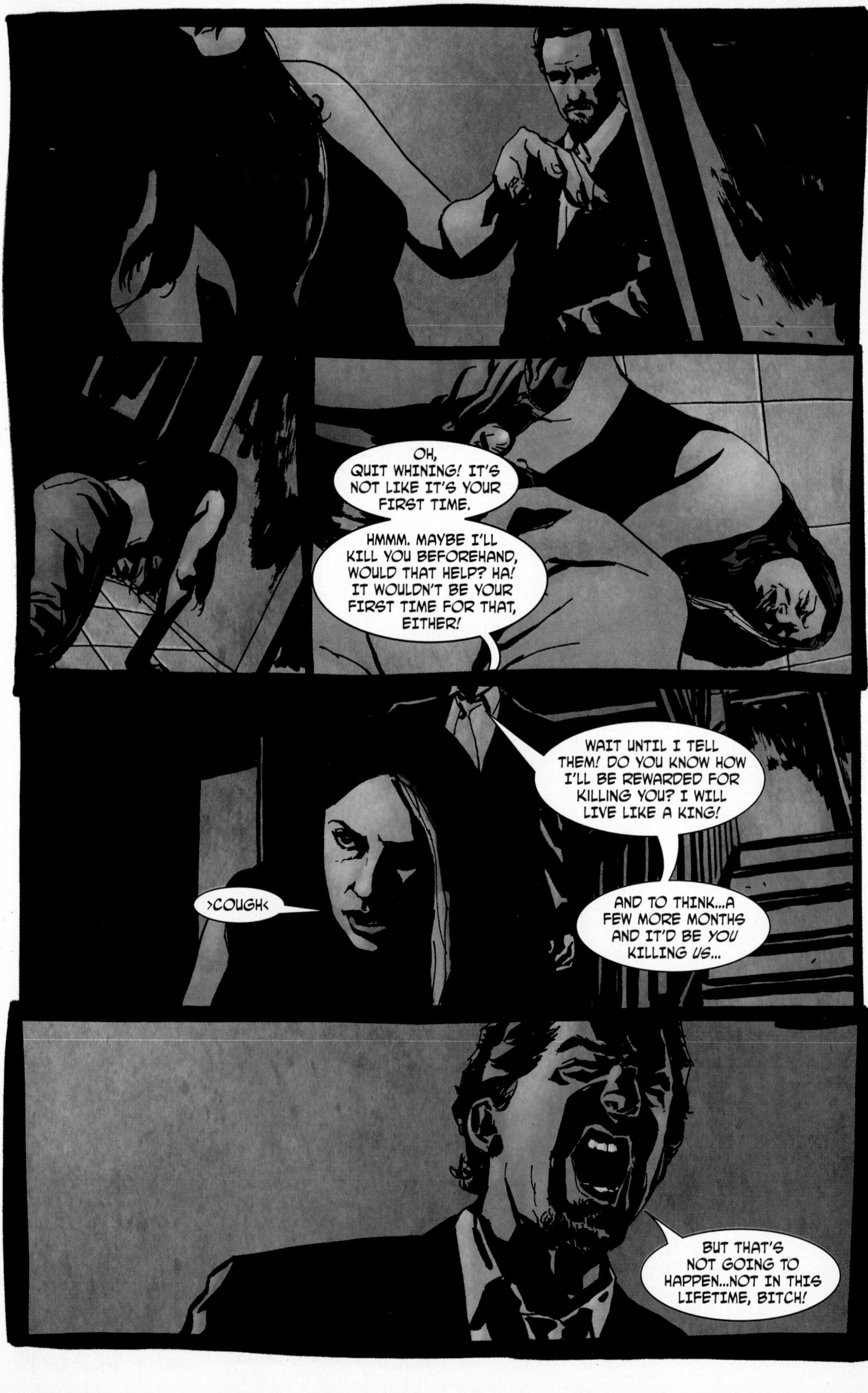
OH, QUIT WHINING! IT'S NOT LIKE IT'S YOUR FIRST TIME.
HMMM. MAYBE I'LL KILL YOU BEFOREHAND, WOULD THAT HELP? HA! IT WOULDN'T BE YOUR FIRST TIME FOR THAT, EITHER!
WAIT UNTIL I TELL THEM! DO YOU KNOW HOW I'LL BE REWARDED FOR KILLING YOU? I WILL LIVE LIKE A KING!
AND TO THINK...A FEW MORE MONTHS AND IT'D BE *YOU* KILLING *US*...
>COUGH<
BUT THAT'S NOT GOING TO HAPPEN...NOT IN THIS LIFETIME, BITCH!

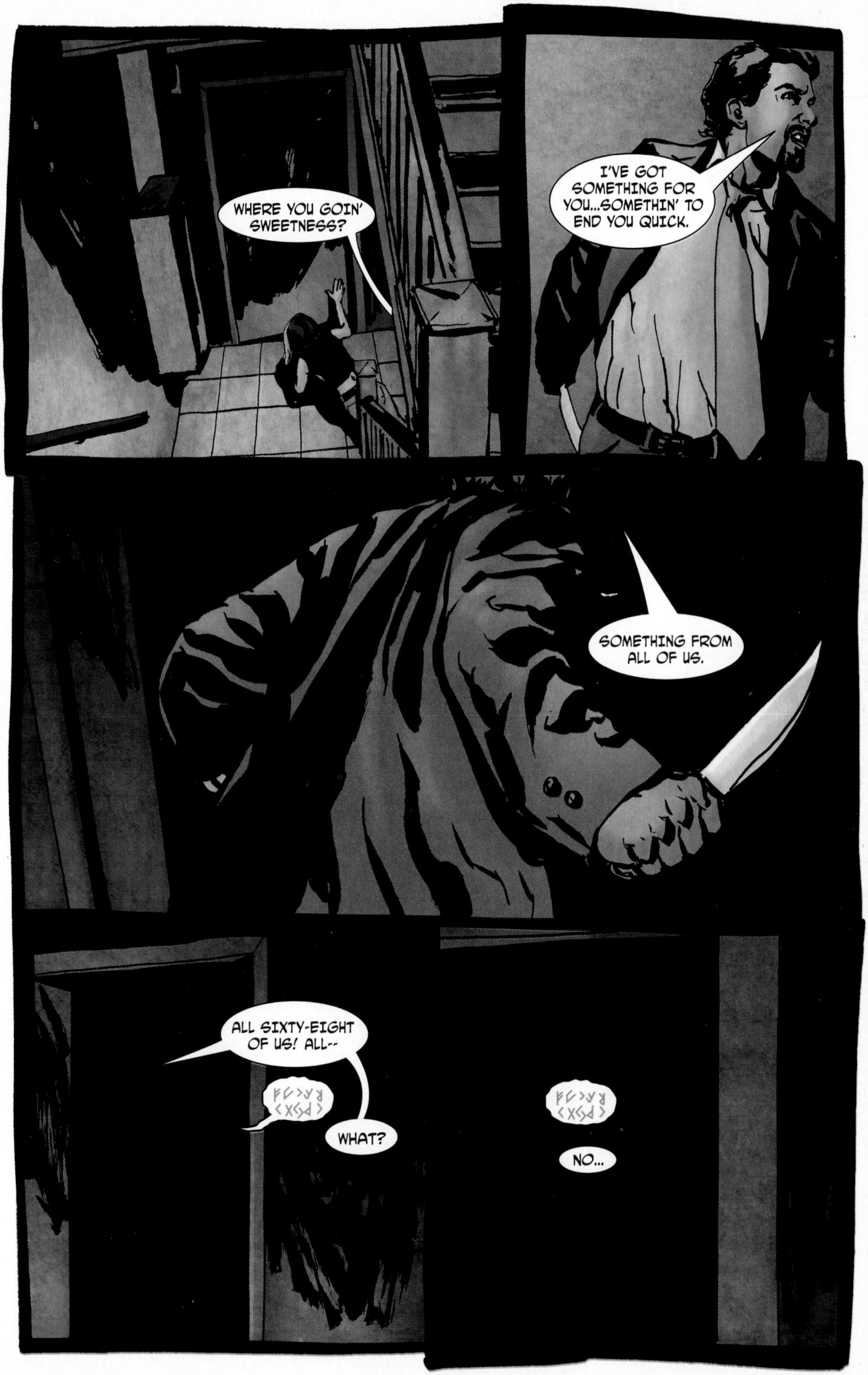
WHERE YOU GOIN' SWEETNESS?
I'VE GOT SOMETHING FOR YOU...SOMETHIN' TO END YOU QUICK.
SOMETHING FROM ALL OF US.
ALL SIXTY-EIGHT OF US! ALL--
WHAT?
NO...

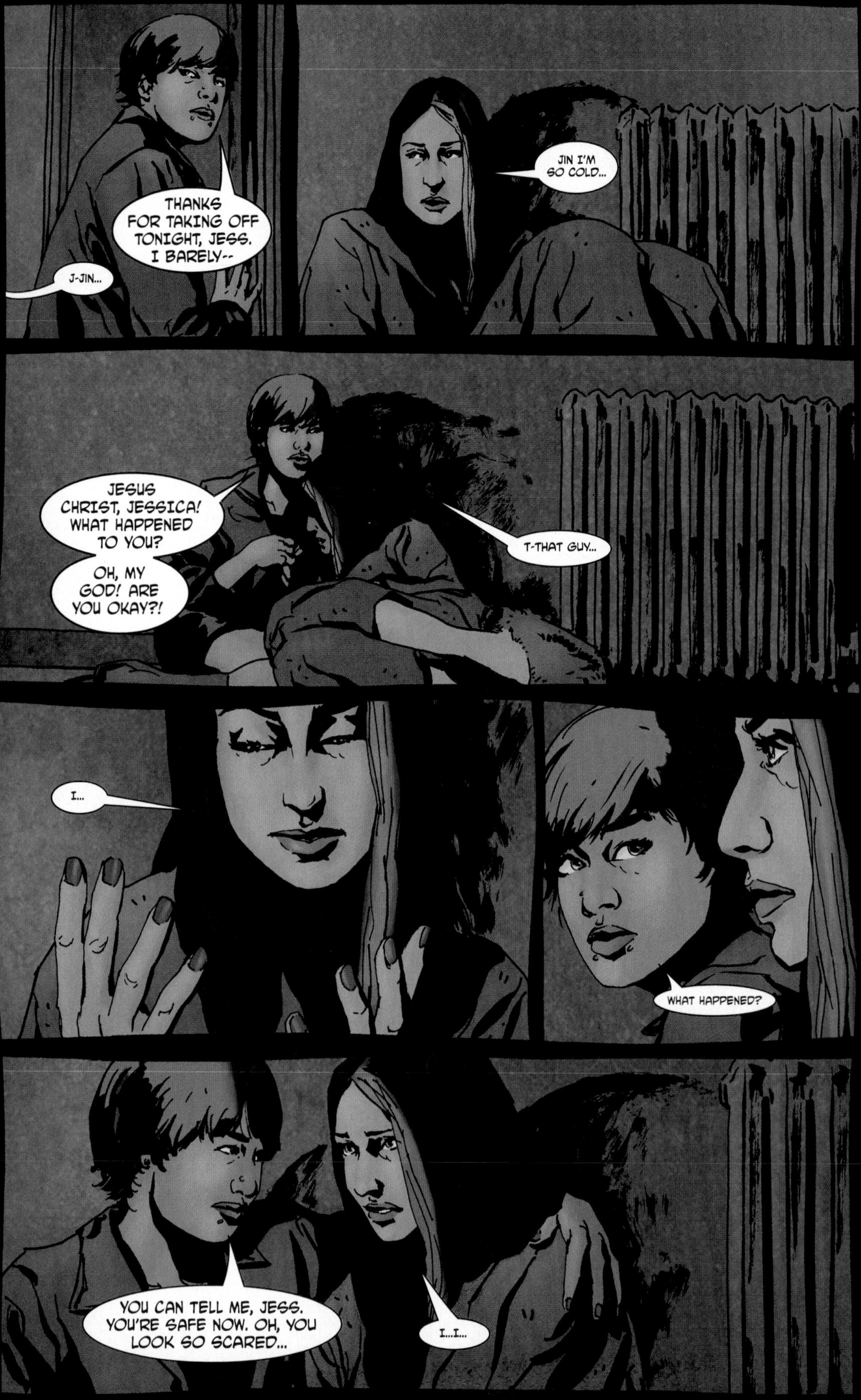
THANKS FOR TAKING OFF TONIGHT, JESS. I BARELY--
J-JIN...
JIN I'M SO COLD...
JESUS CHRIST, JESSICA! WHAT HAPPENED TO YOU?
OH, MY GOD! ARE YOU OKAY?!
T-THAT GUY...
I...
WHAT HAPPENED?
YOU CAN TELL ME, JESS. YOU'RE SAFE NOW. OH, YOU LOOK SO SCARED...
I...I...

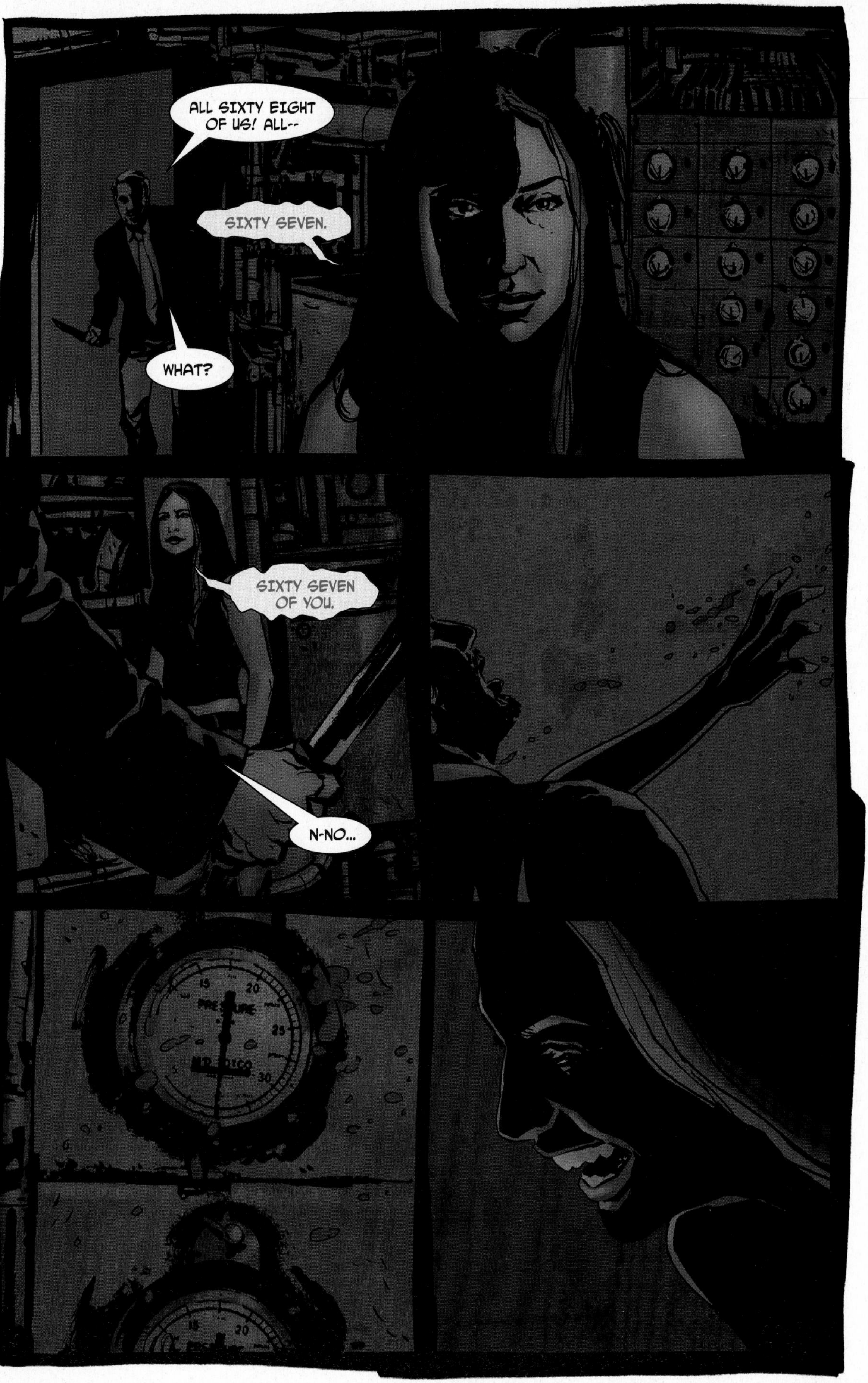
ALL SIXTY EIGHT OF US! ALL--
SIXTY SEVEN.
WHAT?
SIXTY SEVEN OF YOU.
N-NO...

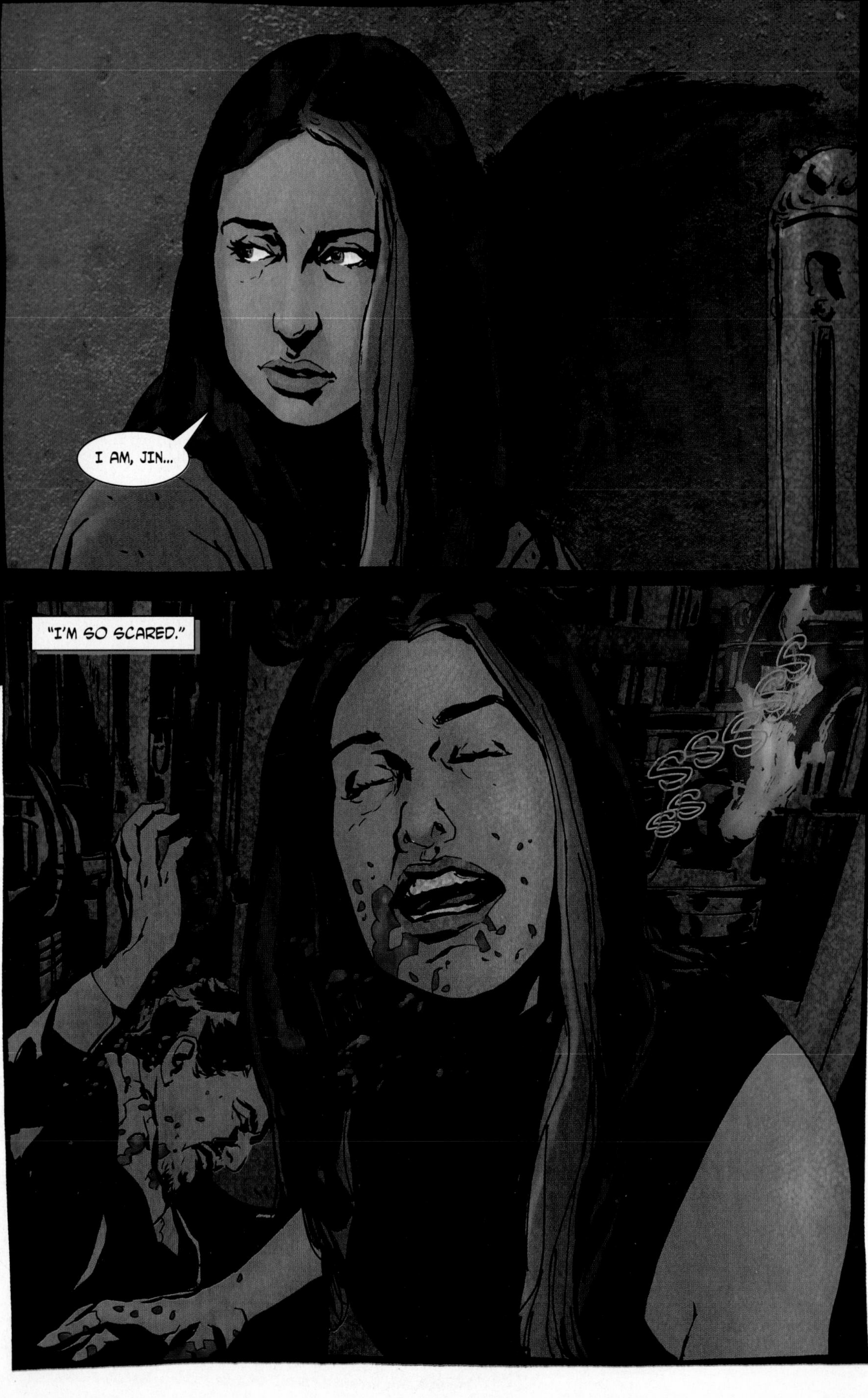
I AM, JIN...
"I'M SO SCARED."
SSSSSSSS

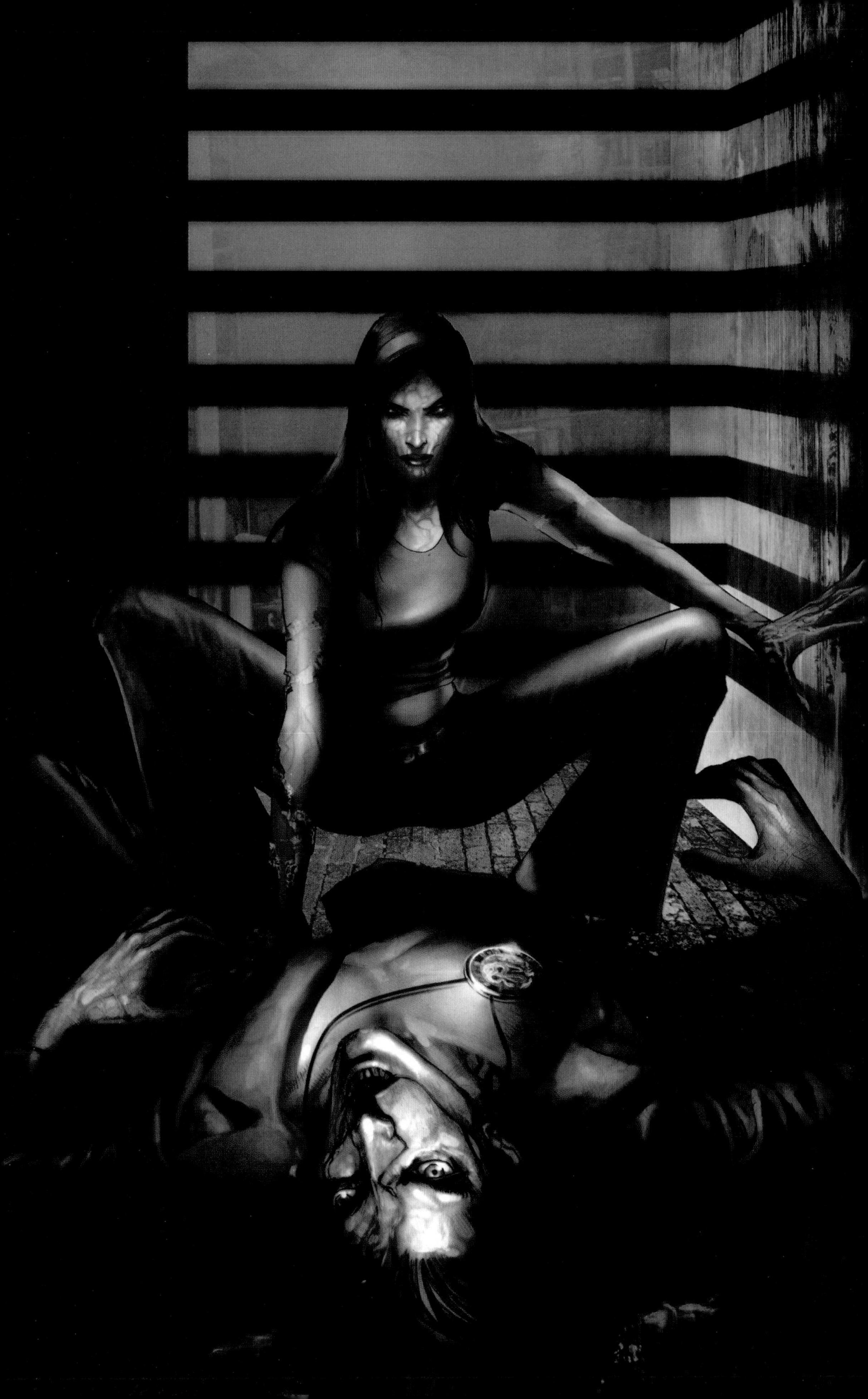

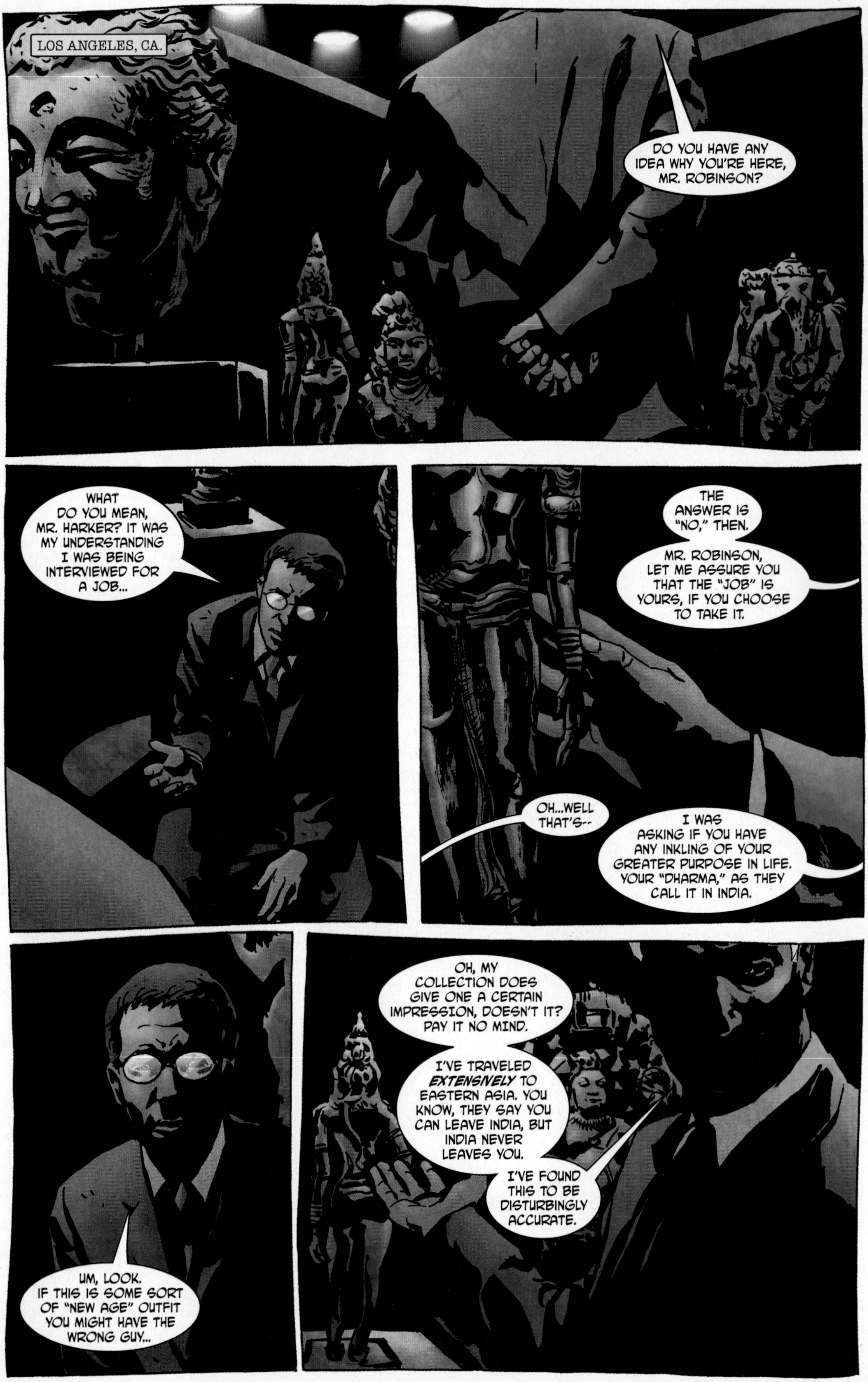
LOS ANGELES, CA.
DO YOU HAVE ANY IDEA WHY YOU'RE HERE, MR. ROBINSON?
WHAT DO YOU MEAN, MR. HARKER? IT WAS MY UNDERSTANDING I WAS BEING INTERVIEWED FOR A JOB...
THE ANSWER IS "NO," THEN.
MR. ROBINSON, LET ME ASSURE YOU THAT THE "JOB" IS YOURS, IF YOU CHOOSE TO TAKE IT.
OH...WELL THAT'S--
I WAS ASKING IF YOU HAVE ANY INKLING OF YOUR GREATER PURPOSE IN LIFE. YOUR "DHARMA," AS THEY CALL IT IN INDIA.
UM, LOOK. IF THIS IS SOME SORT OF "NEW AGE" OUTFIT YOU MIGHT HAVE THE WRONG GUY...
OH, MY COLLECTION DOES GIVE ONE A CERTAIN IMPRESSION, DOESN'T IT? PAY IT NO MIND.
I'VE TRAVELED *EXTENSIVELY* TO EASTERN ASIA. YOU KNOW, THEY SAY YOU CAN LEAVE INDIA, BUT INDIA NEVER LEAVES YOU.
I'VE FOUND THIS TO BE DISTURBINGLY ACCURATE.

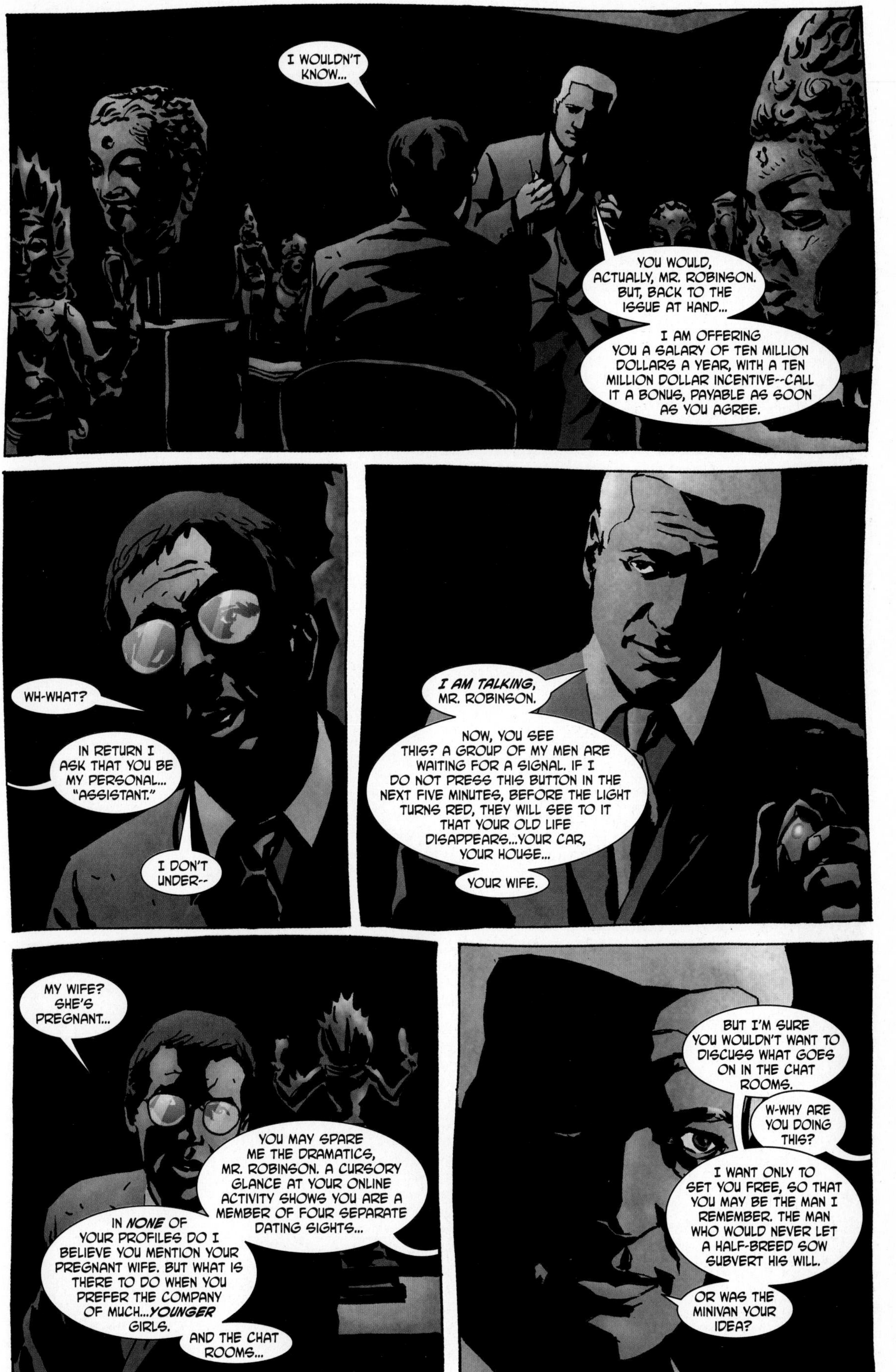
I WOULDN'T KNOW...
YOU WOULD, ACTUALLY, MR. ROBINSON. BUT, BACK TO THE ISSUE AT HAND...
I AM OFFERING YOU A SALARY OF TEN MILLION DOLLARS A YEAR, WITH A TEN MILLION DOLLAR INCENTIVE--CALL IT A BONUS, PAYABLE AS SOON AS YOU AGREE.
WH-WHAT?
IN RETURN I ASK THAT YOU BE MY PERSONAL... "ASSISTANT."
I DON'T UNDER--
I AM TALKING, MR. ROBINSON.
NOW, YOU SEE THIS? A GROUP OF MY MEN ARE WAITING FOR A SIGNAL. IF I DO NOT PRESS THIS BUTTON IN THE NEXT FIVE MINUTES, BEFORE THE LIGHT TURNS RED, THEY WILL SEE TO IT THAT YOUR OLD LIFE DISAPPEARS...YOUR CAR, YOUR HOUSE...
YOUR WIFE.
MY WIFE? SHE'S PREGNANT...
YOU MAY SPARE ME THE DRAMATICS, MR. ROBINSON. A CURSORY GLANCE AT YOUR ONLINE ACTIVITY SHOWS YOU ARE A MEMBER OF FOUR SEPARATE DATING SIGHTS...
IN *NONE* OF YOUR PROFILES DO I BELIEVE YOU MENTION YOUR PREGNANT WIFE. BUT WHAT IS THERE TO DO WHEN YOU PREFER THE COMPANY OF MUCH...*YOUNGER* GIRLS.
AND THE CHAT ROOMS...
BUT I'M SURE YOU WOULDN'T WANT TO DISCUSS WHAT GOES ON IN THE CHAT ROOMS.
W-WHY ARE YOU DOING THIS?
I WANT ONLY TO SET YOU FREE, SO THAT YOU MAY BE THE MAN I REMEMBER. THE MAN WHO WOULD NEVER LET A HALF-BREED SOW SUBVERT HIS WILL.
OR WAS THE MINIVAN YOUR IDEA?

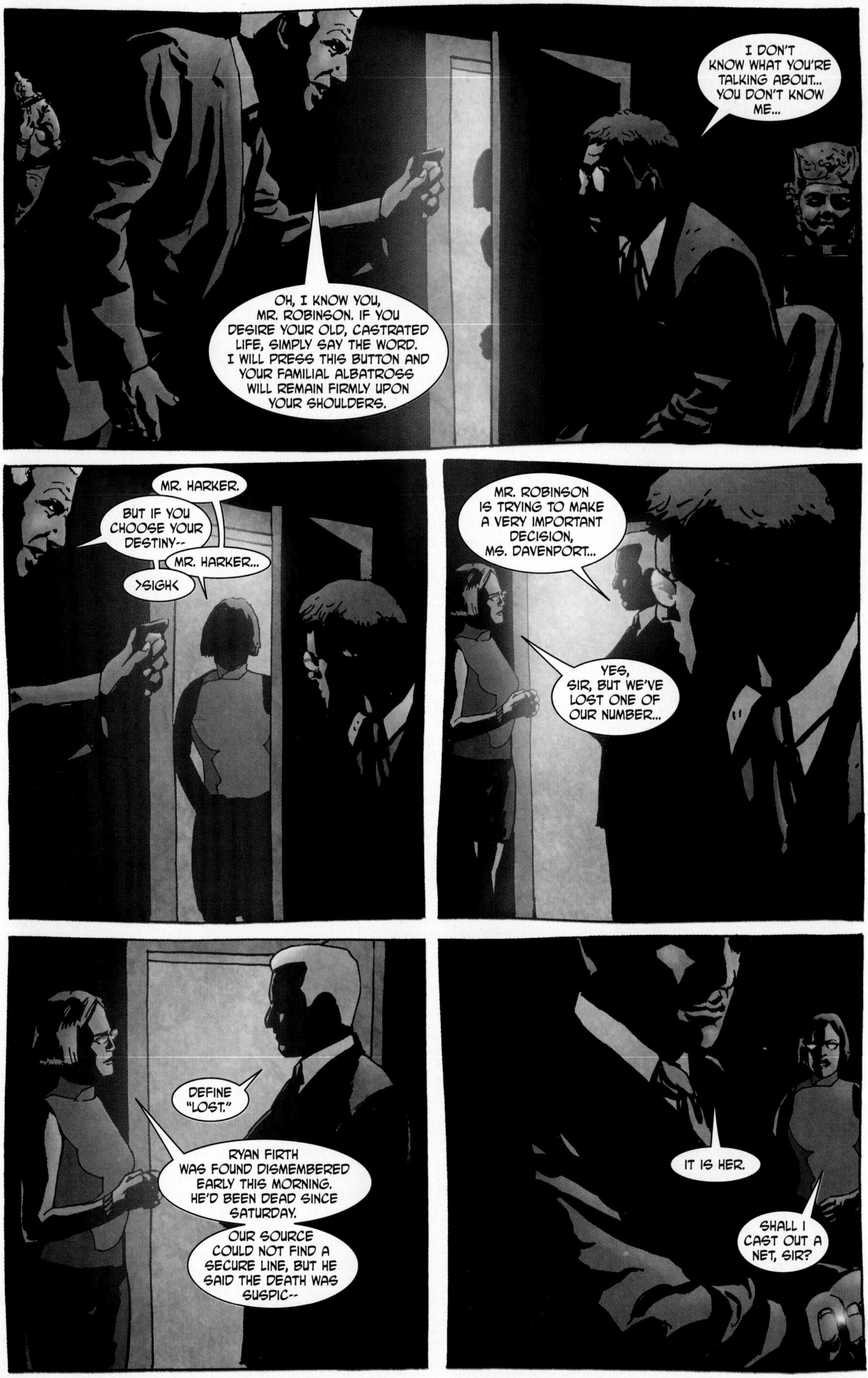
I DON'T KNOW WHAT YOU'RE TALKING ABOUT... YOU DON'T KNOW ME...
OH, I KNOW YOU, MR. ROBINSON. IF YOU DESIRE YOUR OLD, CASTRATED LIFE, SIMPLY SAY THE WORD. I WILL PRESS THIS BUTTON AND YOUR FAMILIAL ALBATROSS WILL REMAIN FIRMLY UPON YOUR SHOULDERS.
MR. HARKER.
BUT IF YOU CHOOSE YOUR DESTINY--
MR. HARKER...
>SIGH<
MR. ROBINSON IS TRYING TO MAKE A VERY IMPORTANT DECISION, MS. DAVENPORT...
YES, SIR, BUT WE'VE LOST ONE OF OUR NUMBER...
DEFINE "LOST."
RYAN FIRTH WAS FOUND DISMEMBERED EARLY THIS MORNING. HE'D BEEN DEAD SINCE SATURDAY.
OUR SOURCE COULD NOT FIND A SECURE LINE, BUT HE SAID THE DEATH WAS SUSPIC--
IT IS HER.
SHALL I CAST OUT A NET, SIR?

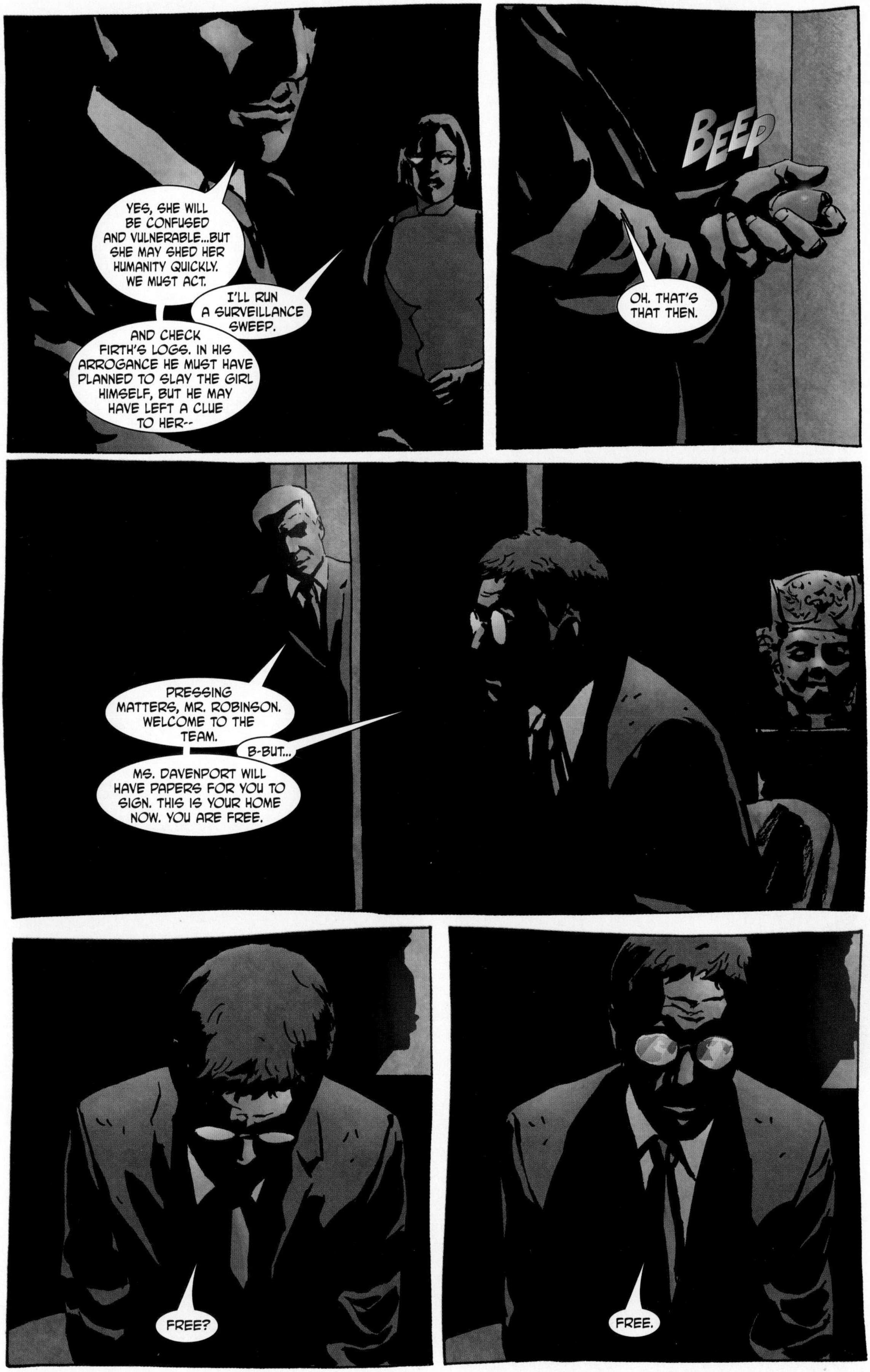
YES, SHE WILL BE CONFUSED AND VULNERABLE...BUT SHE MAY SHED HER HUMANITY QUICKLY. WE MUST ACT.
I'LL RUN A SURVEILLANCE SWEEP.
AND CHECK FIRTH'S LOGS. IN HIS ARROGANCE HE MUST HAVE PLANNED TO SLAY THE GIRL HIMSELF, BUT HE MAY HAVE LEFT A CLUE TO HER--
BEEP
OH. THAT'S THAT THEN.
PRESSING MATTERS, MR. ROBINSON. WELCOME TO THE TEAM.
B-BUT...
MS. DAVENPORT WILL HAVE PAPERS FOR YOU TO SIGN. THIS IS YOUR HOME NOW. YOU ARE FREE.
FREE?
FREE.

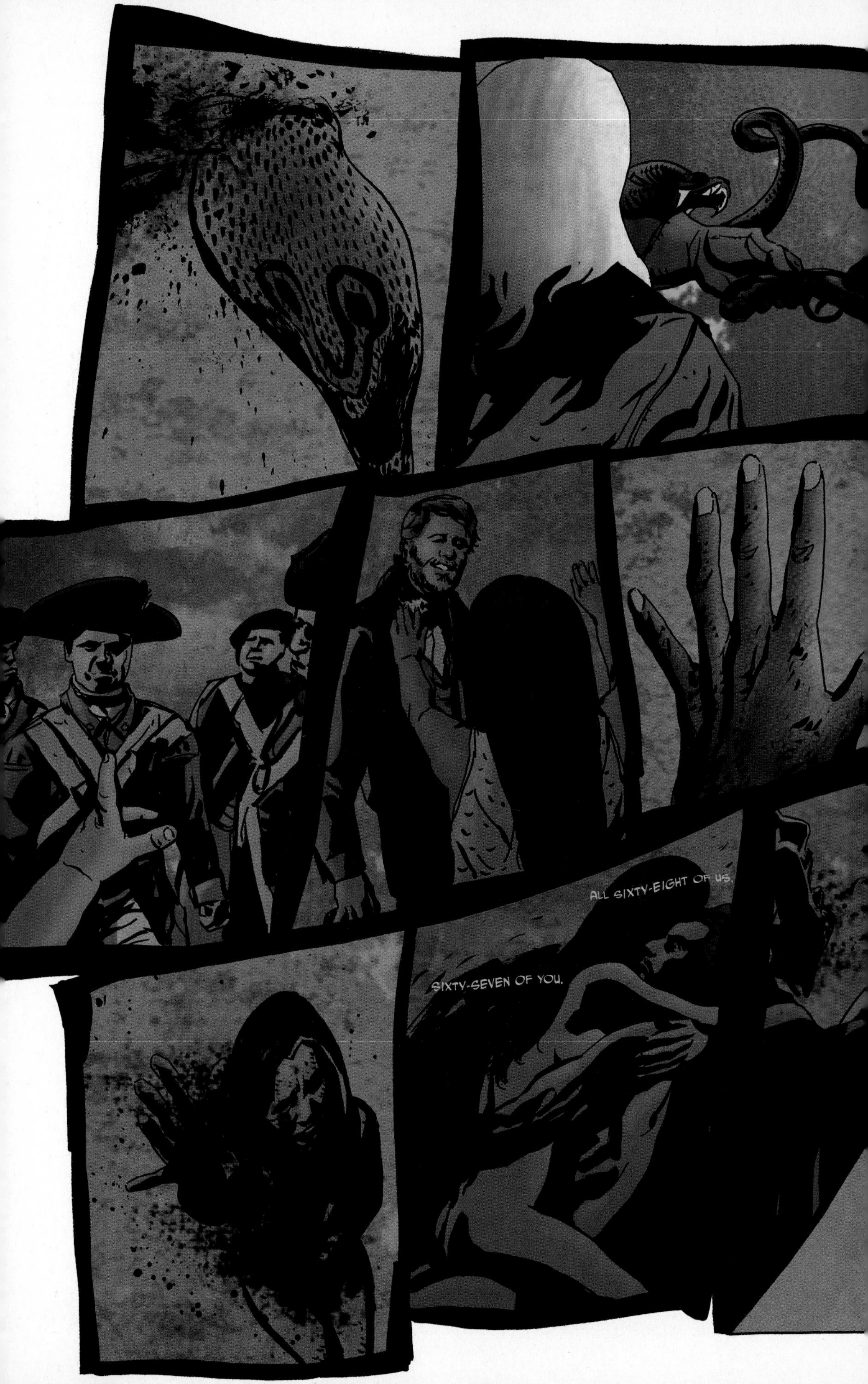
ALL SIXTY-EIGHT OF US.
SIXTY-SEVEN OF YOU.

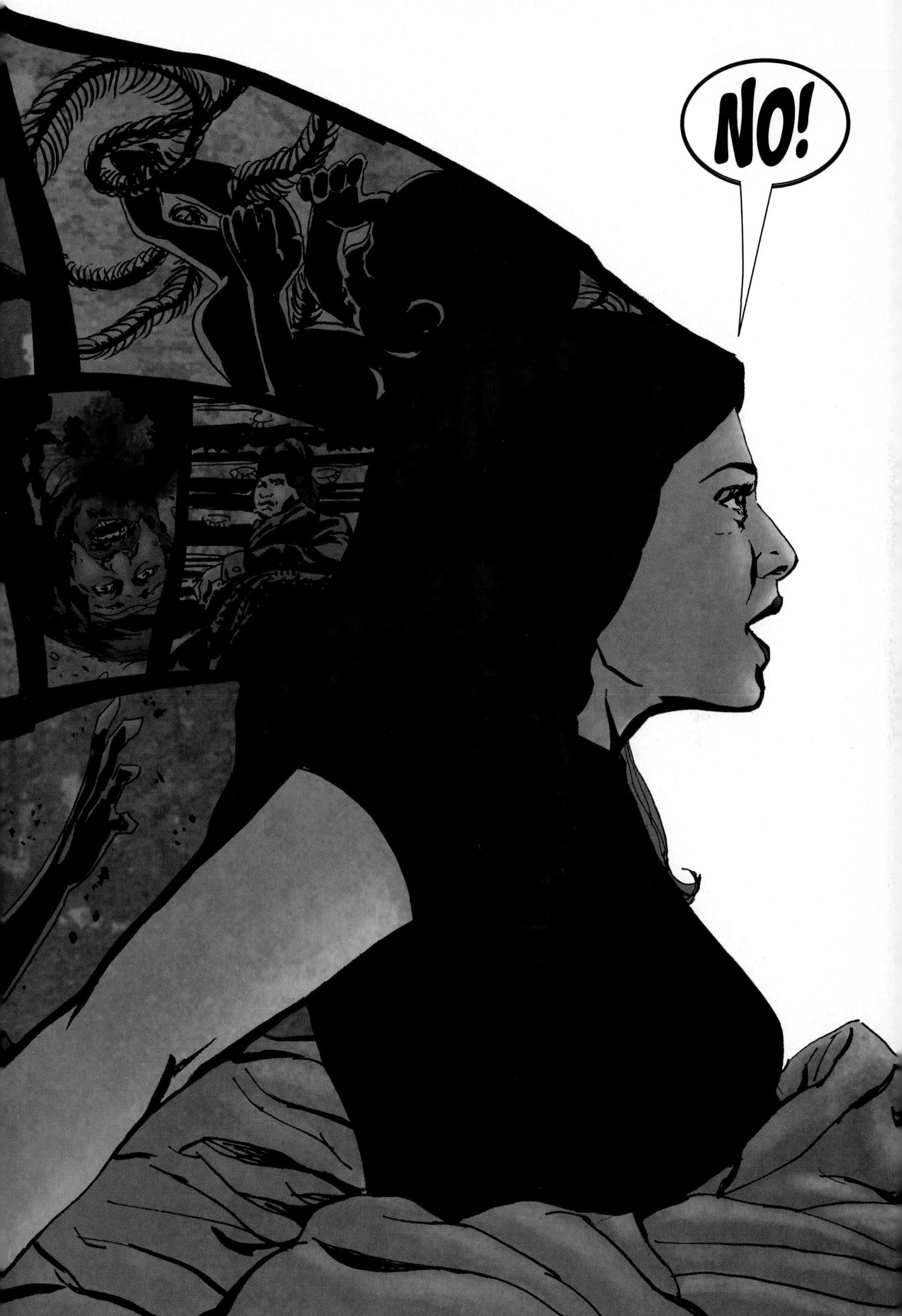
NO!

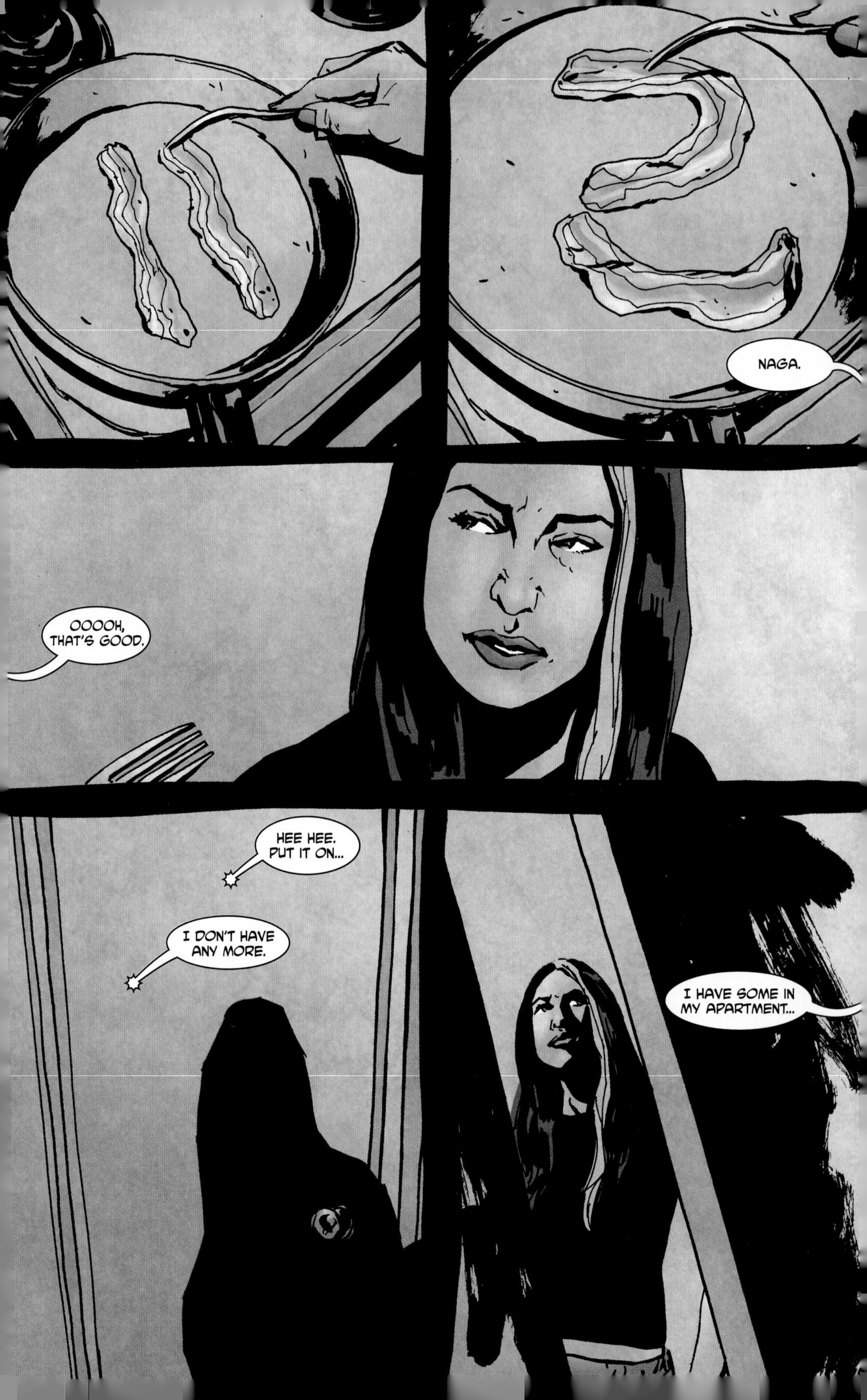
NAGA.
OOOOH, THAT'S GOOD.
HEE HEE. PUT IT ON...
I DON'T HAVE ANY MORE.
I HAVE SOME IN MY APARTMENT...

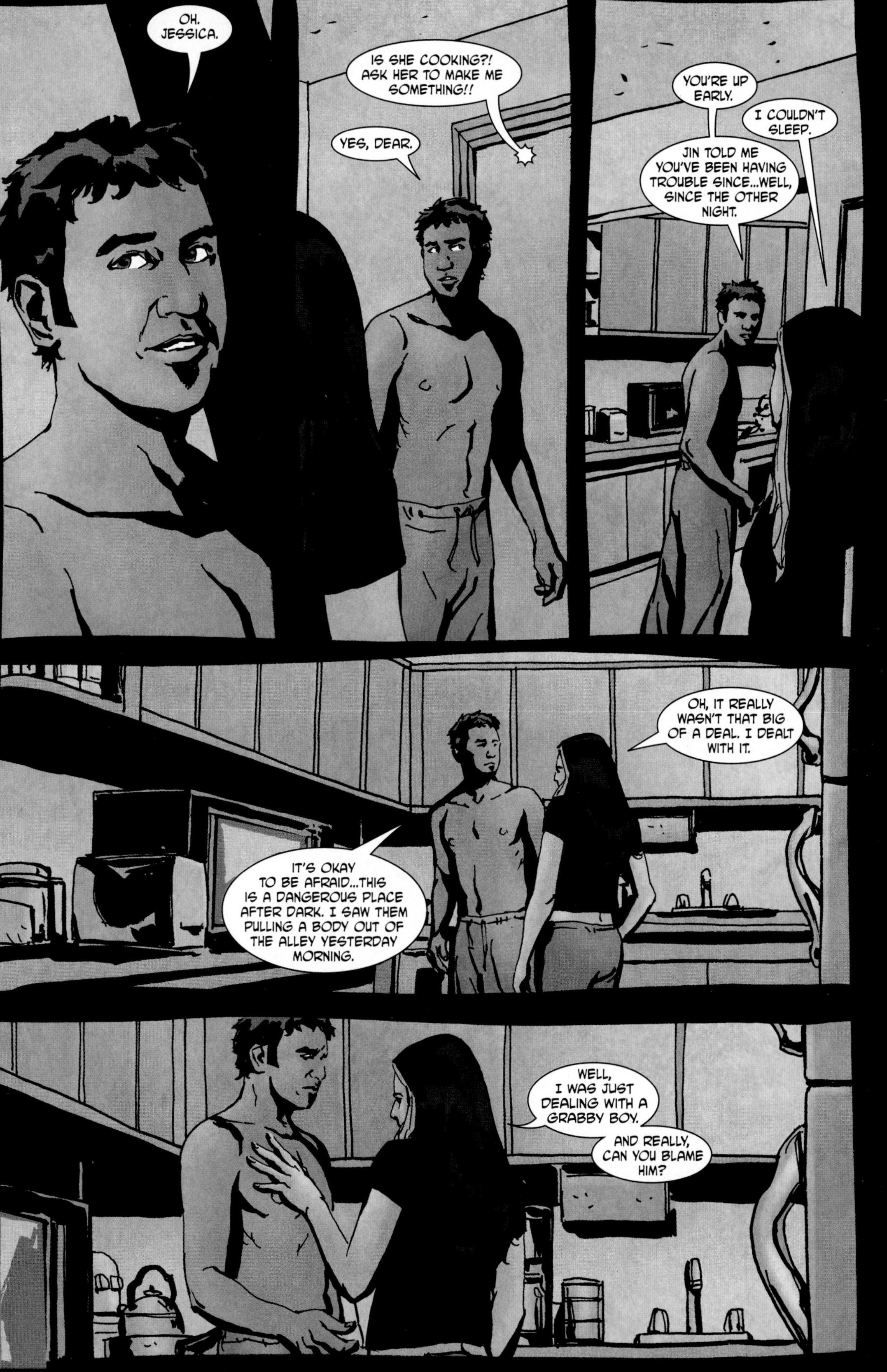
OH. JESSICA.
IS SHE COOKING?! ASK HER TO MAKE ME SOMETHING!!
YES, DEAR.
YOU'RE UP EARLY.
I COULDN'T SLEEP.
JIN TOLD ME YOU'VE BEEN HAVING TROUBLE SINCE...WELL, SINCE THE OTHER NIGHT.
OH, IT REALLY WASN'T THAT BIG OF A DEAL. I DEALT WITH IT.
IT'S OKAY TO BE AFRAID...THIS IS A DANGEROUS PLACE AFTER DARK. I SAW THEM PULLING A BODY OUT OF THE ALLEY YESTERDAY MORNING.
WELL, I WAS JUST DEALING WITH A GRABBY BOY.
AND REALLY, CAN YOU BLAME HIM?

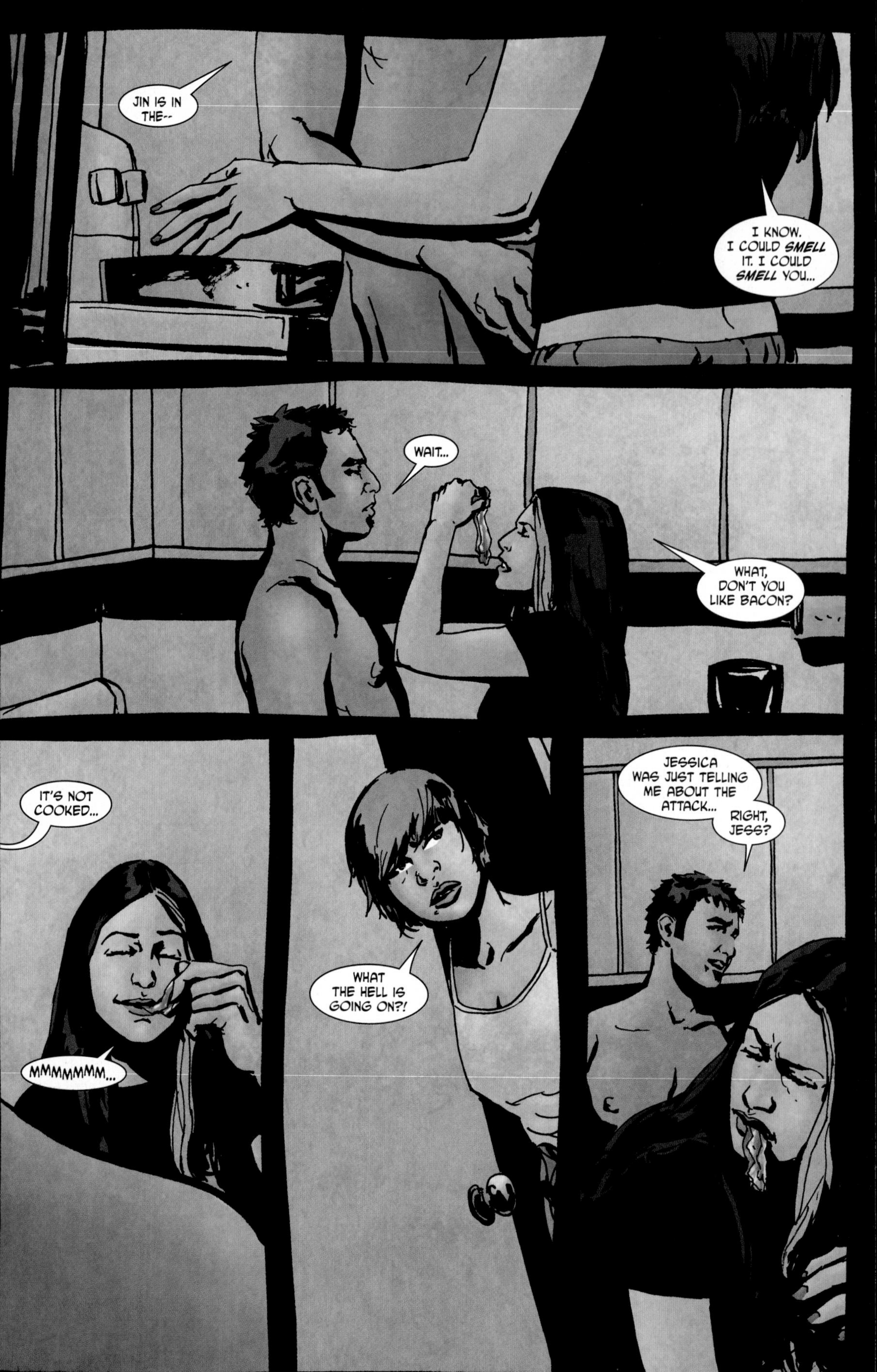
JIN IS IN THE--
I KNOW. I COULD SMELL IT. I COULD SMELL YOU...
WAIT...
WHAT, DON'T YOU LIKE BACON?
IT'S NOT COOKED...
MMMMMMM...
WHAT THE HELL IS GOING ON?!
JESSICA WAS JUST TELLING ME ABOUT THE ATTACK...
RIGHT, JESS?

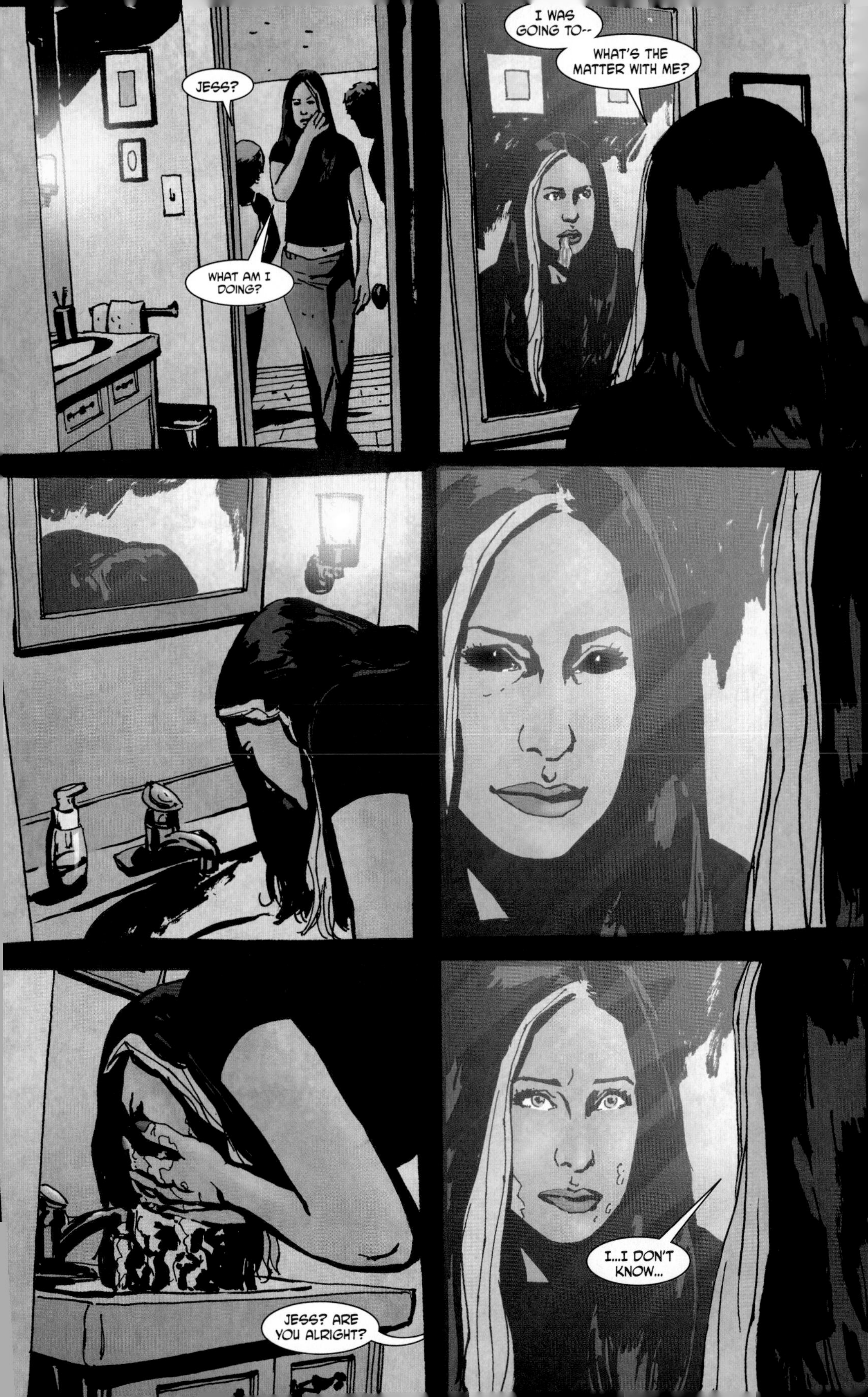
JESS?
WHAT AM I DOING?
I WAS GOING TO--
WHAT'S THE MATTER WITH ME?
I...I DON'T KNOW...
JESS? ARE YOU ALRIGHT?

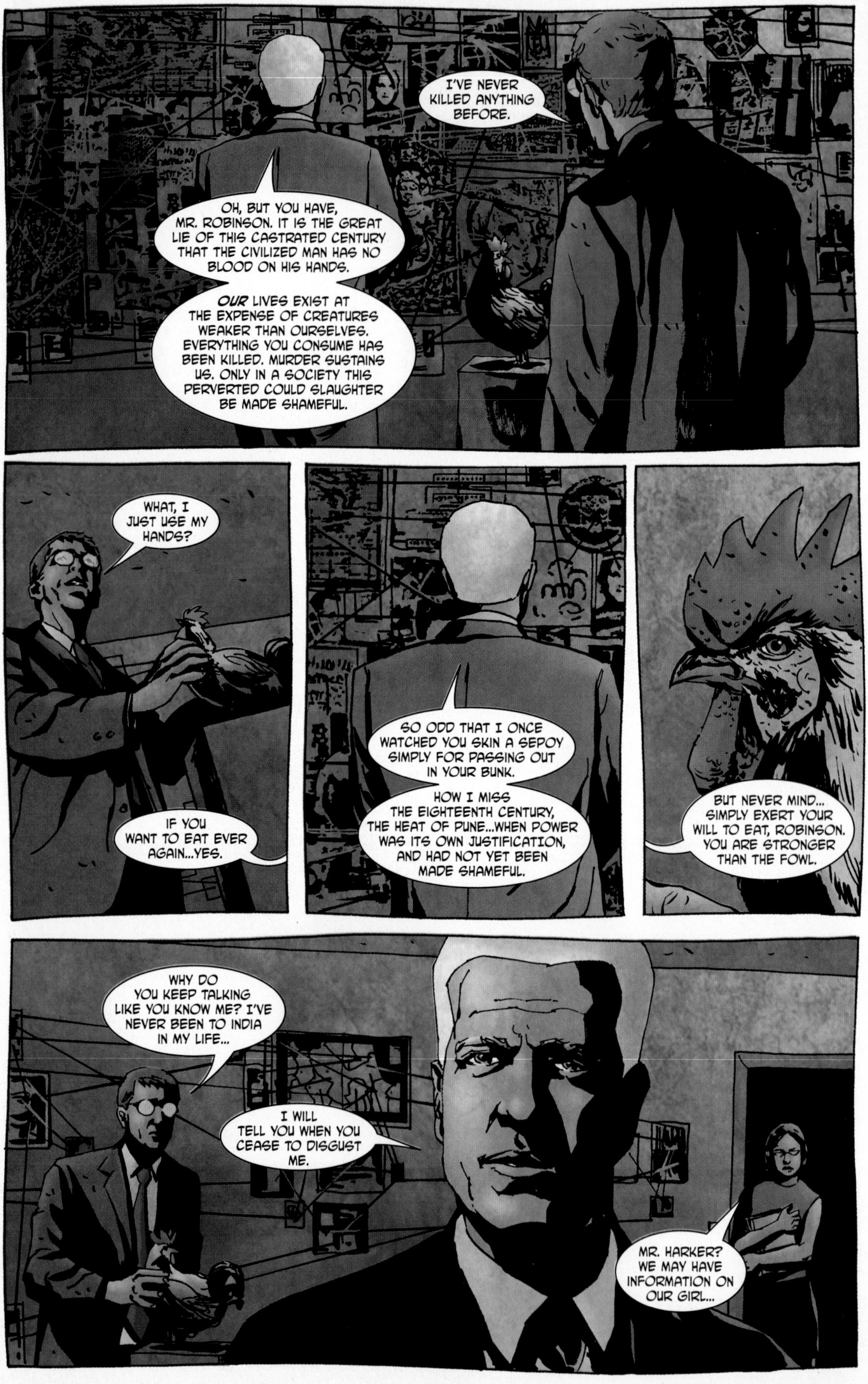
I'VE NEVER KILLED ANYTHING BEFORE.
OH, BUT YOU HAVE, MR. ROBINSON. IT IS THE GREAT LIE OF THIS CASTRATED CENTURY THAT THE CIVILIZED MAN HAS NO BLOOD ON HIS HANDS.
OUR LIVES EXIST AT THE EXPENSE OF CREATURES WEAKER THAN OURSELVES. EVERYTHING YOU CONSUME HAS BEEN KILLED. MURDER SUSTAINS US. ONLY IN A SOCIETY THIS PERVERTED COULD SLAUGHTER BE MADE SHAMEFUL.
WHAT, I JUST USE MY HANDS?
IF YOU WANT TO EAT EVER AGAIN...YES.
SO ODD THAT I ONCE WATCHED YOU SKIN A SEPOY SIMPLY FOR PASSING OUT IN YOUR BUNK.
HOW I MISS THE EIGHTEENTH CENTURY, THE HEAT OF PUNE...WHEN POWER WAS ITS OWN JUSTIFICATION, AND HAD NOT YET BEEN MADE SHAMEFUL.
BUT NEVER MIND... SIMPLY EXERT YOUR WILL TO EAT, ROBINSON. YOU ARE STRONGER THAN THE FOWL.
WHY DO YOU KEEP TALKING LIKE YOU KNOW ME? I'VE NEVER BEEN TO INDIA IN MY LIFE...
I WILL TELL YOU WHEN YOU CEASE TO DISGUST ME.
MR. HARKER? WE MAY HAVE INFORMATION ON OUR GIRL...

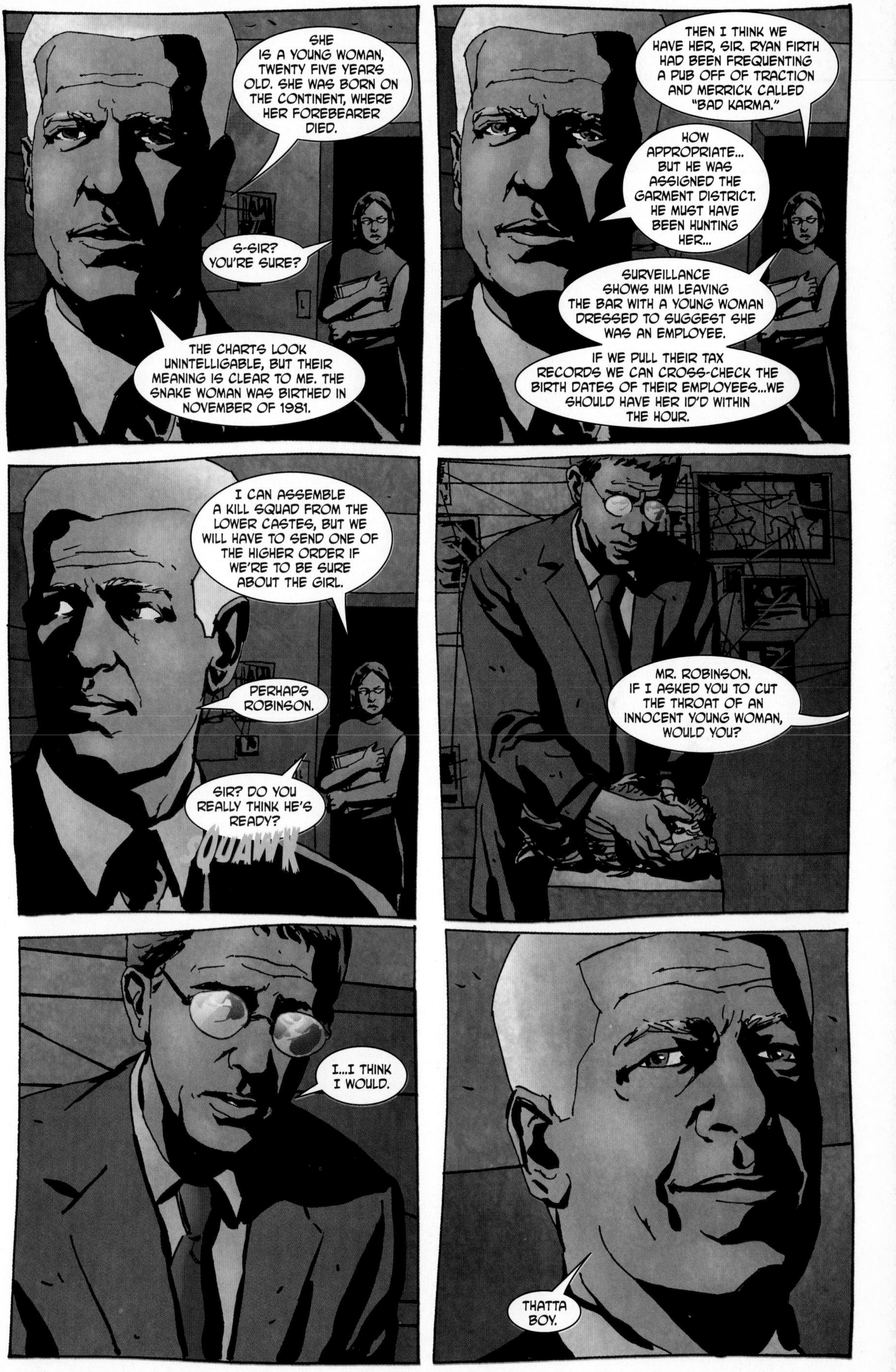
SHE IS A YOUNG WOMAN, TWENTY FIVE YEARS OLD. SHE WAS BORN ON THE CONTINENT, WHERE HER FOREBEARER DIED.
S-SIR? YOU'RE SURE?
THE CHARTS LOOK UNINTELLIGABLE, BUT THEIR MEANING IS CLEAR TO ME. THE SNAKE WOMAN WAS BIRTHED IN NOVEMBER OF 1981.
THEN I THINK WE HAVE HER, SIR. RYAN FIRTH HAD BEEN FREQUENTING A PUB OFF OF TRACTION AND MERRICK CALLED "BAD KARMA."
HOW APPROPRIATE... BUT HE WAS ASSIGNED THE GARMENT DISTRICT. HE MUST HAVE BEEN HUNTING HER...
SURVEILLANCE SHOWS HIM LEAVING THE BAR WITH A YOUNG WOMAN DRESSED TO SUGGEST SHE WAS AN EMPLOYEE.
IF WE PULL THEIR TAX RECORDS WE CAN CROSS-CHECK THE BIRTH DATES OF THEIR EMPLOYEES...WE SHOULD HAVE HER ID'D WITHIN THE HOUR.
I CAN ASSEMBLE A KILL SQUAD FROM THE LOWER CASTES, BUT WE WILL HAVE TO SEND ONE OF THE HIGHER ORDER IF WE'RE TO BE SURE ABOUT THE GIRL.
PERHAPS ROBINSON.
SIR? DO YOU REALLY THINK HE'S READY?
SQUAWK
MR. ROBINSON. IF I ASKED YOU TO CUT THE THROAT OF AN INNOCENT YOUNG WOMAN, WOULD YOU?
I...I THINK I WOULD.
THATTA BOY.

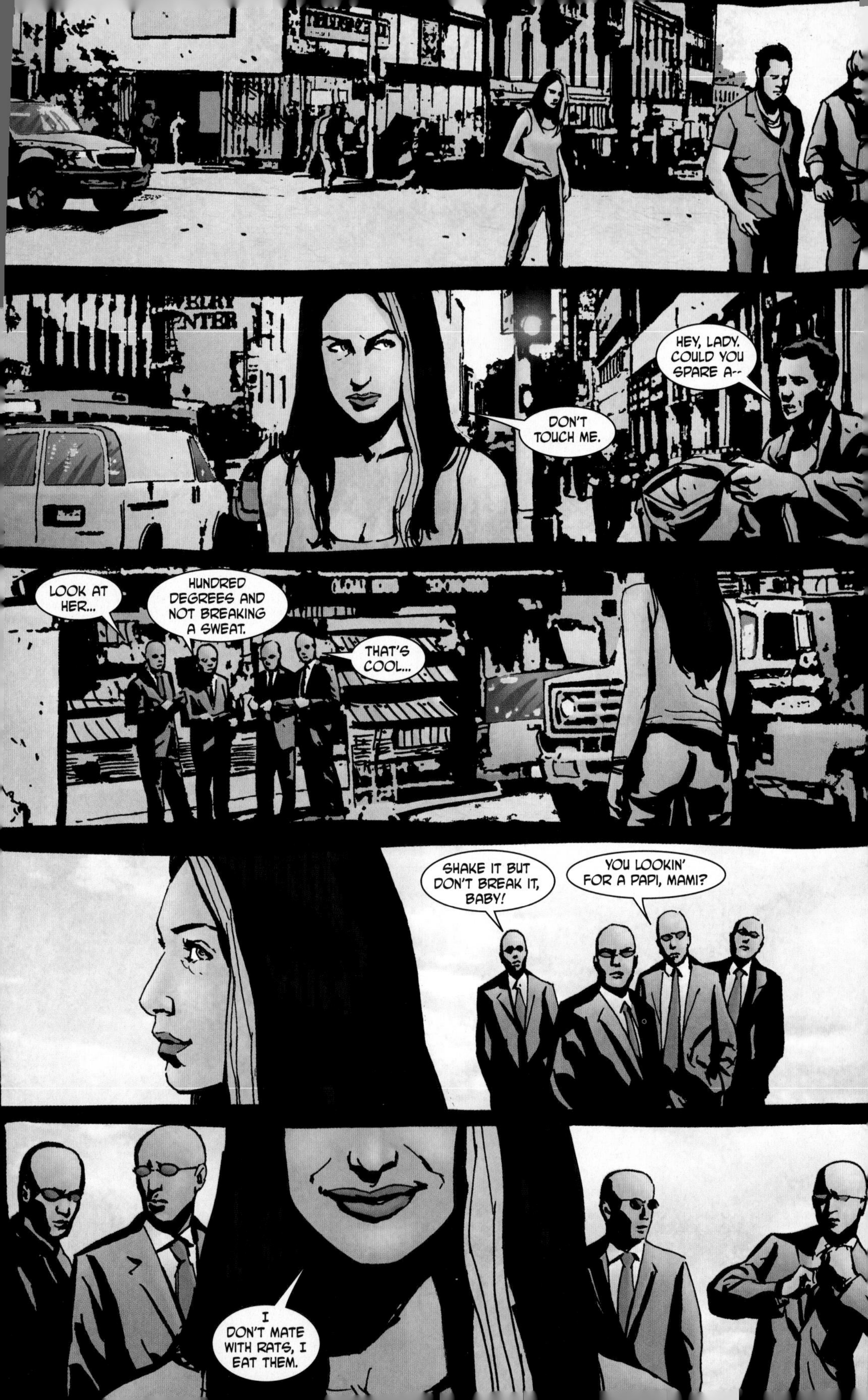
HEY, LADY. COULD YOU SPARE A--
DON'T TOUCH ME.
LOOK AT HER...
HUNDRED DEGREES AND NOT BREAKING A SWEAT.
THAT'S COOL...
SHAKE IT BUT DON'T BREAK IT, BABY!
YOU LOOKIN' FOR A PAPI, MAMI?
I DON'T MATE WITH RATS, I EAT THEM.

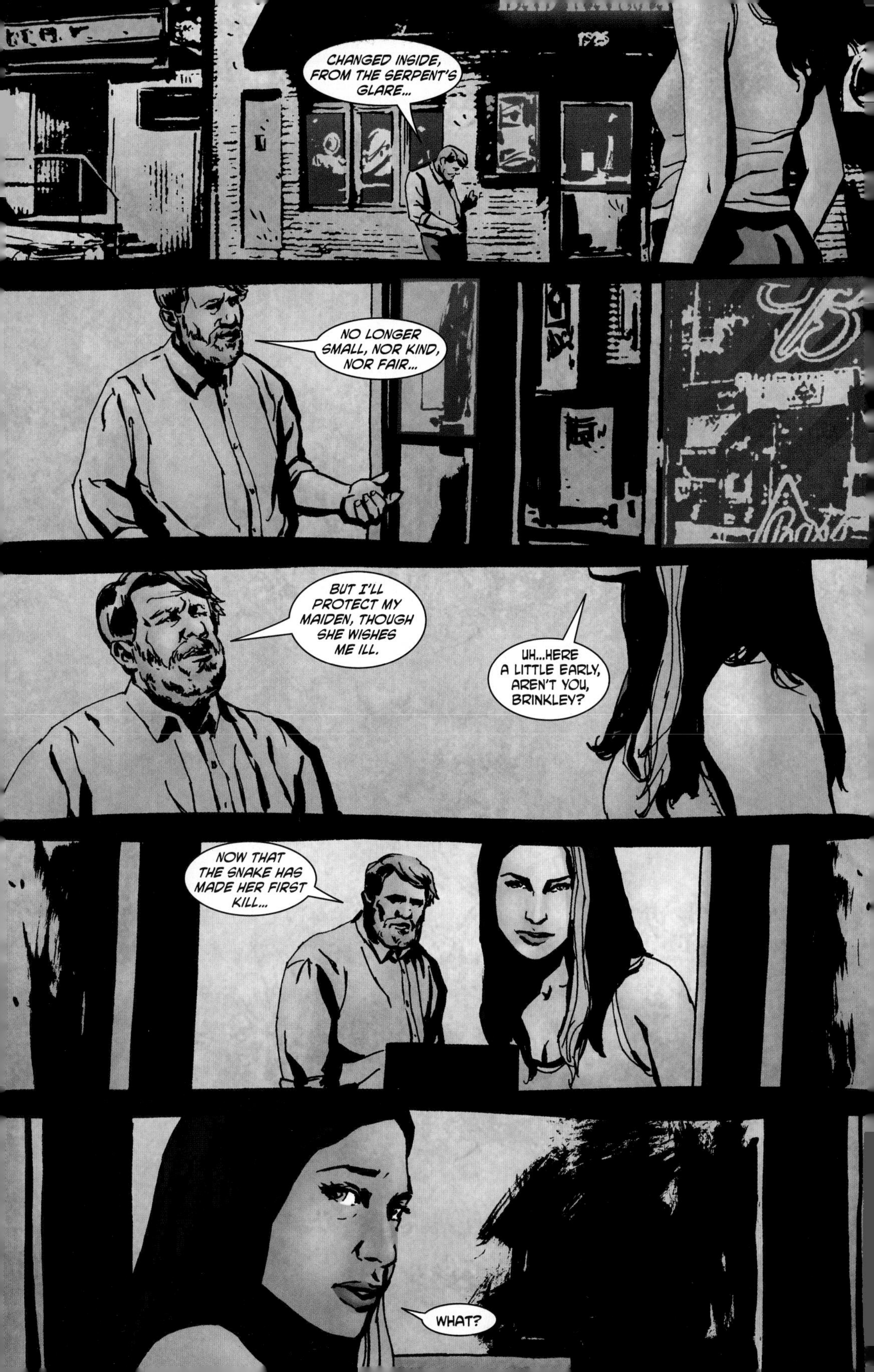
CHANGED INSIDE, FROM THE SERPENT'S GLARE...
NO LONGER SMALL, NOR KIND, NOR FAIR...
BUT I'LL PROTECT MY MAIDEN, THOUGH SHE WISHES ME ILL.
UH...HERE A LITTLE EARLY, AREN'T YOU, BRINKLEY?
NOW THAT THE SNAKE HAS MADE HER FIRST KILL...
WHAT?

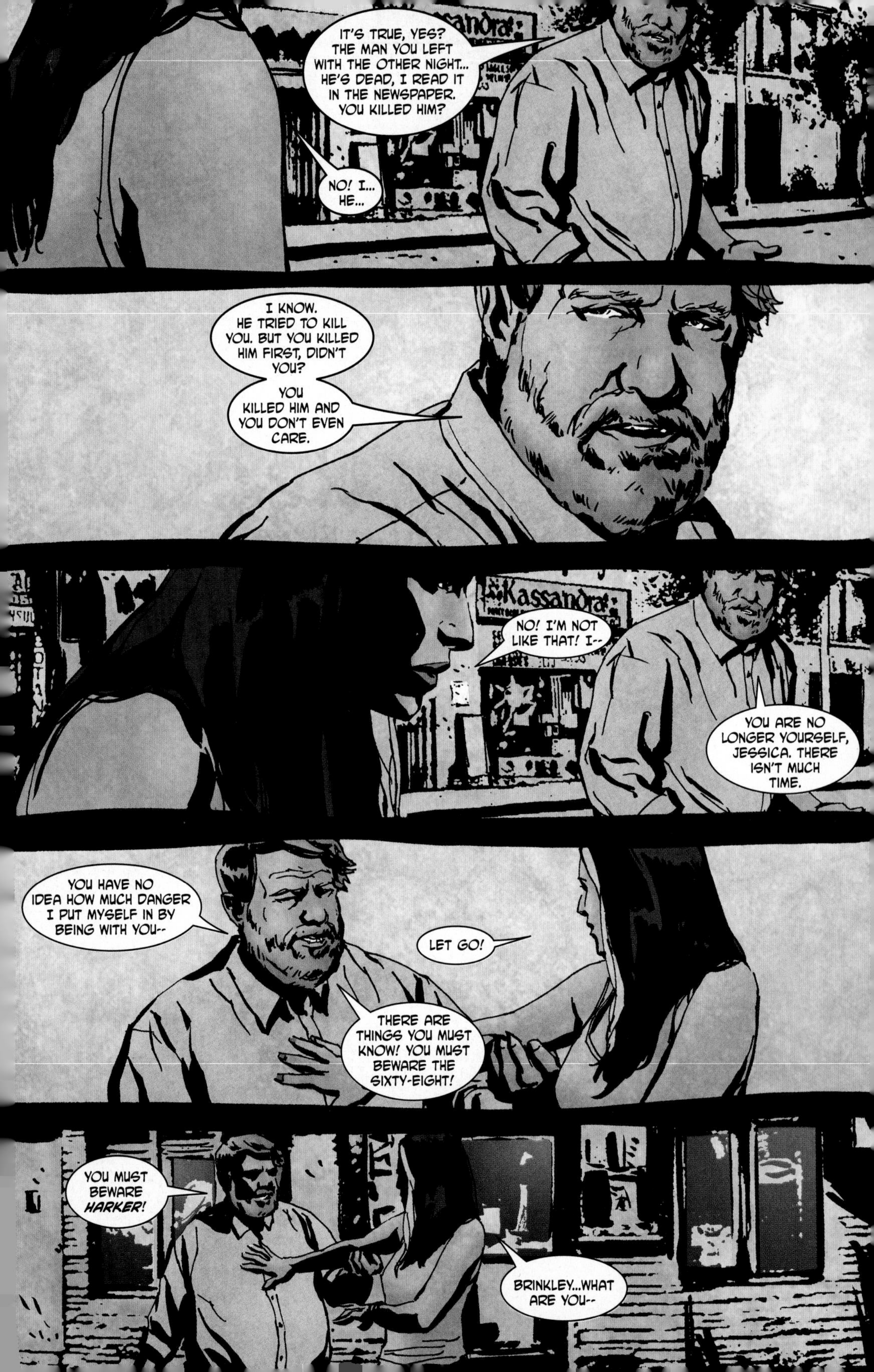
IT'S TRUE, YES? THE MAN YOU LEFT WITH THE OTHER NIGHT... HE'S DEAD, I READ IT IN THE NEWSPAPER. YOU KILLED HIM?
NO! I... HE...
I KNOW. HE TRIED TO KILL YOU. BUT YOU KILLED HIM FIRST, DIDN'T YOU?
YOU KILLED HIM AND YOU DON'T EVEN CARE.
NO! I'M NOT LIKE THAT! I--
YOU ARE NO LONGER YOURSELF, JESSICA. THERE ISN'T MUCH TIME.
YOU HAVE NO IDEA HOW MUCH DANGER I PUT MYSELF IN BY BEING WITH YOU--
LET GO!
THERE ARE THINGS YOU MUST KNOW! YOU MUST BEWARE THE SIXTY-EIGHT!
YOU MUST BEWARE *HARKER!*
BRINKLEY...WHAT ARE YOU--

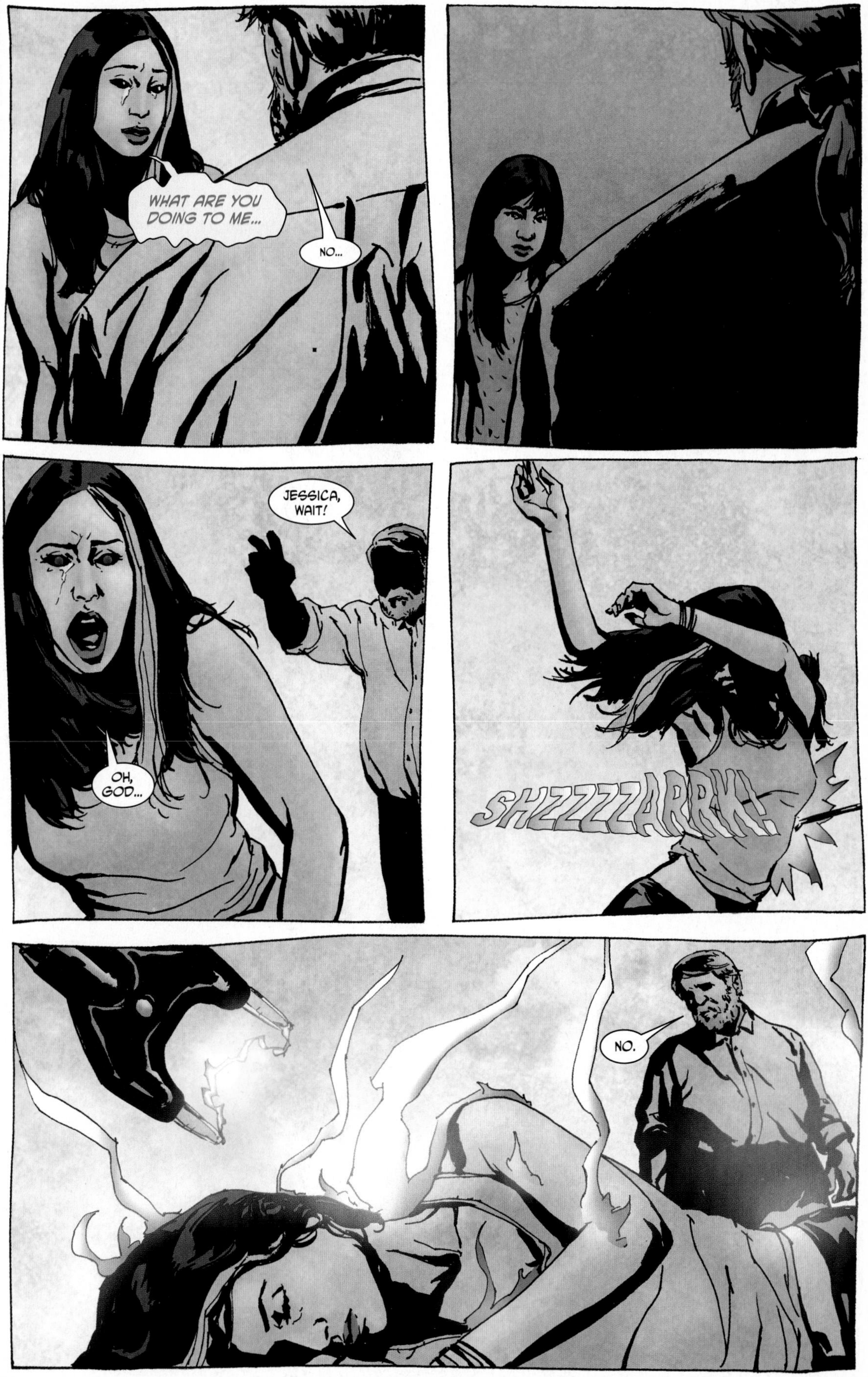
WHAT ARE YOU DOING TO ME...
NO...
JESSICA, WAIT!
OH, GOD...
SHZZZZZARRRK!
NO.

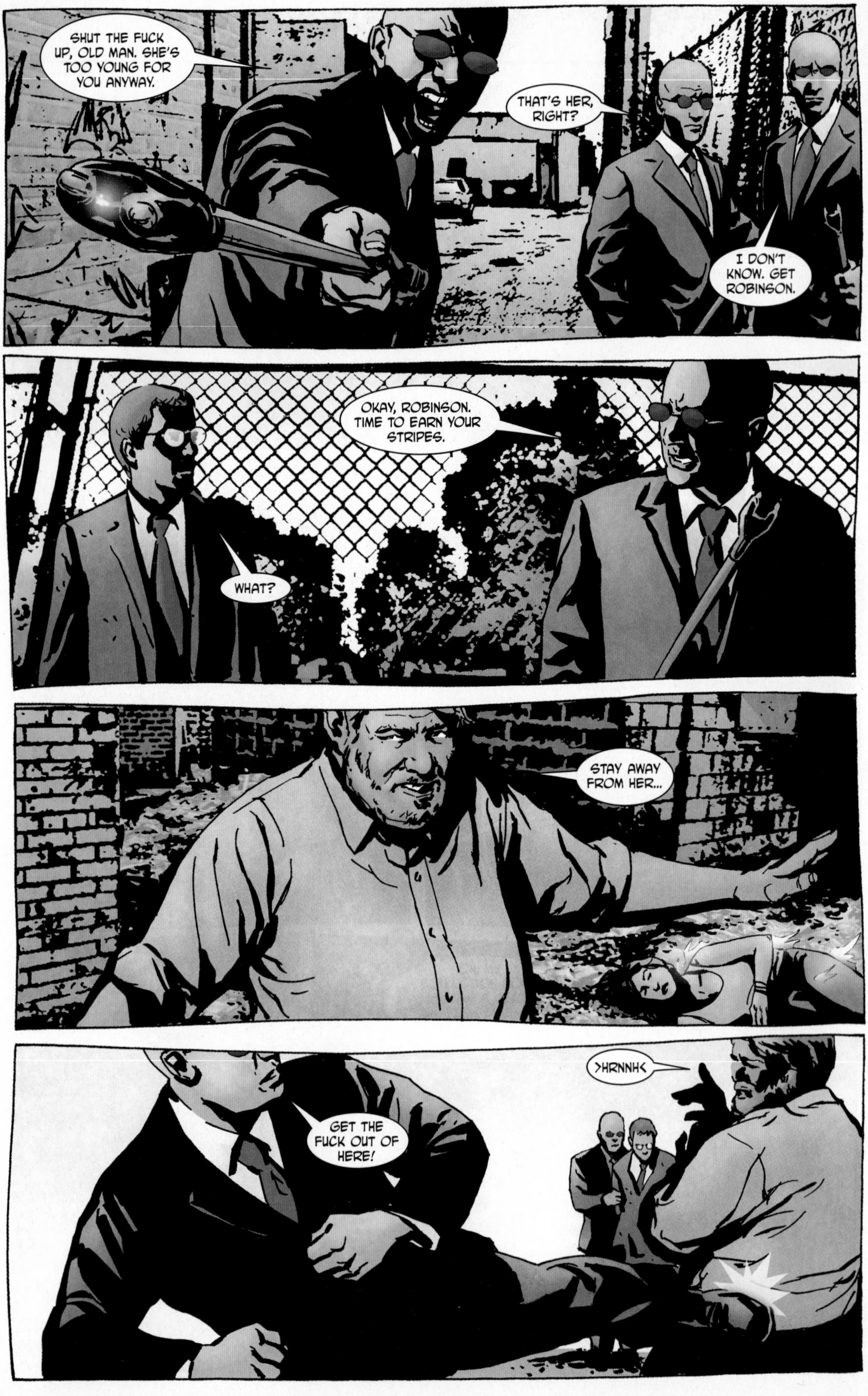
SHUT THE FUCK UP, OLD MAN. SHE'S TOO YOUNG FOR YOU ANYWAY.
THAT'S HER, RIGHT?
I DON'T KNOW. GET ROBINSON.
OKAY, ROBINSON. TIME TO EARN YOUR STRIPES.
WHAT?
STAY AWAY FROM HER...
GET THE FUCK OUT OF HERE!
>HRNNH<

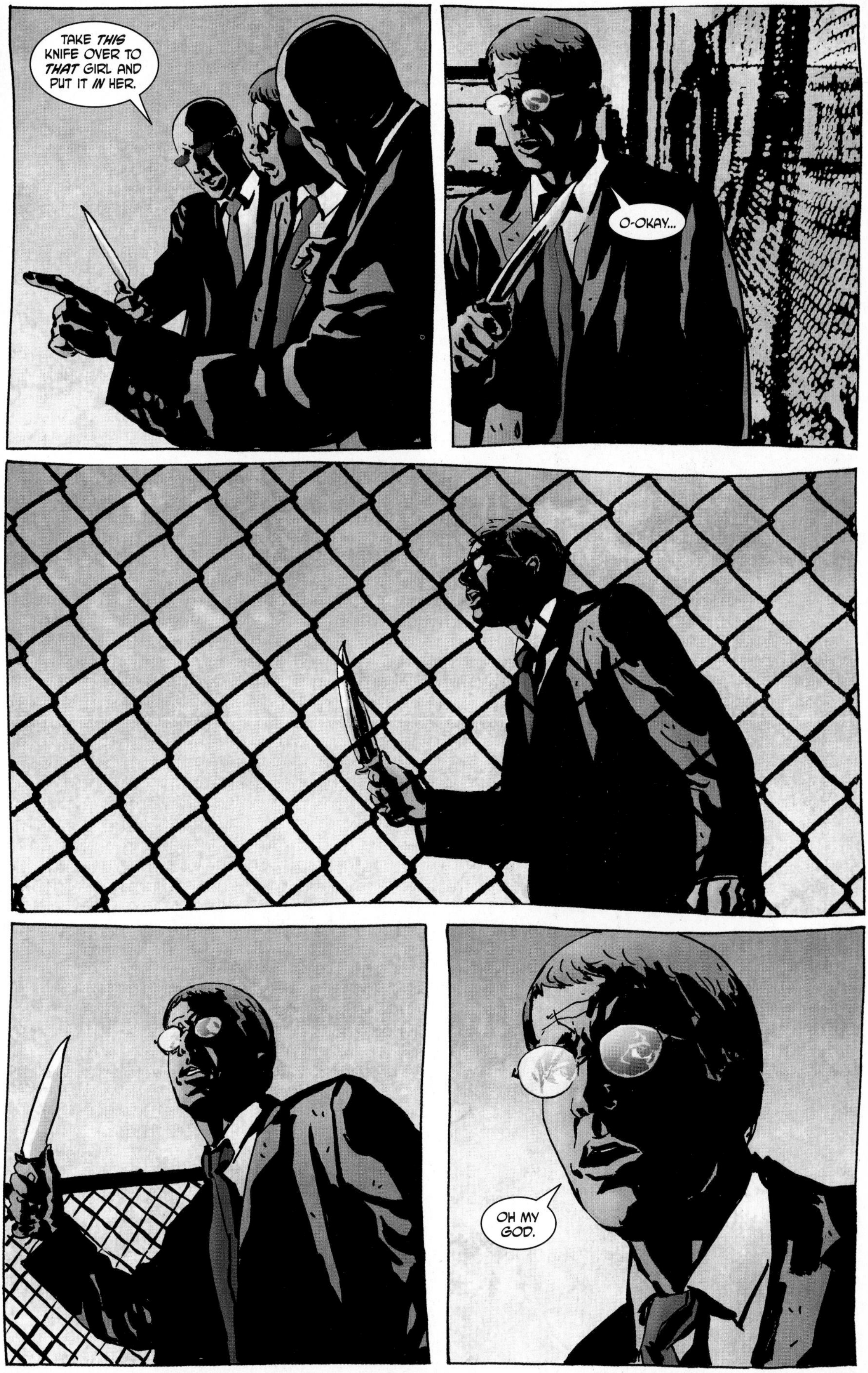
TAKE *THIS* KNIFE OVER TO *THAT* GIRL AND PUT IT *IN* HER.
O-OKAY...
OH MY GOD.

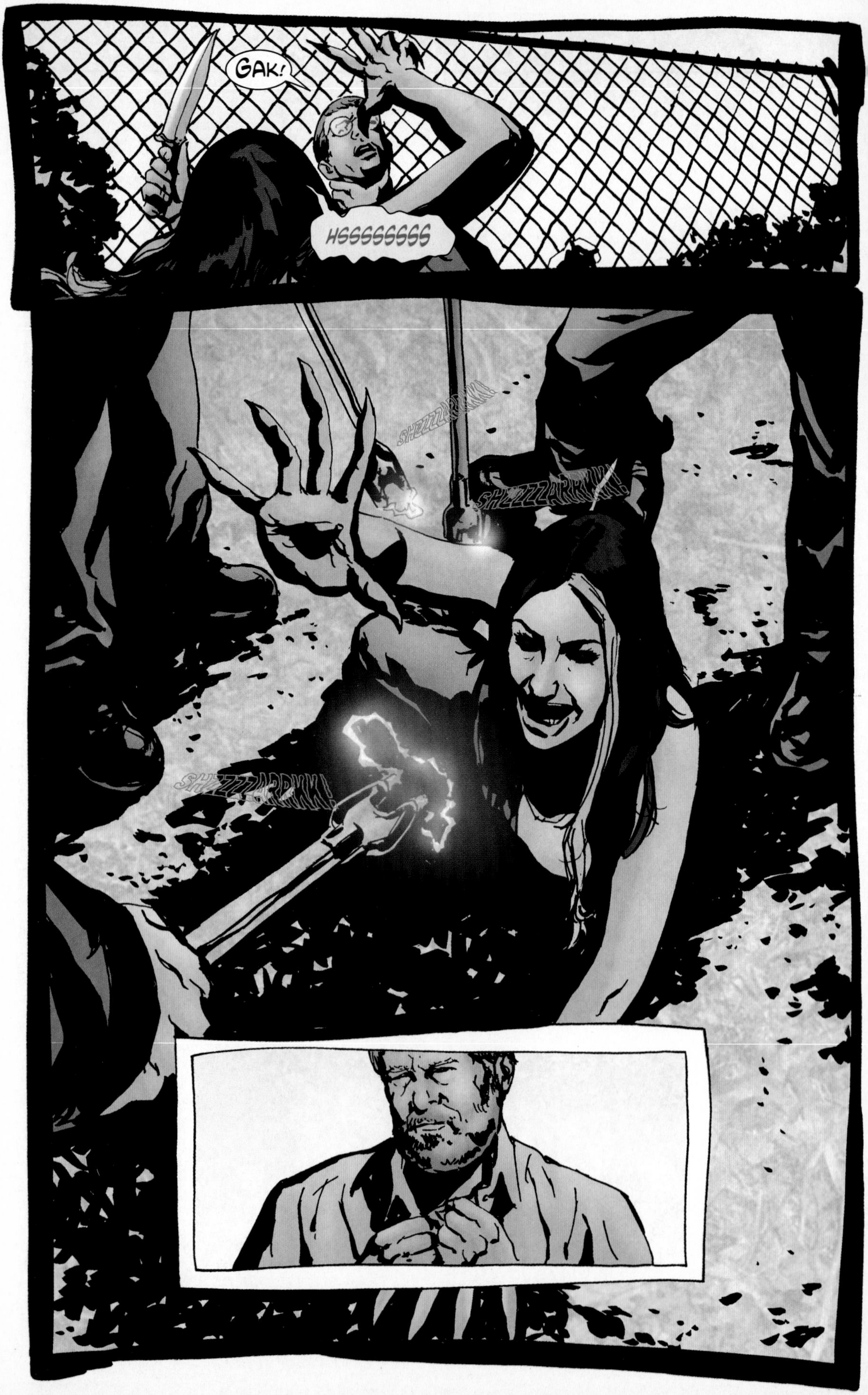
GAK!
HSSSSSSSS
SHZZZZARRKK!
SHZZZZARRKK!
SHZZZZARRKK!

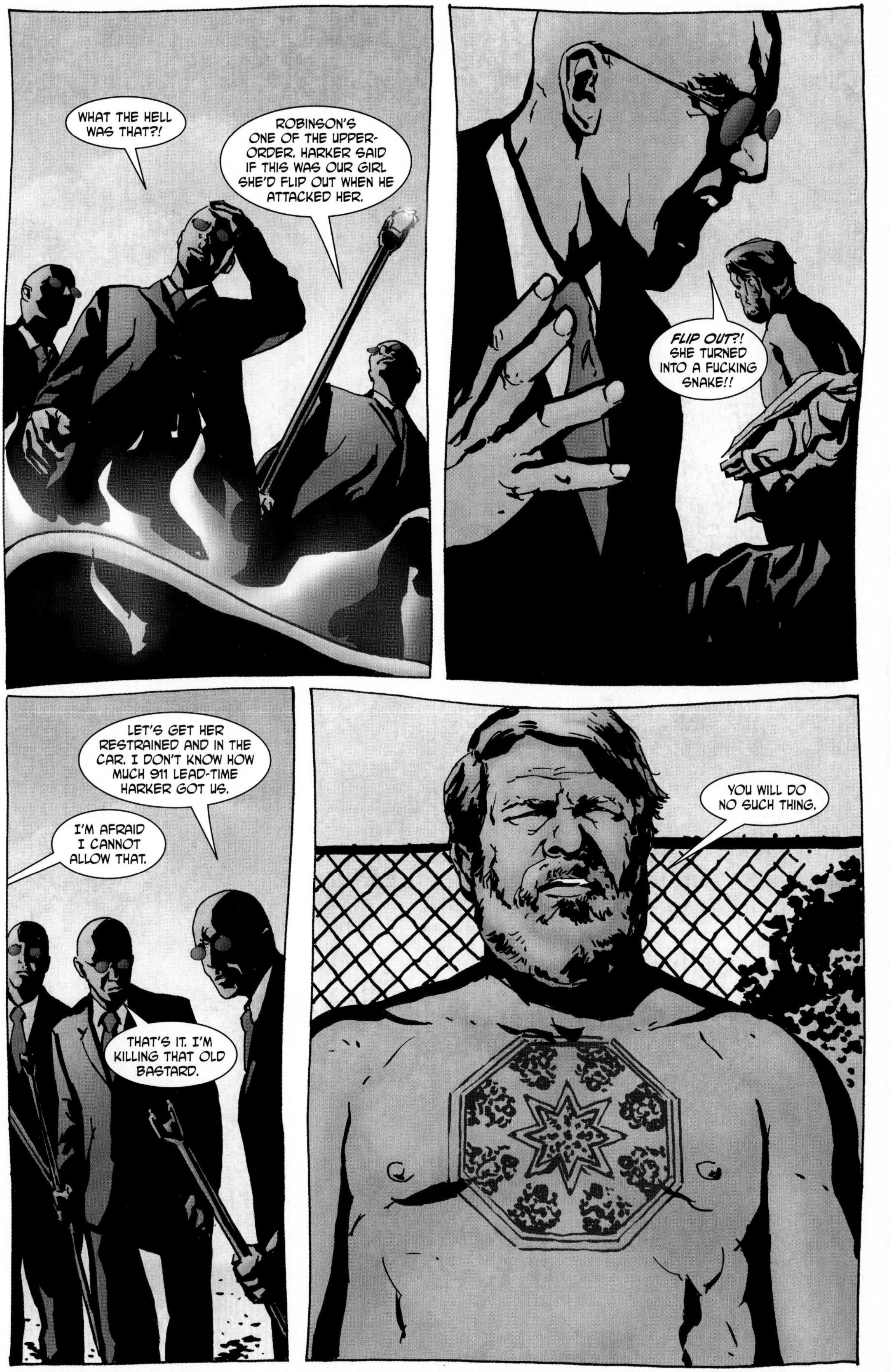
WHAT THE HELL WAS THAT?!
ROBINSON'S ONE OF THE UPPER-ORDER. HARKER SAID IF THIS WAS OUR GIRL SHE'D FLIP OUT WHEN HE ATTACKED HER.
FLIP OUT?! SHE TURNED INTO A FUCKING SNAKE!!
LET'S GET HER RESTRAINED AND IN THE CAR. I DON'T KNOW HOW MUCH 911 LEAD-TIME HARKER GOT US.
I'M AFRAID I CANNOT ALLOW THAT.
THAT'S IT. I'M KILLING THAT OLD BASTARD.
YOU WILL DO NO SUCH THING.

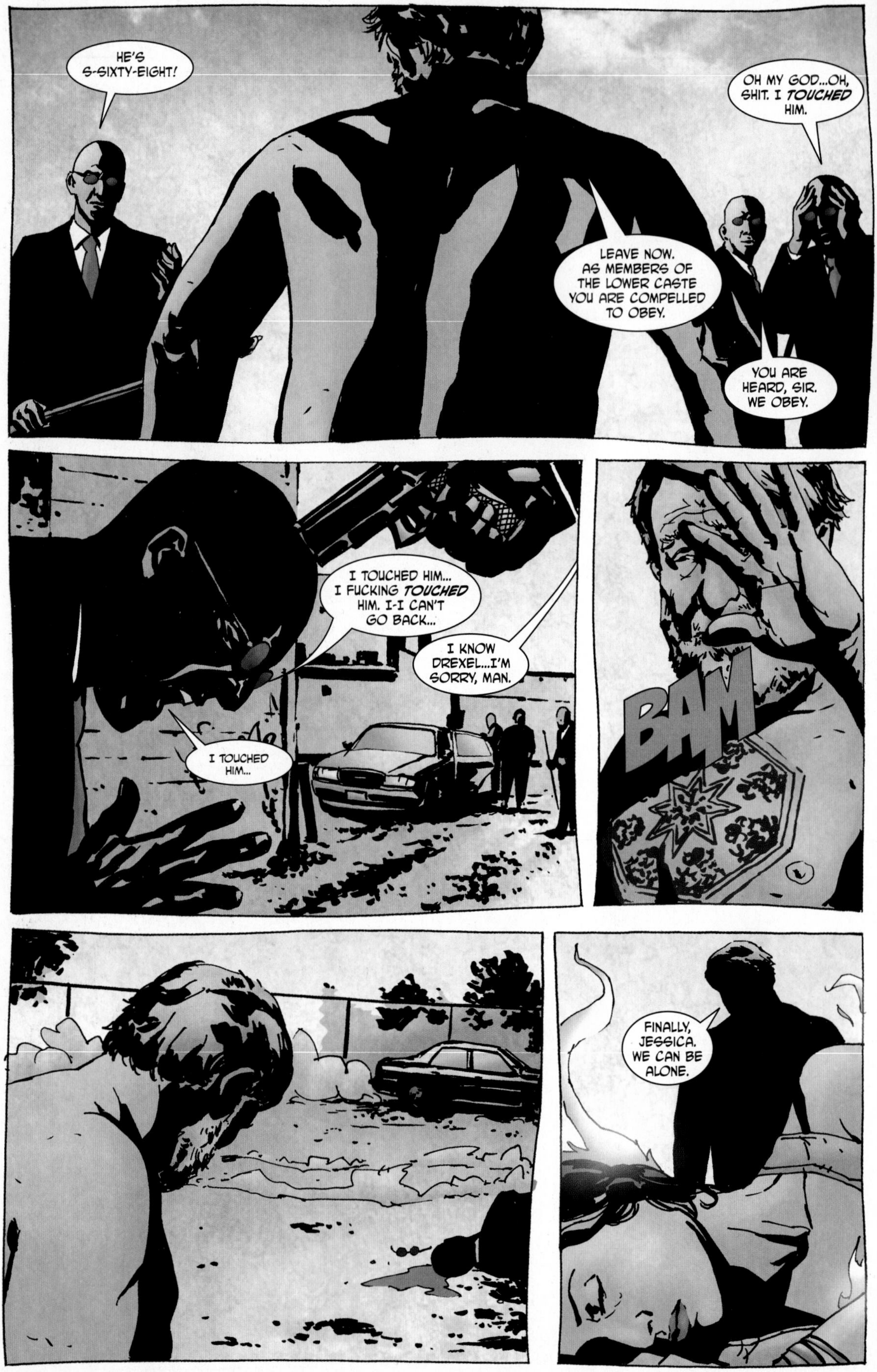
HE'S S-SIXTY-EIGHT!
OH MY GOD...OH, SHIT. I *TOUCHED* HIM.
LEAVE NOW. AS MEMBERS OF THE LOWER CASTE YOU ARE COMPELLED TO OBEY.
YOU ARE HEARD, SIR. WE OBEY.
I TOUCHED HIM... I FUCKING *TOUCHED* HIM. I-I CAN'T GO BACK...
I KNOW DREXEL...I'M SORRY, MAN.
I TOUCHED HIM...
BAM
FINALLY, JESSICA. WE CAN BE ALONE.

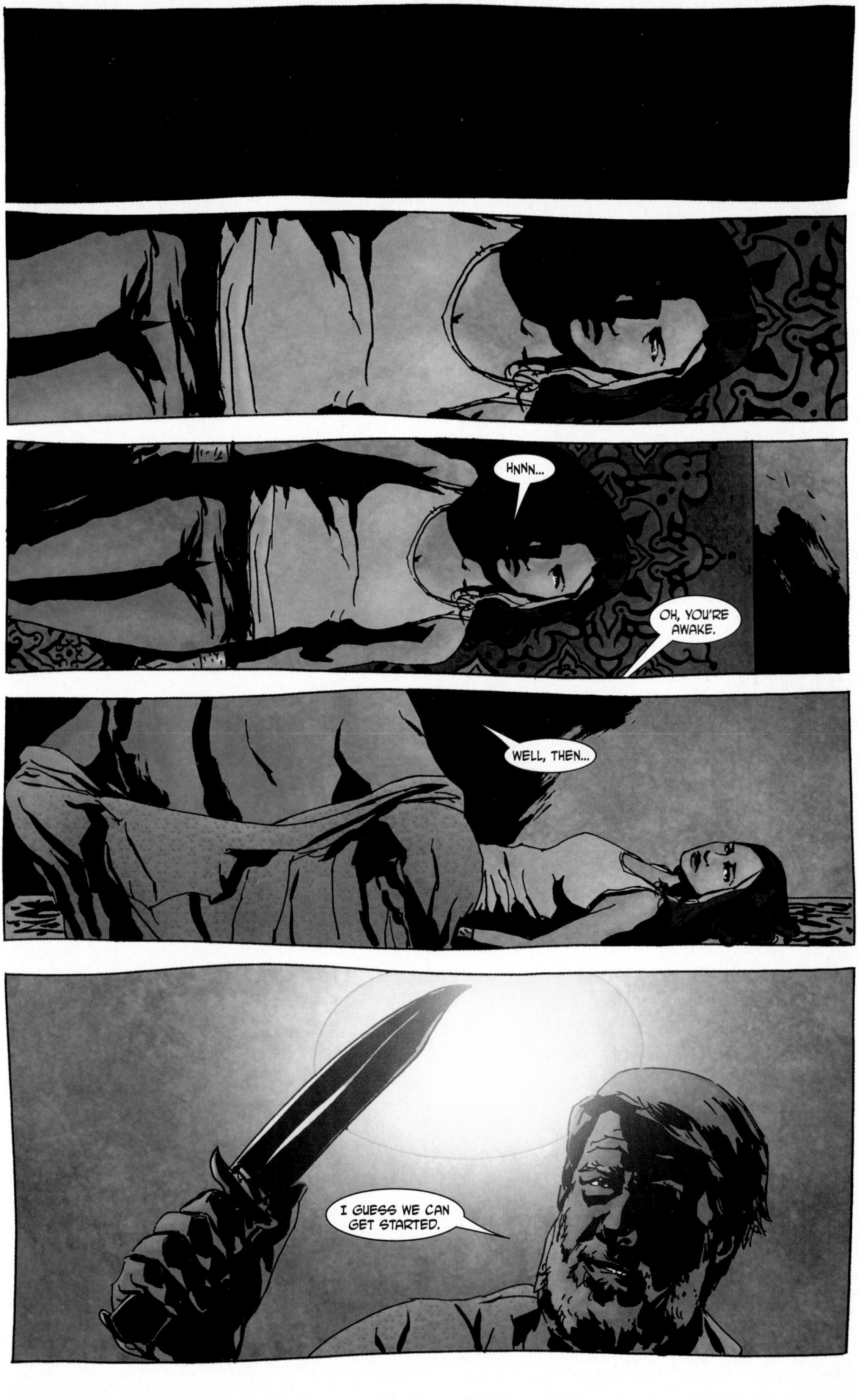
HNNN...
OH, YOU'RE AWAKE.
WELL, THEN...
I GUESS WE CAN GET STARTED.

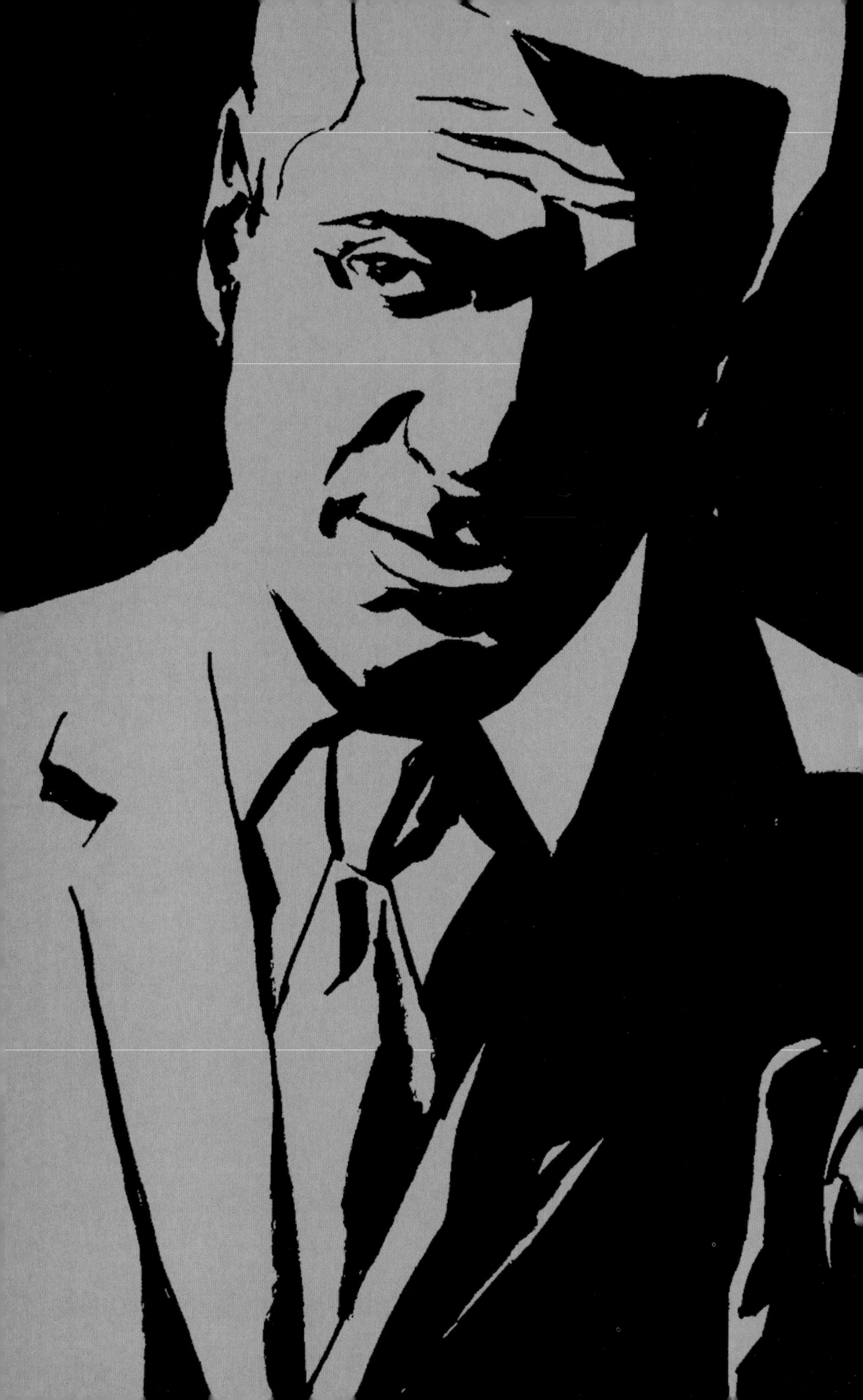

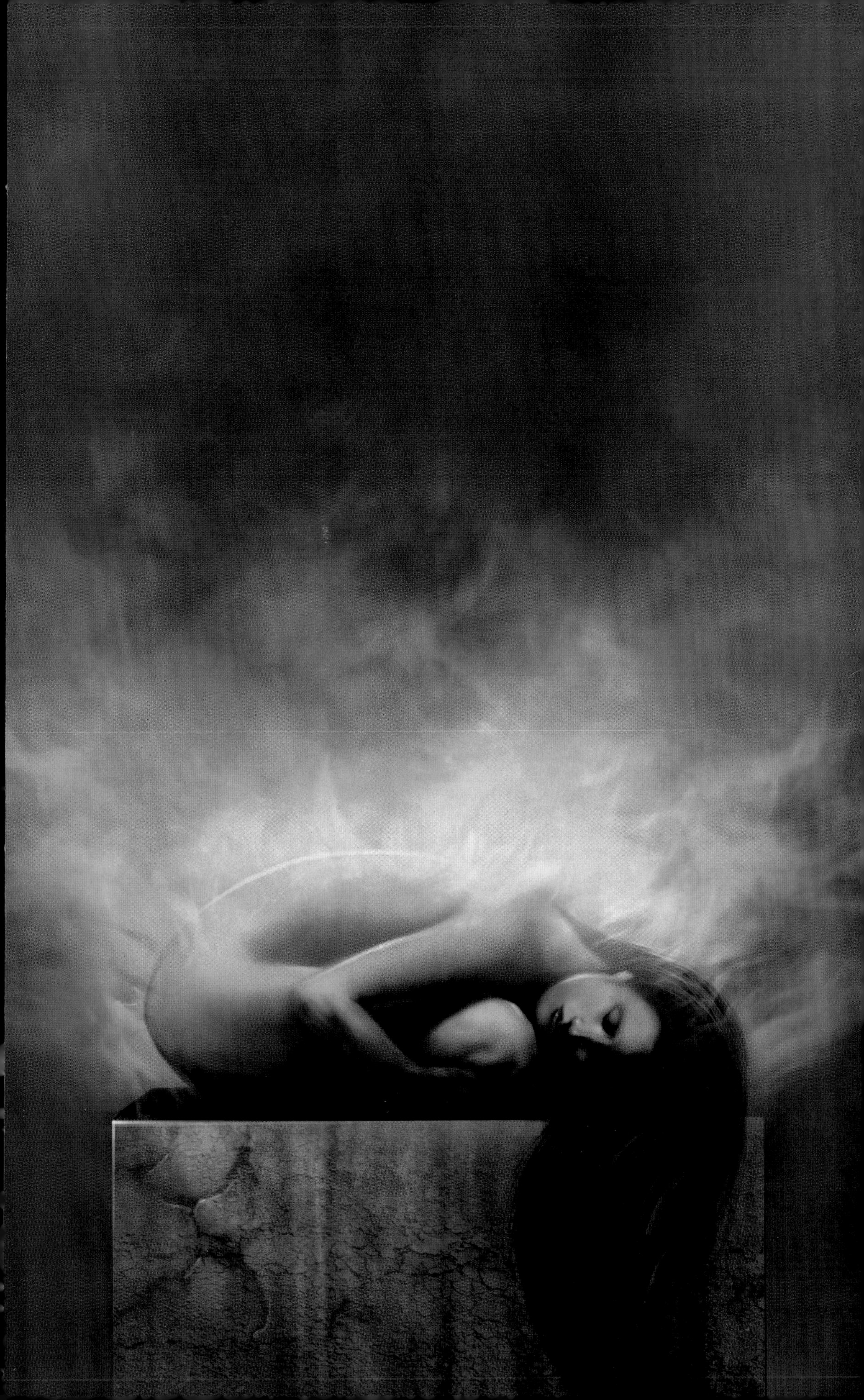

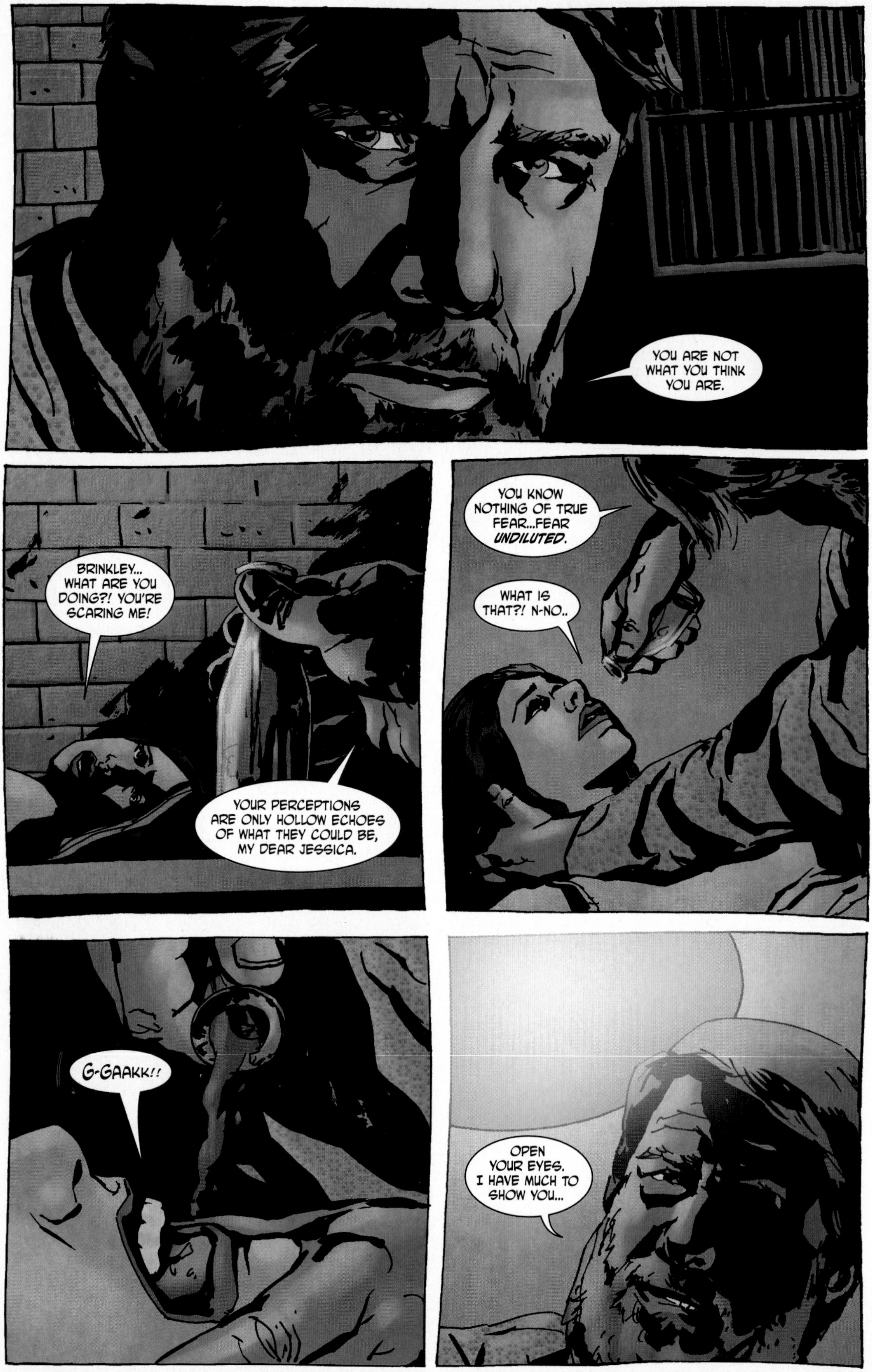
YOU ARE NOT WHAT YOU THINK YOU ARE.
BRINKLEY... WHAT ARE YOU DOING?! YOU'RE SCARING ME!
YOUR PERCEPTIONS ARE ONLY HOLLOW ECHOES OF WHAT THEY COULD BE, MY DEAR JESSICA.
YOU KNOW NOTHING OF TRUE FEAR...FEAR *UNDILUTED*.
WHAT IS THAT?! N-NO..
G-GAAKK!!
OPEN YOUR EYES. I HAVE MUCH TO SHOW YOU...

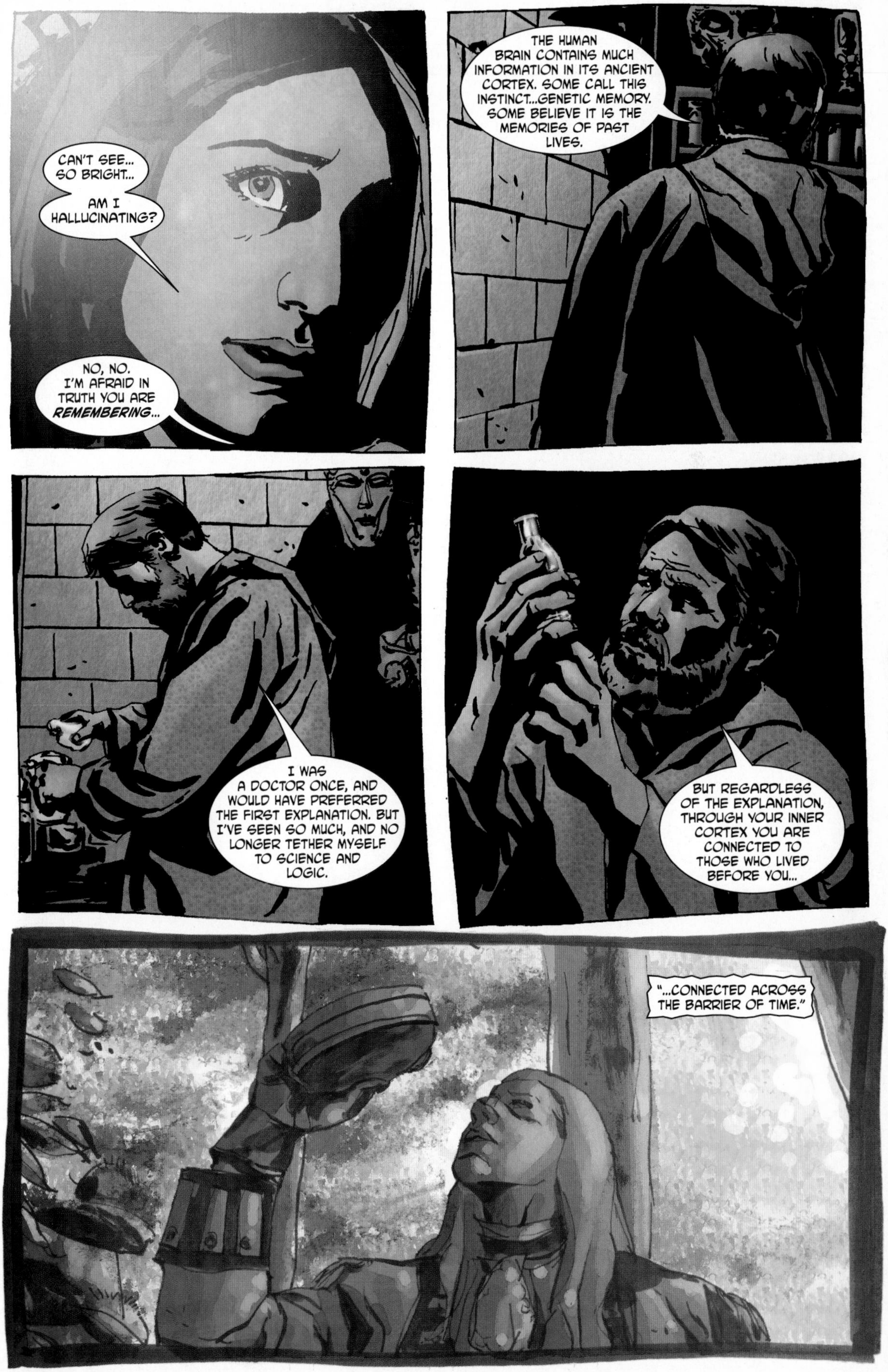
CAN'T SEE... SO BRIGHT...
AM I HALLUCINATING?
NO, NO. I'M AFRAID IN TRUTH YOU ARE *REMEMBERING*...
THE HUMAN BRAIN CONTAINS MUCH INFORMATION IN ITS ANCIENT CORTEX. SOME CALL THIS INSTINCT...GENETIC MEMORY. SOME BELIEVE IT IS THE MEMORIES OF PAST LIVES.
I WAS A DOCTOR ONCE, AND WOULD HAVE PREFERRED THE FIRST EXPLANATION. BUT I'VE SEEN SO MUCH, AND NO LONGER TETHER MYSELF TO SCIENCE AND LOGIC.
BUT REGARDLESS OF THE EXPLANATION, THROUGH YOUR INNER CORTEX YOU ARE CONNECTED TO THOSE WHO LIVED BEFORE YOU...
"...CONNECTED ACROSS THE BARRIER OF TIME."

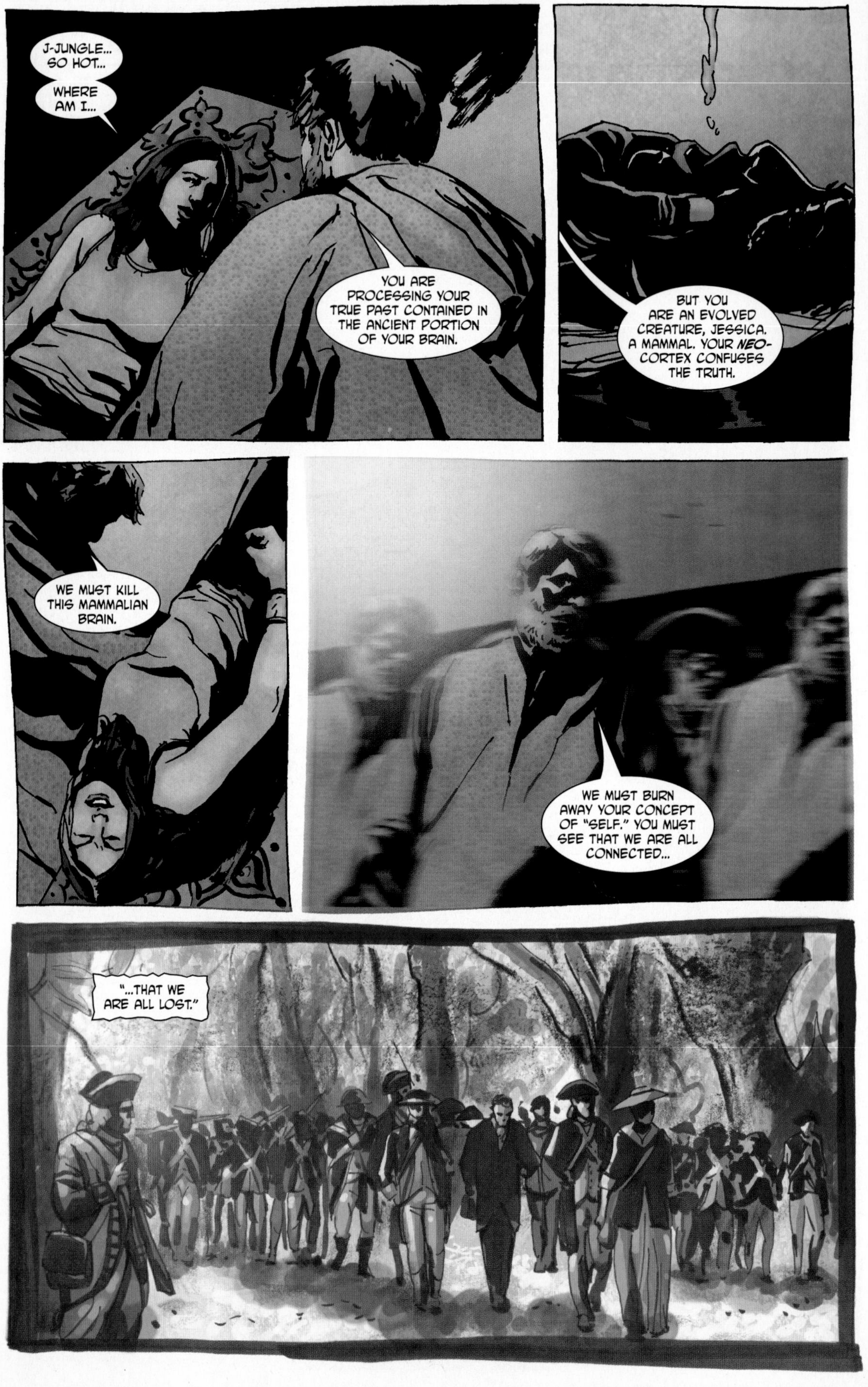
J-JUNGLE... SO HOT...
WHERE AM I...
YOU ARE PROCESSING YOUR TRUE PAST CONTAINED IN THE ANCIENT PORTION OF YOUR BRAIN.
BUT YOU ARE AN EVOLVED CREATURE, JESSICA. A MAMMAL. YOUR *NEO*-CORTEX CONFUSES THE TRUTH.
WE MUST KILL THIS MAMMALIAN BRAIN.
WE MUST BURN AWAY YOUR CONCEPT OF "SELF." YOU MUST SEE THAT WE ARE ALL CONNECTED...
"...THAT WE ARE ALL LOST."

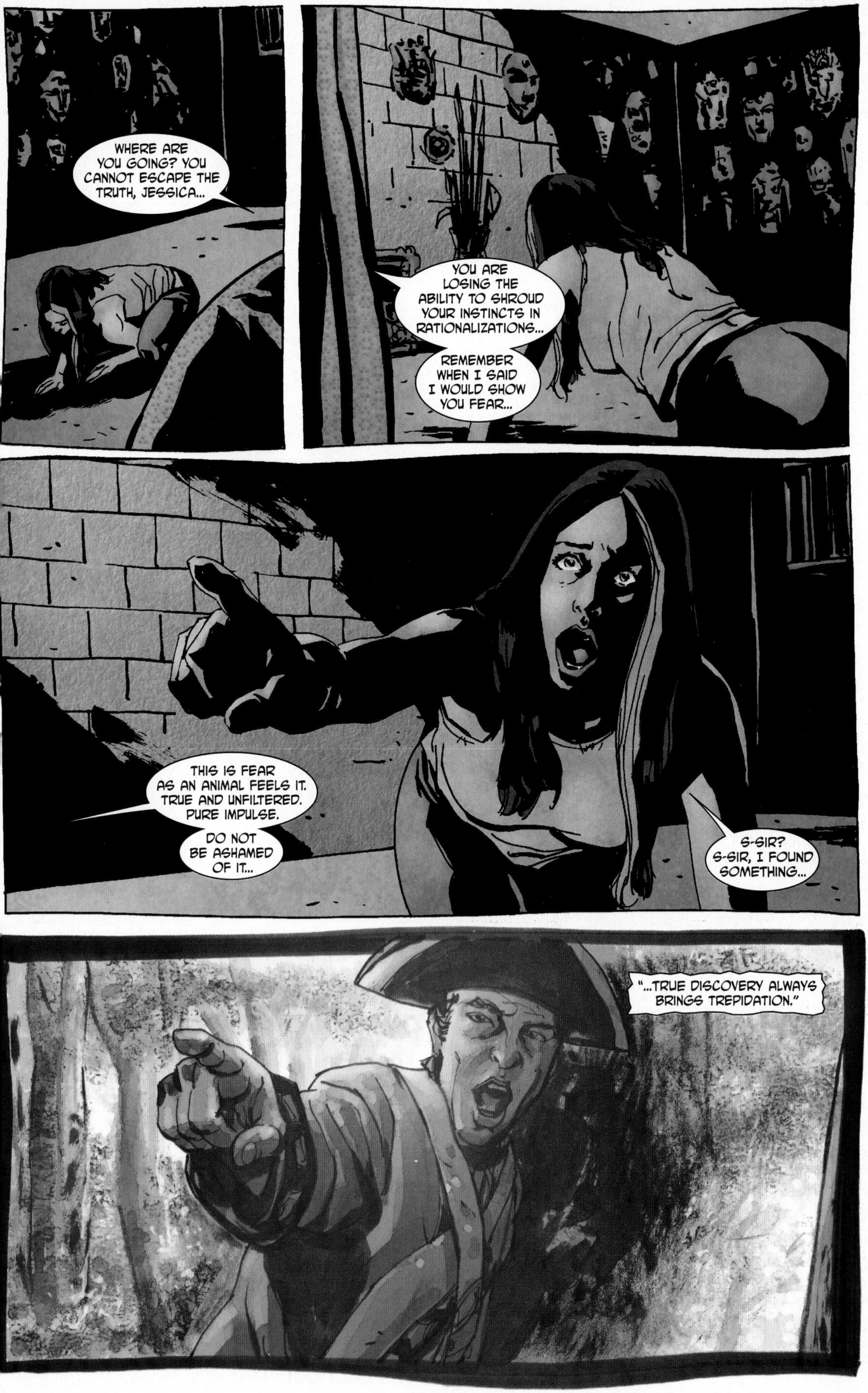
WHERE ARE YOU GOING? YOU CANNOT ESCAPE THE TRUTH, JESSICA...
YOU ARE LOSING THE ABILITY TO SHROUD YOUR INSTINCTS IN RATIONALIZATIONS...
REMEMBER WHEN I SAID I WOULD SHOW YOU FEAR...
THIS IS FEAR AS AN ANIMAL FEELS IT. TRUE AND UNFILTERED. PURE IMPULSE.
DO NOT BE ASHAMED OF IT...
S-SIR? S-SIR, I FOUND SOMETHING...
"...TRUE DISCOVERY ALWAYS BRINGS TREPIDATION."

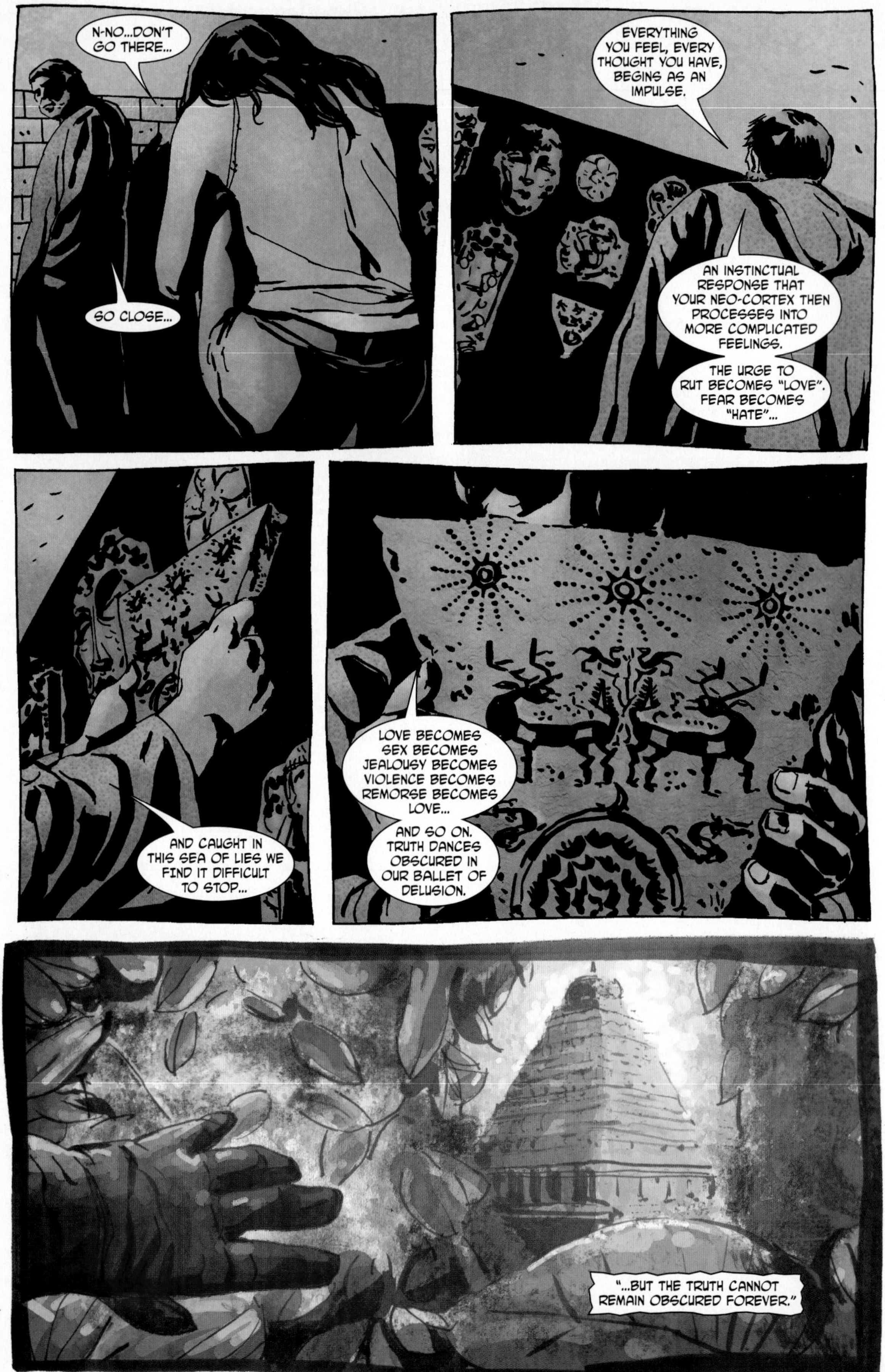
N-NO...DON'T GO THERE...
SO CLOSE...
EVERYTHING YOU FEEL, EVERY THOUGHT YOU HAVE, BEGINS AS AN IMPULSE.
AN INSTINCTUAL RESPONSE THAT YOUR NEO-CORTEX THEN PROCESSES INTO MORE COMPLICATED FEELINGS.
THE URGE TO RUT BECOMES "LOVE". FEAR BECOMES "HATE"...
AND CAUGHT IN THIS SEA OF LIES WE FIND IT DIFFICULT TO STOP...
LOVE BECOMES SEX BECOMES JEALOUSY BECOMES VIOLENCE BECOMES REMORSE BECOMES LOVE...
AND SO ON. TRUTH DANCES OBSCURED IN OUR BALLET OF DELUSION.
"...BUT THE TRUTH CANNOT REMAIN OBSCURED FOREVER."

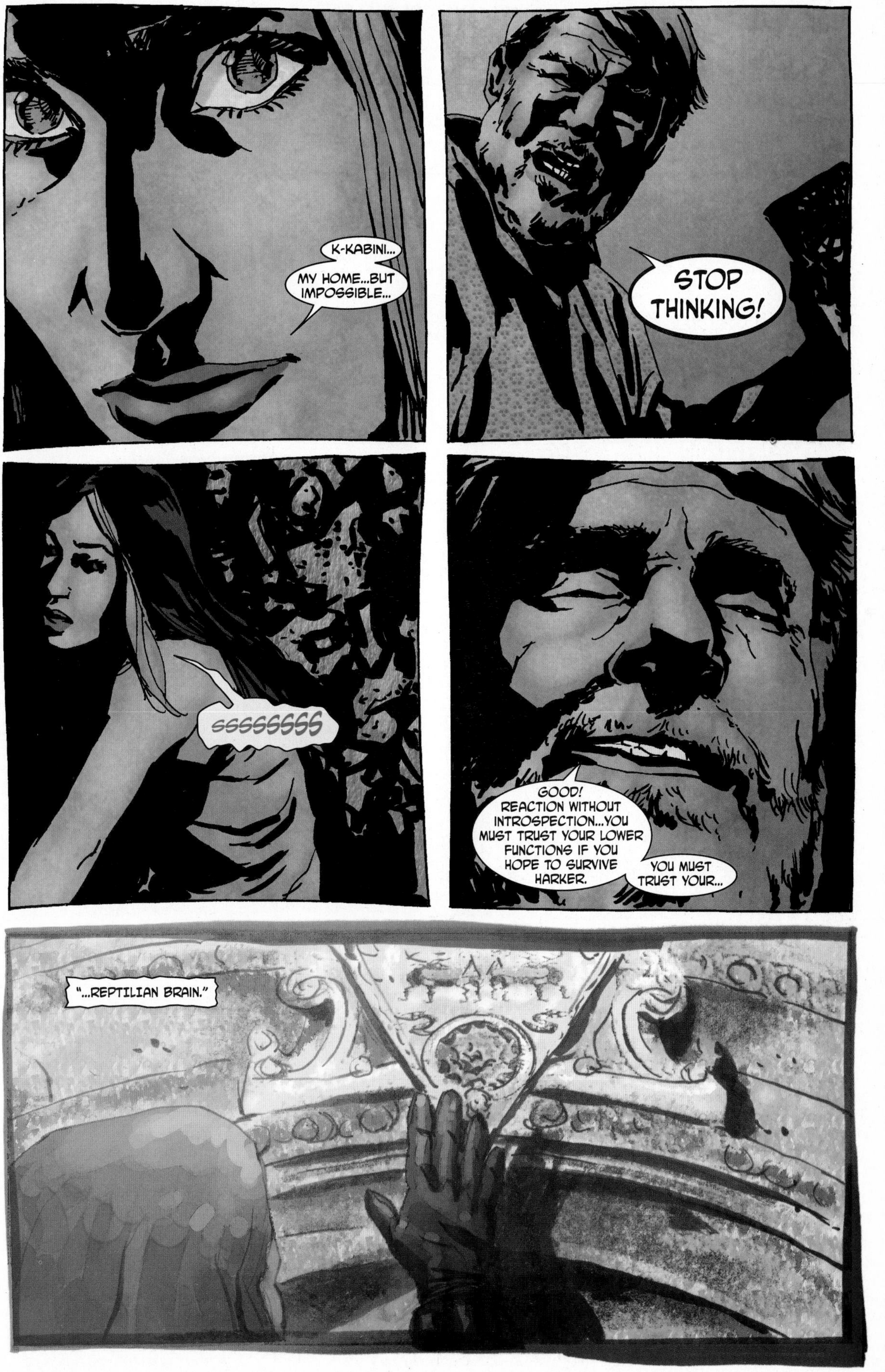
K-KABINI...
MY HOME...BUT IMPOSSIBLE...
STOP THINKING!
SSSSSSSS
GOOD! REACTION WITHOUT INTROSPECTION...YOU MUST TRUST YOUR LOWER FUNCTIONS IF YOU HOPE TO SURVIVE HARKER.
YOU MUST TRUST YOUR...
"...REPTILIAN BRAIN."

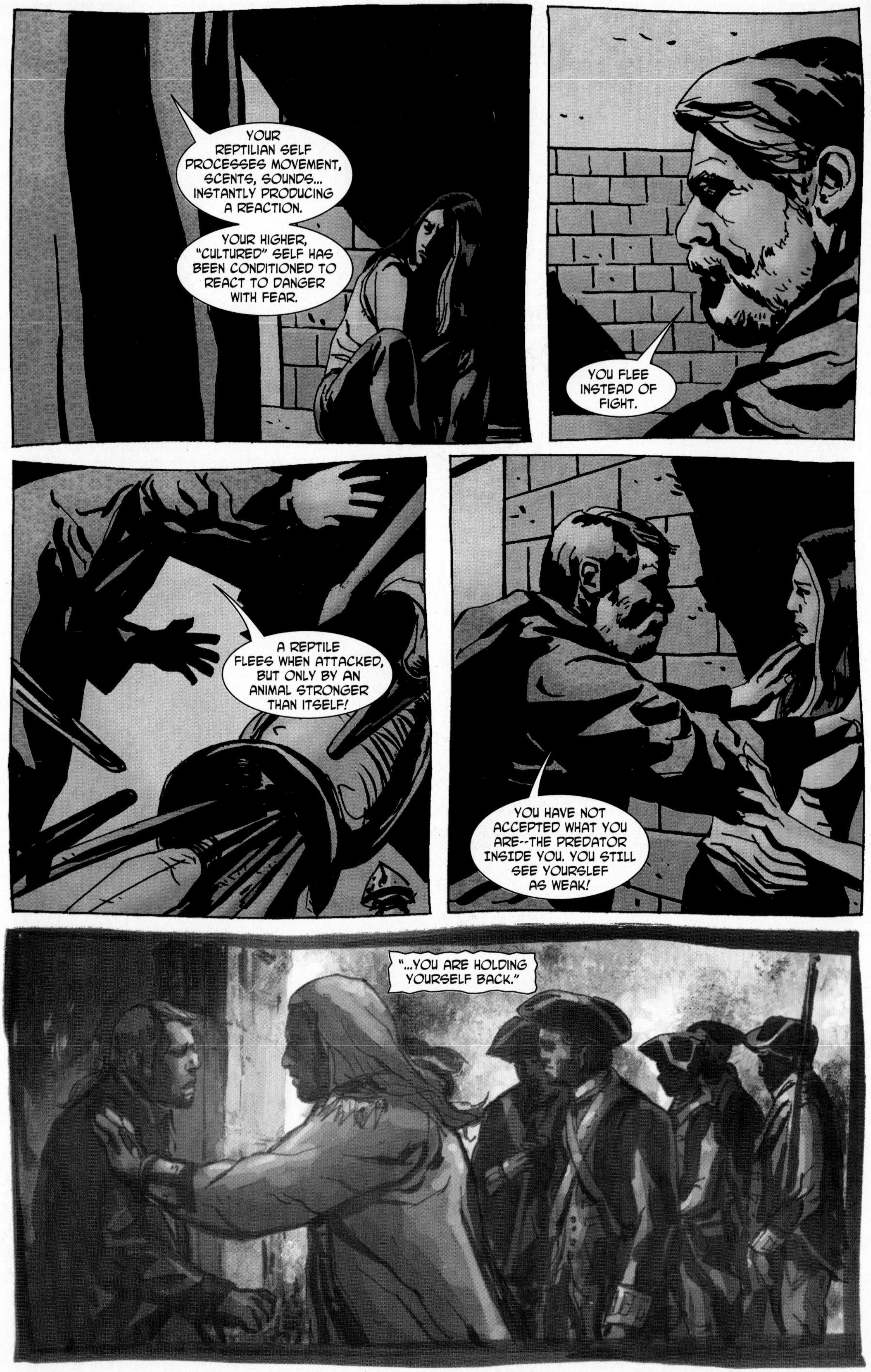
YOUR REPTILIAN SELF PROCESSES MOVEMENT, SCENTS, SOUNDS... INSTANTLY PRODUCING A REACTION.
YOUR HIGHER, "CULTURED" SELF HAS BEEN CONDITIONED TO REACT TO DANGER WITH FEAR.
YOU FLEE INSTEAD OF FIGHT.
A REPTILE FLEES WHEN ATTACKED, BUT ONLY BY AN ANIMAL STRONGER THAN ITSELF!
YOU HAVE NOT ACCEPTED WHAT YOU ARE--THE PREDATOR INSIDE YOU. YOU STILL SEE YOURSLEF AS WEAK!
"...YOU ARE HOLDING YOURSELF BACK."

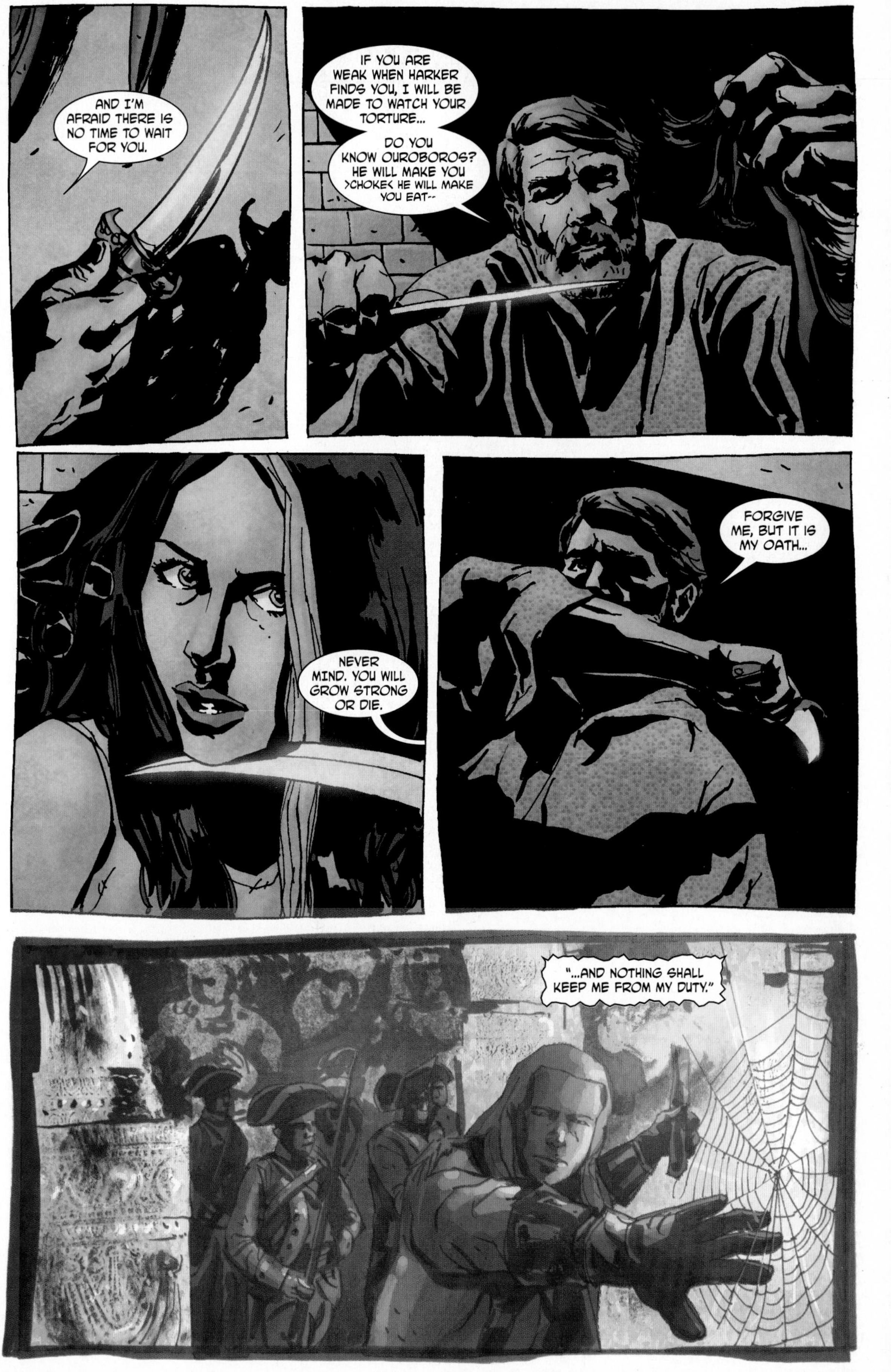
AND I'M AFRAID THERE IS NO TIME TO WAIT FOR YOU.
IF YOU ARE WEAK WHEN HARKER FINDS YOU, I WILL BE MADE TO WATCH YOUR TORTURE...
DO YOU KNOW OUROBOROS? HE WILL MAKE YOU >CHOKE< HE WILL MAKE YOU EAT--
NEVER MIND. YOU WILL GROW STRONG OR DIE.
FORGIVE ME, BUT IT IS MY OATH...
"...AND NOTHING SHALL KEEP ME FROM MY DUTY."

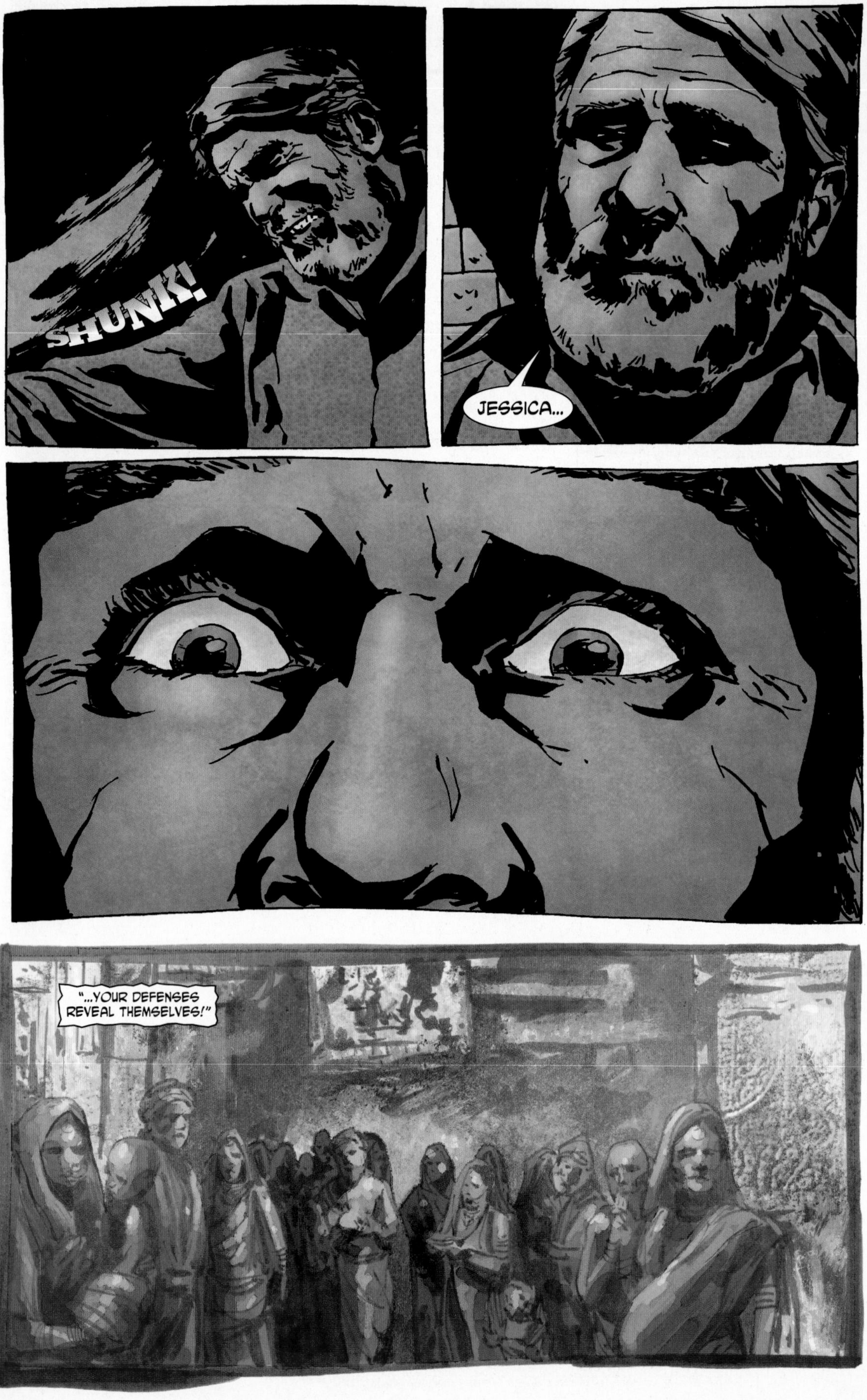
SHUNK!
JESSICA...
"...YOUR DEFENSES REVEAL THEMSELVES!"

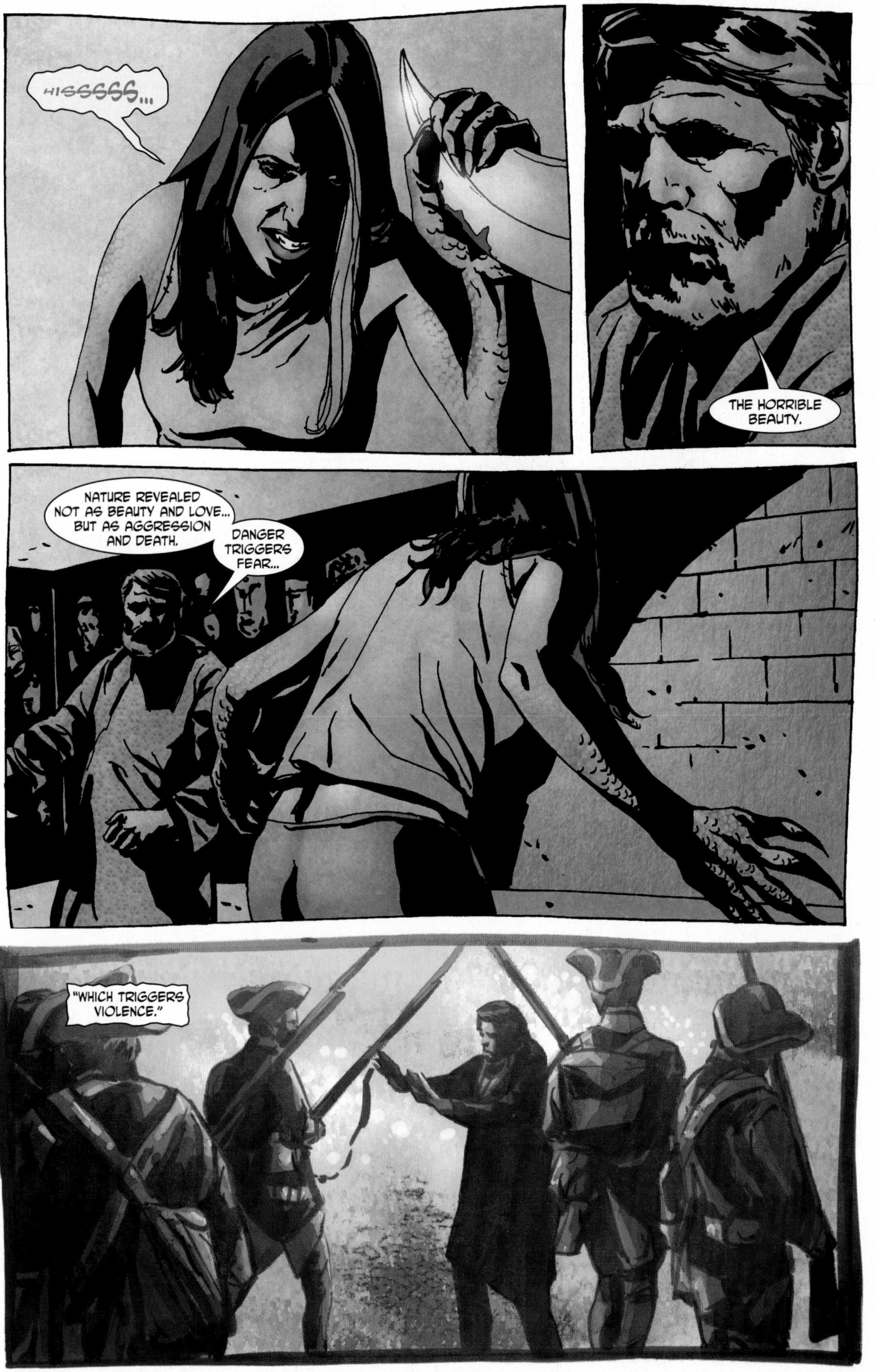
HISSSSS...
THE HORRIBLE BEAUTY.
NATURE REVEALED NOT AS BEAUTY AND LOVE... BUT AS AGGRESSION AND DEATH.
DANGER TRIGGERS FEAR...
"WHICH TRIGGERS VIOLENCE."

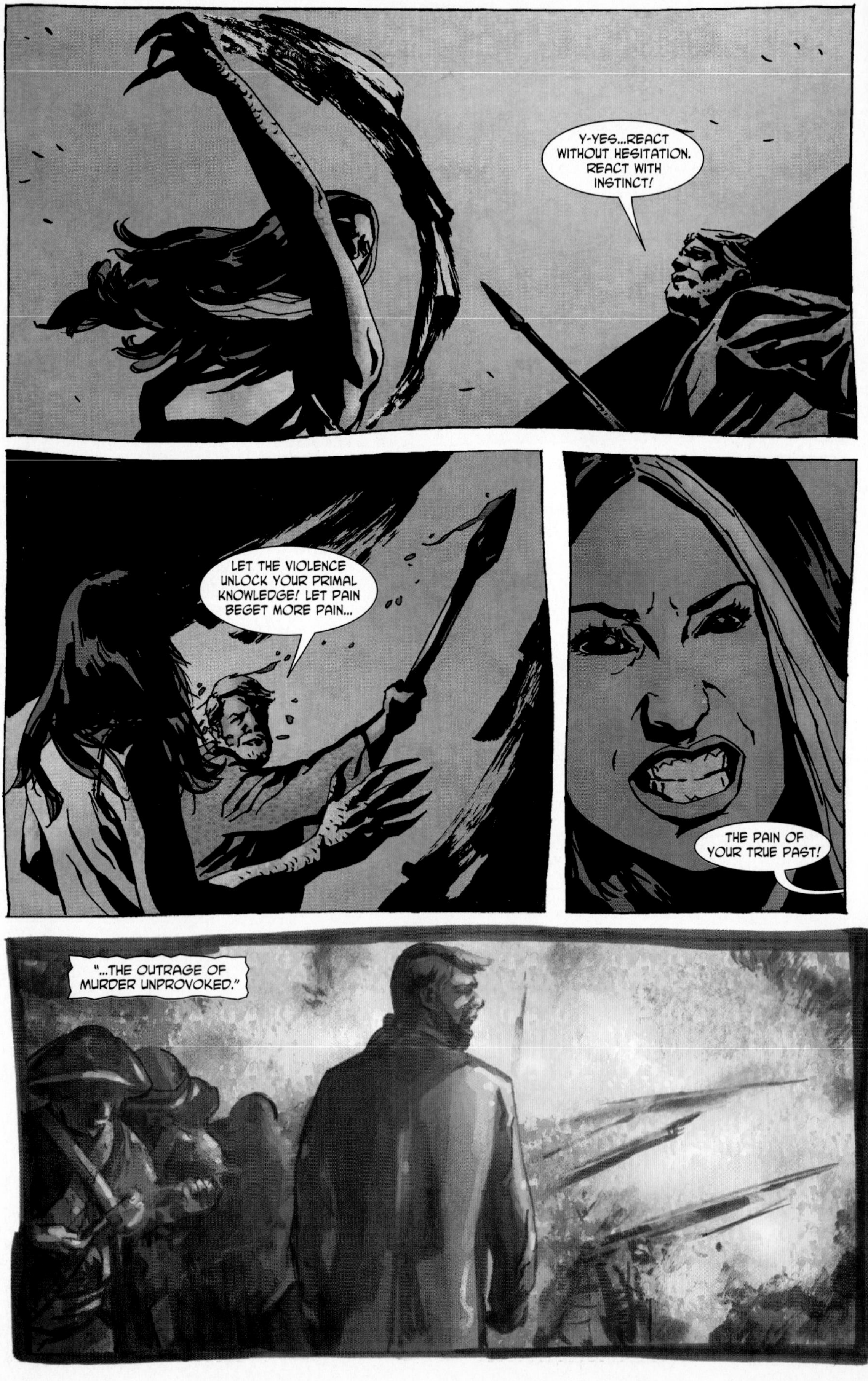
Y-YES...REACT WITHOUT HESITATION. REACT WITH INSTINCT!
LET THE VIOLENCE UNLOCK YOUR PRIMAL KNOWLEDGE! LET PAIN BEGET MORE PAIN...
THE PAIN OF YOUR TRUE PAST!
"...THE OUTRAGE OF MURDER UNPROVOKED."

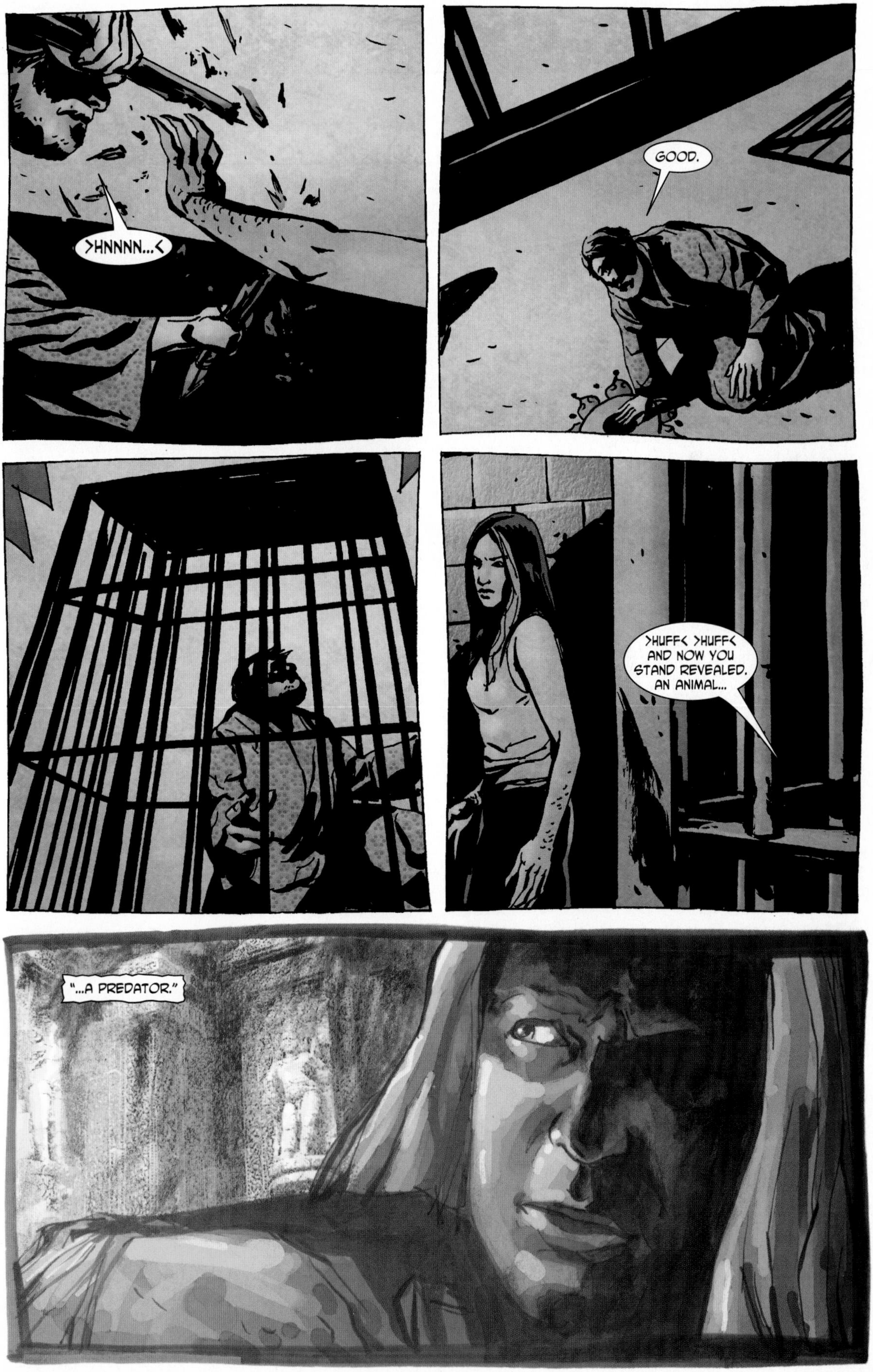

>HNNNN...<
GOOD.
>HUFF< >HUFF< AND NOW YOU STAND REVEALED. AN ANIMAL...
"...A PREDATOR."

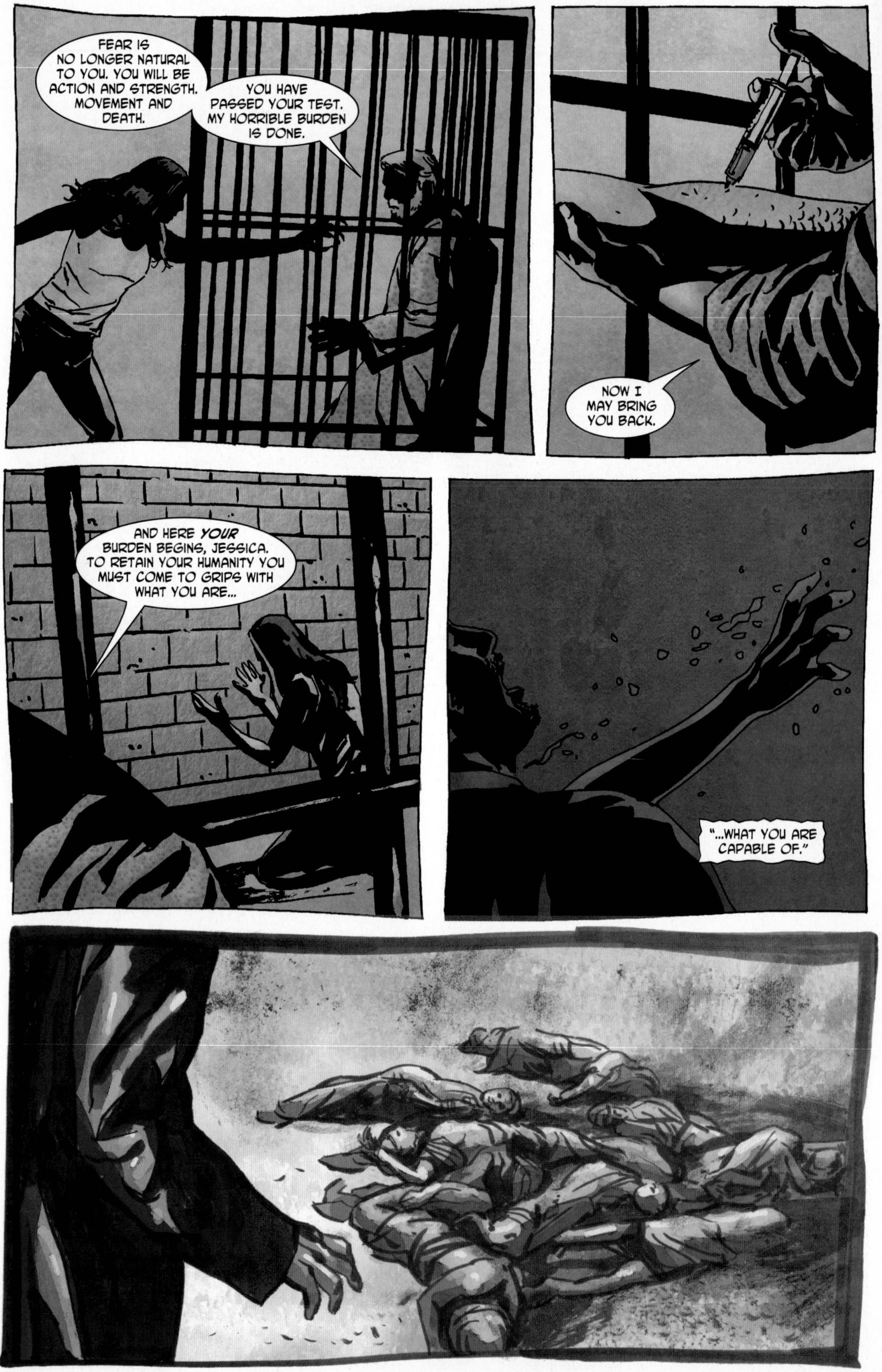
FEAR IS NO LONGER NATURAL TO YOU. YOU WILL BE ACTION AND STRENGTH. MOVEMENT AND DEATH.
YOU HAVE PASSED YOUR TEST. MY HORRIBLE BURDEN IS DONE.
NOW I MAY BRING YOU BACK.
AND HERE *YOUR* BURDEN BEGINS, JESSICA. TO RETAIN YOUR HUMANITY YOU MUST COME TO GRIPS WITH WHAT YOU ARE...
"...WHAT YOU ARE CAPABLE OF."

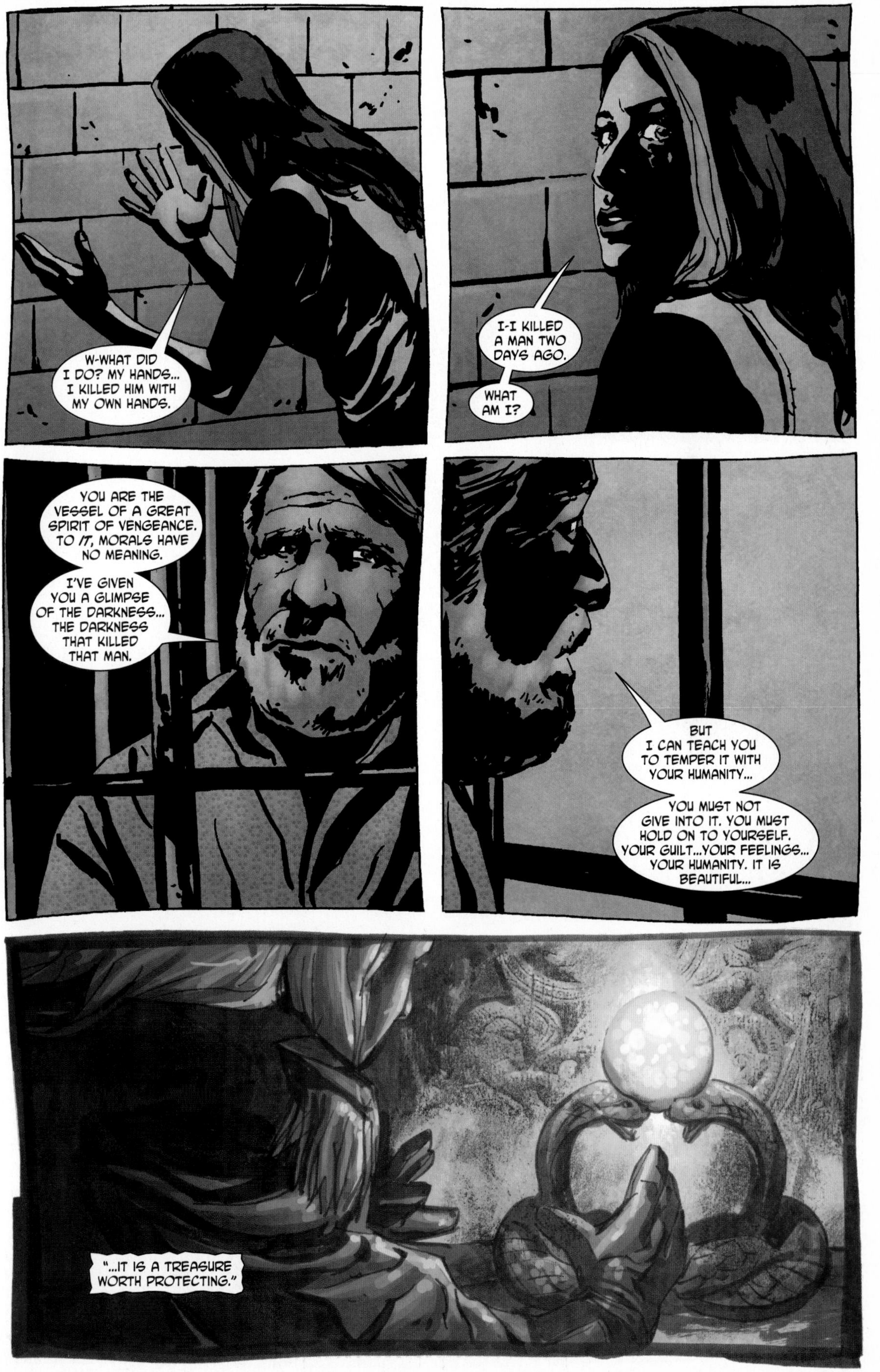
W-WHAT DID I DO? MY HANDS... I KILLED HIM WITH MY OWN HANDS.
I-I KILLED A MAN TWO DAYS AGO.
WHAT AM I?
YOU ARE THE VESSEL OF A GREAT SPIRIT OF VENGEANCE. TO *IT*, MORALS HAVE NO MEANING.
I'VE GIVEN YOU A GLIMPSE OF THE DARKNESS... THE DARKNESS THAT KILLED THAT MAN.
BUT I CAN TEACH YOU TO TEMPER IT WITH YOUR HUMANITY...
YOU MUST NOT GIVE INTO IT. YOU MUST HOLD ON TO YOURSELF. YOUR GUILT...YOUR FEELINGS... YOUR HUMANITY. IT IS BEAUTIFUL...
"...IT IS A TREASURE WORTH PROTECTING."

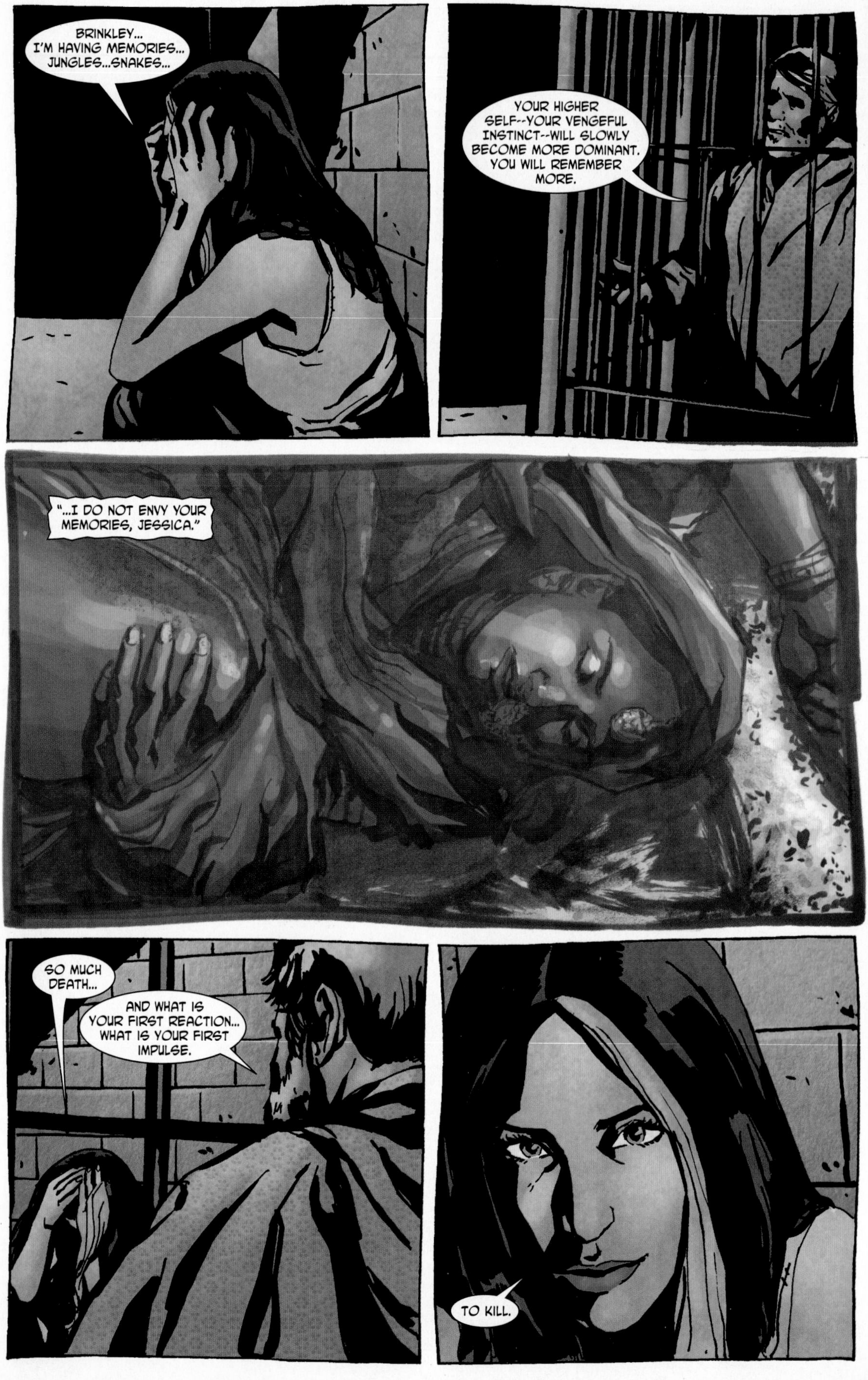
BRINKLEY... I'M HAVING MEMORIES... JUNGLES...SNAKES...
YOUR HIGHER SELF--YOUR VENGEFUL INSTINCT--WILL SLOWLY BECOME MORE DOMINANT. YOU WILL REMEMBER MORE.
"...I DO NOT ENVY YOUR MEMORIES, JESSICA."
SO MUCH DEATH...
AND WHAT IS YOUR FIRST REACTION... WHAT IS YOUR FIRST IMPULSE.
TO KILL.

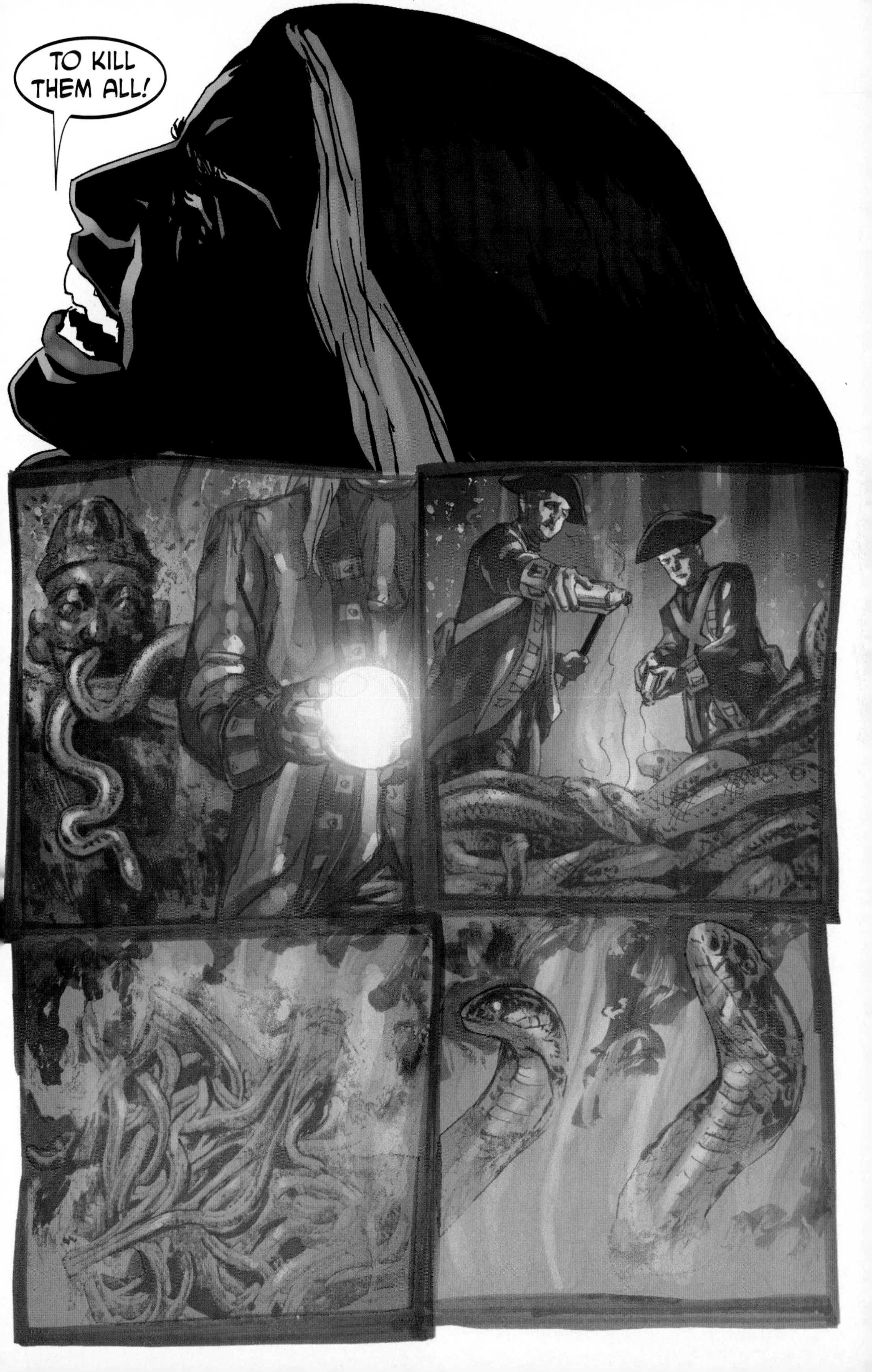
TO KILL THEM ALL!

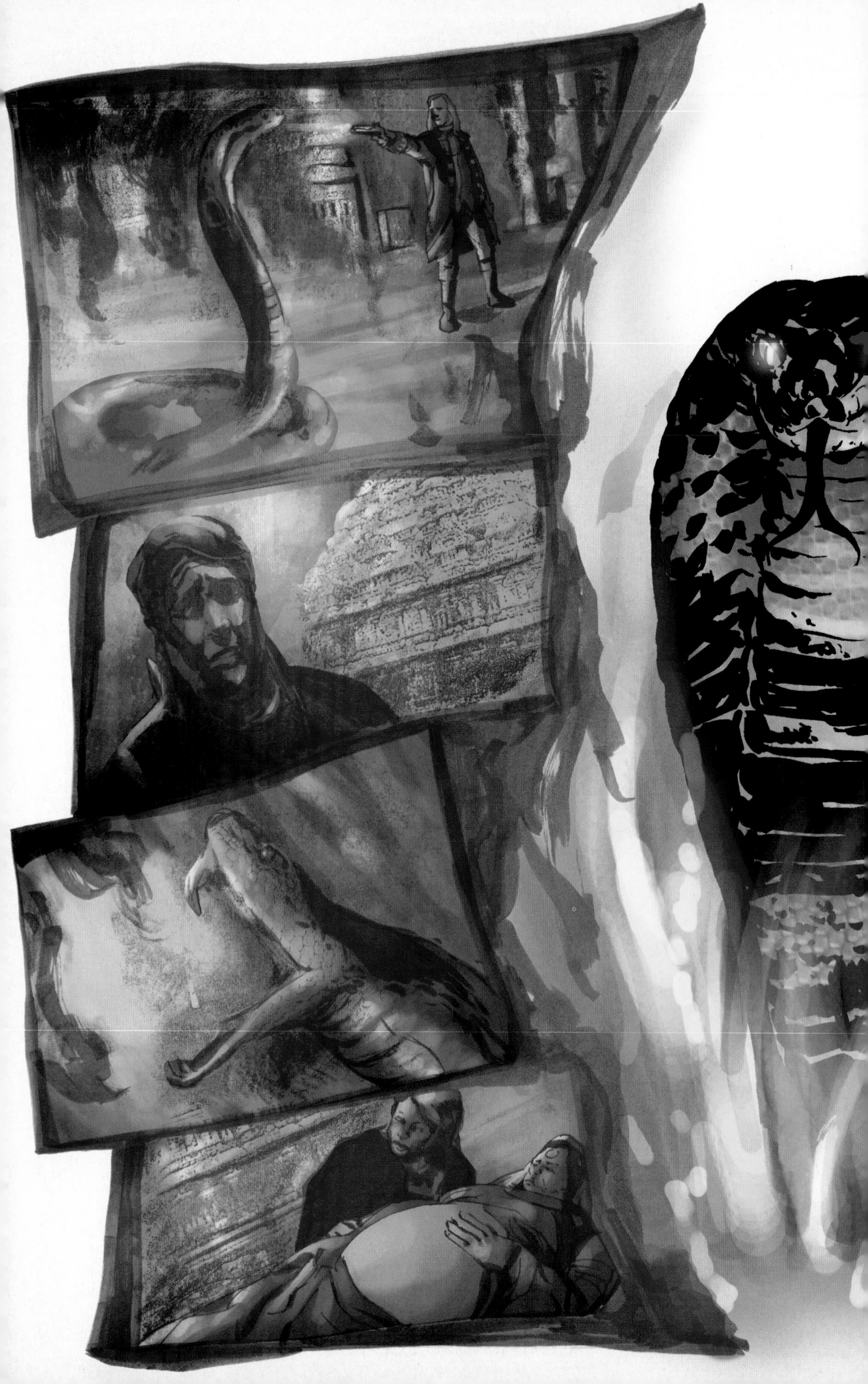

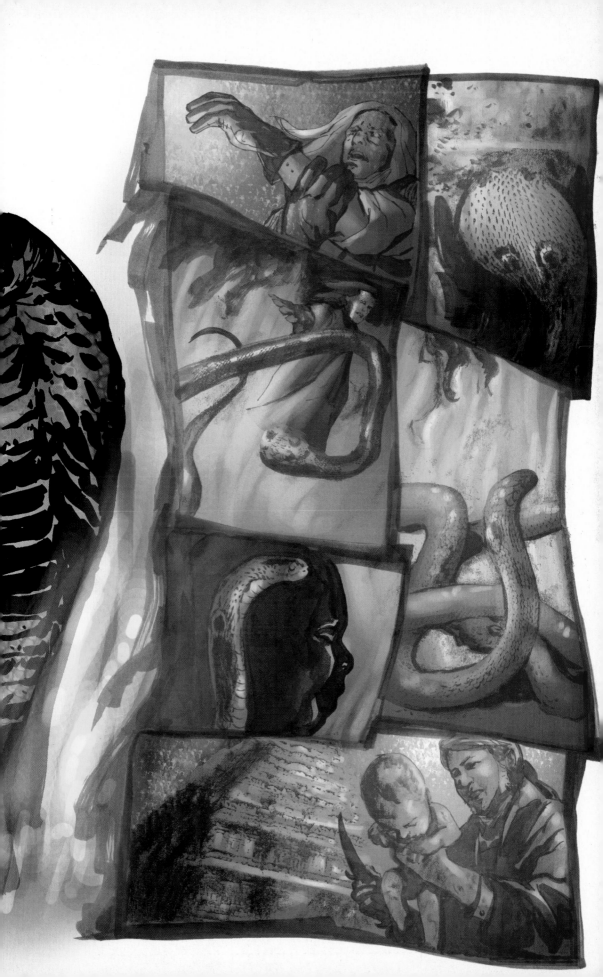

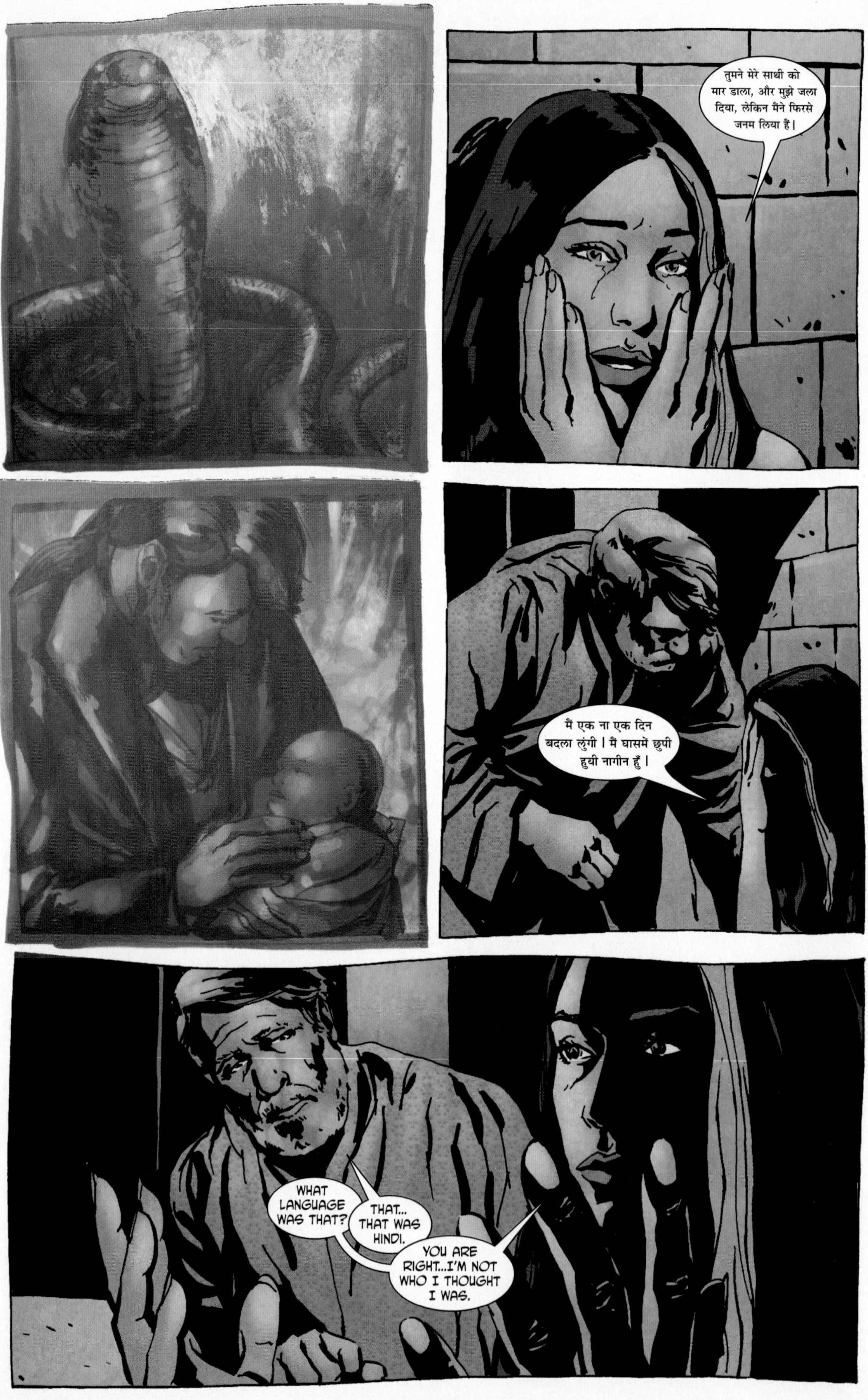
तुमने मेरे साथी को मार डाला, और मुझे जला दिया, लेकिन मैंने फिरसे जनम लिया हैं।
मैं एक ना एक दिन बदला लुंगी। मैं घासमें छुपी हुयी नागीन हुँ।
WHAT LANGUAGE WAS THAT?
THAT... THAT WAS HINDI.
YOU ARE RIGHT...I'M NOT WHO I THOUGHT I WAS.

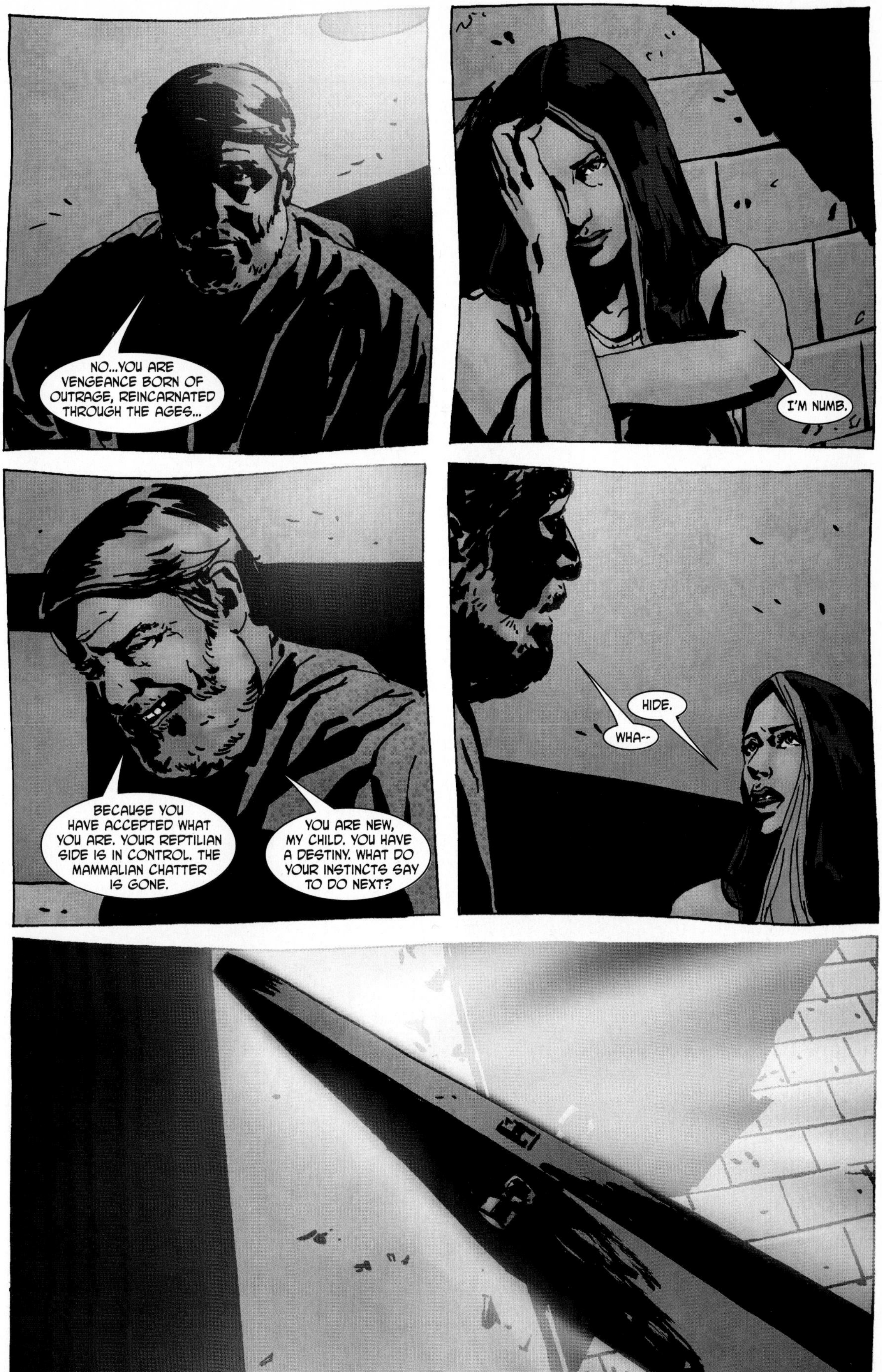
NO...YOU ARE VENGEANCE BORN OF OUTRAGE, REINCARNATED THROUGH THE AGES...
I'M NUMB.
BECAUSE YOU HAVE ACCEPTED WHAT YOU ARE. YOUR REPTILIAN SIDE IS IN CONTROL. THE MAMMALIAN CHATTER IS GONE.
YOU ARE NEW, MY CHILD. YOU HAVE A DESTINY. WHAT DO YOUR INSTINCTS SAY TO DO NEXT?
WHA--
HIDE.

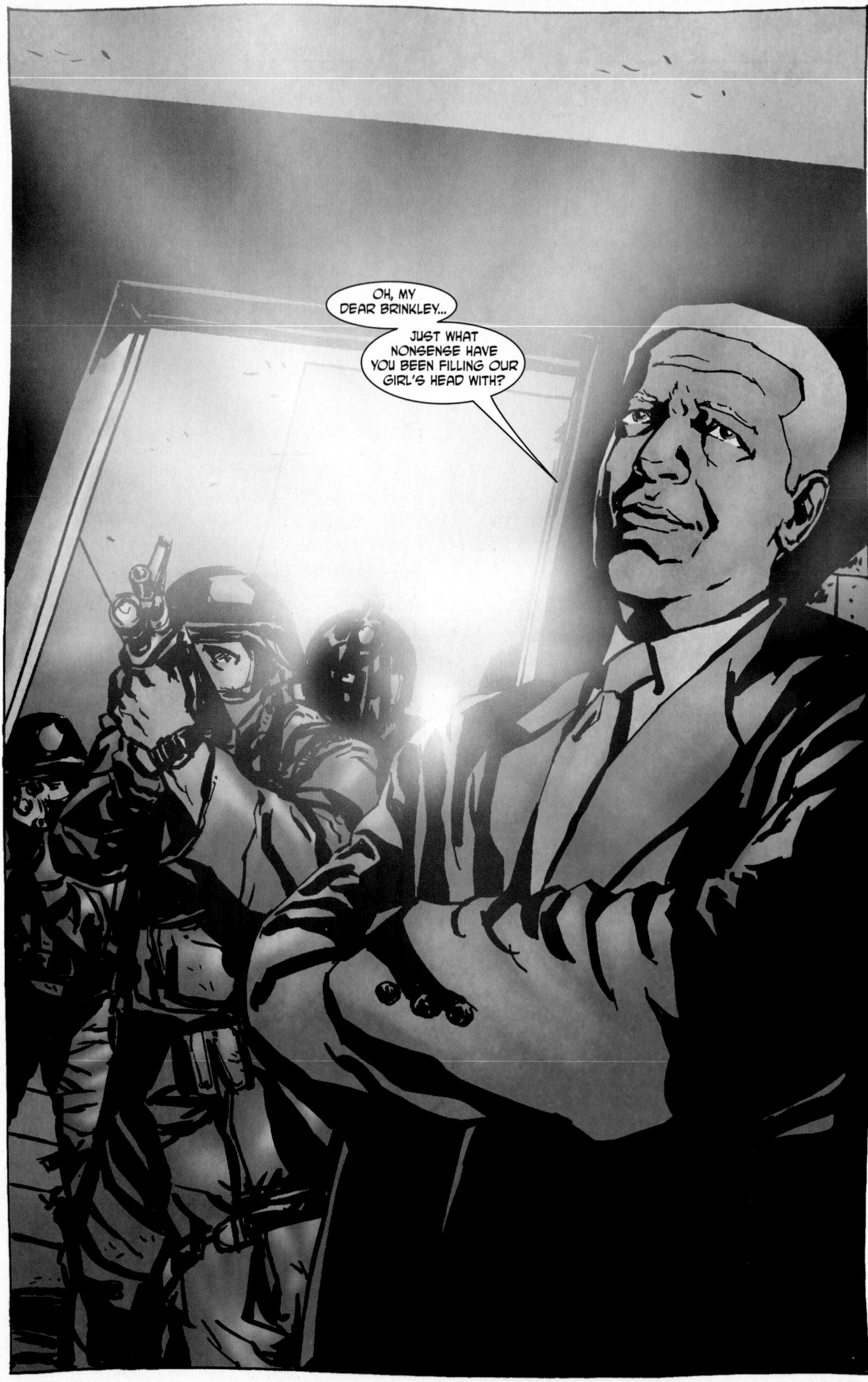
OH, MY DEAR BRINKLEY...
JUST WHAT NONSENSE HAVE YOU BEEN FILLING OUR GIRL'S HEAD WITH?

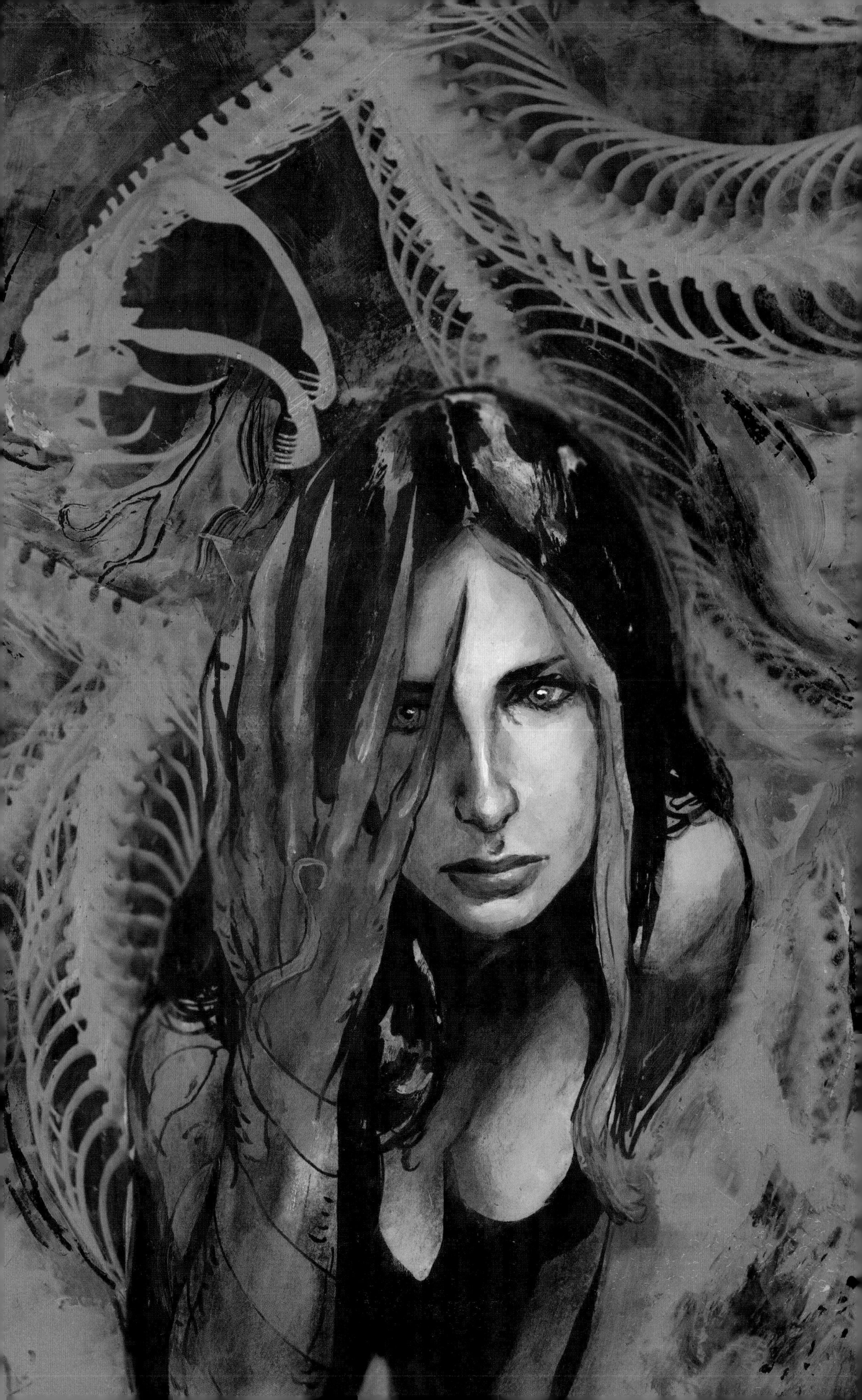

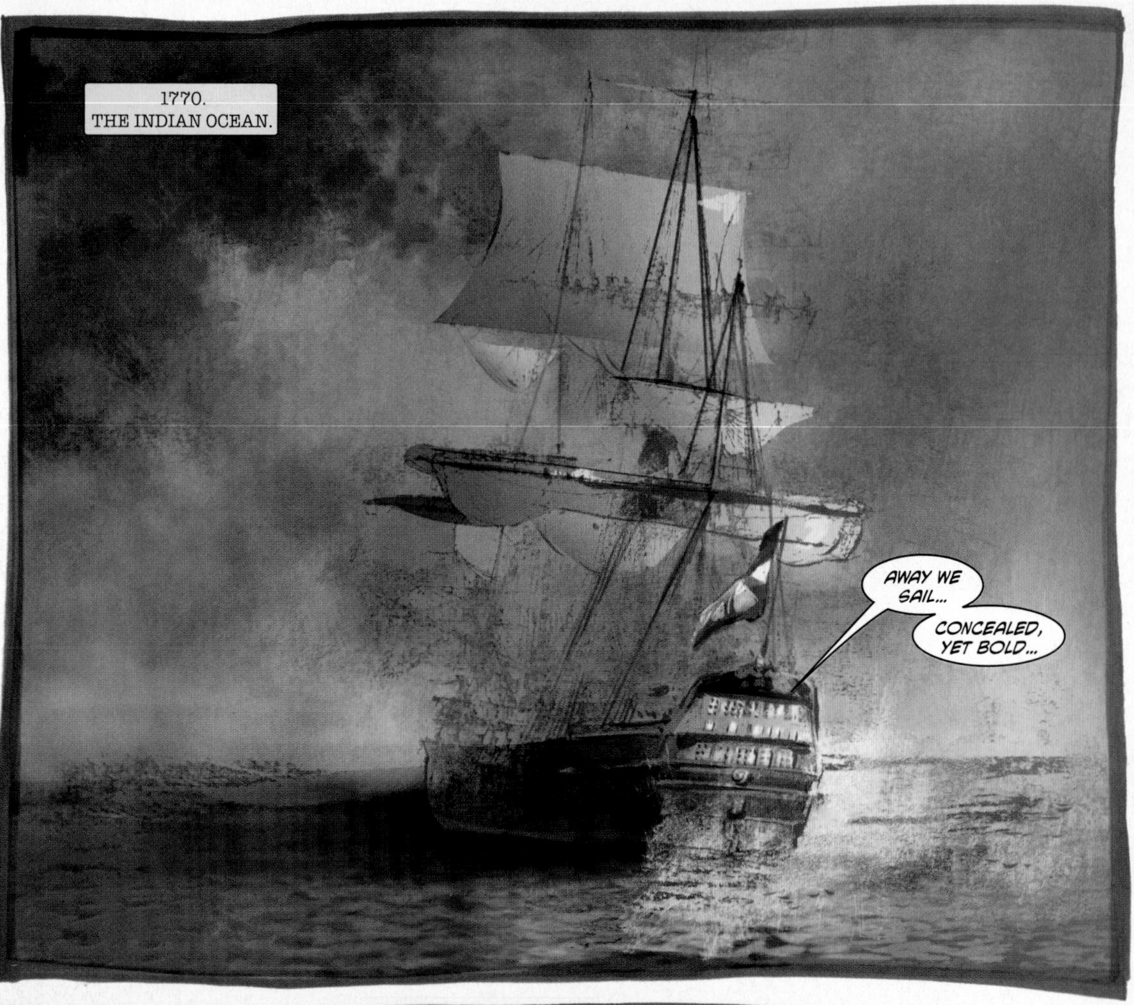
1770.
THE INDIAN OCEAN.
AWAY WE SAIL...
CONCEALED, YET BOLD...

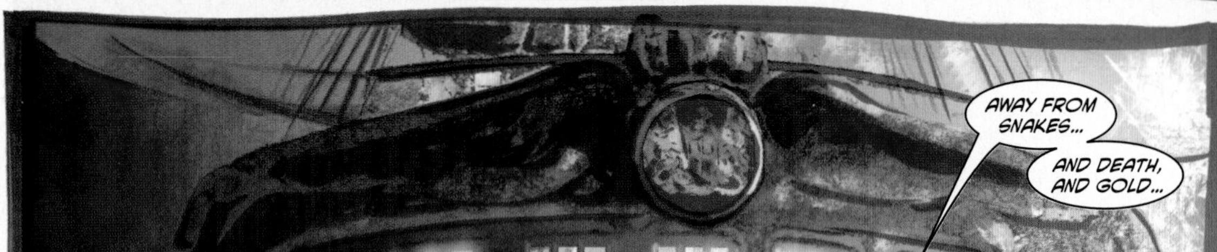
AWAY FROM SNAKES...
AND DEATH, AND GOLD...

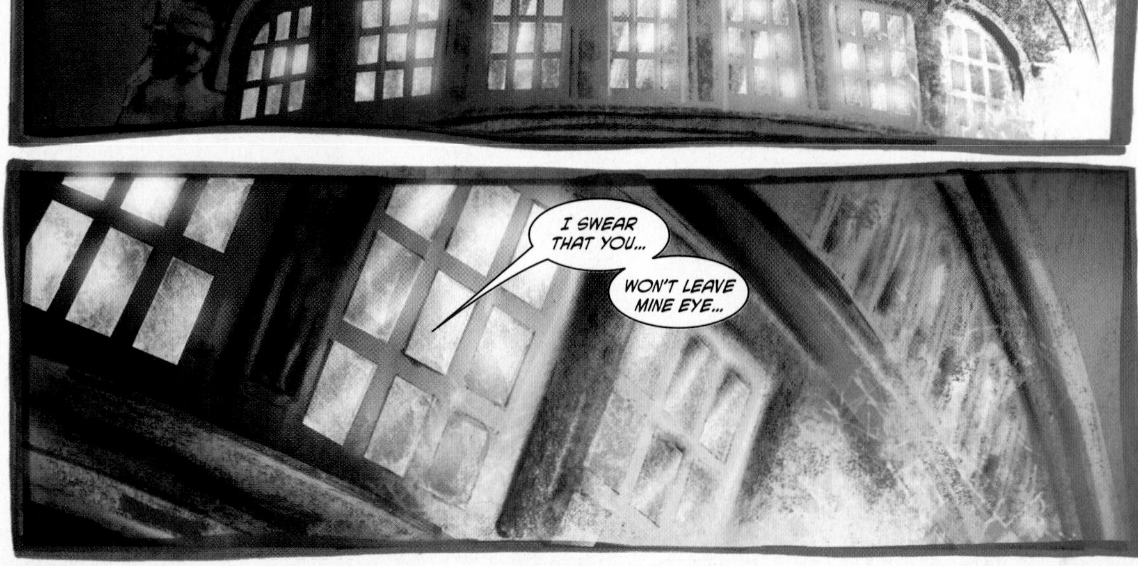
I SWEAR THAT YOU...
WON'T LEAVE MINE EYE...

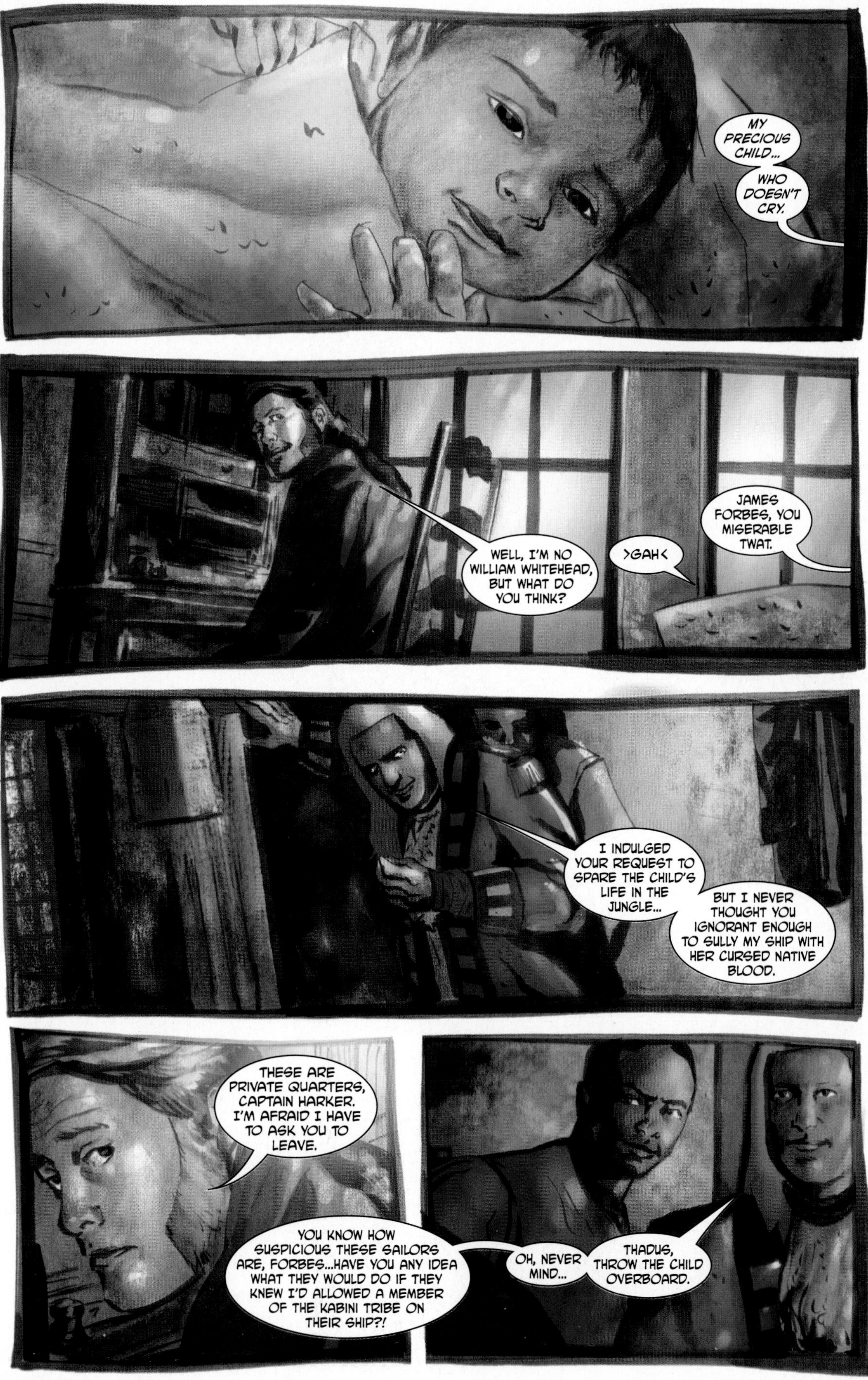
MY PRECIOUS CHILD...
WHO DOESN'T CRY.
WELL, I'M NO WILLIAM WHITEHEAD, BUT WHAT DO YOU THINK?
>GAH<
JAMES FORBES, YOU MISERABLE TWAT.
I INDULGED YOUR REQUEST TO SPARE THE CHILD'S LIFE IN THE JUNGLE...
BUT I NEVER THOUGHT YOU IGNORANT ENOUGH TO SULLY MY SHIP WITH HER CURSED NATIVE BLOOD.
THESE ARE PRIVATE QUARTERS, CAPTAIN HARKER. I'M AFRAID I HAVE TO ASK YOU TO LEAVE.
YOU KNOW HOW SUSPICIOUS THESE SAILORS ARE, FORBES...HAVE YOU ANY IDEA WHAT THEY WOULD DO IF THEY KNEW I'D ALLOWED A MEMBER OF THE KABINI TRIBE ON THEIR SHIP?!
OH, NEVER MIND...
THADUS, THROW THE CHILD OVERBOARD.

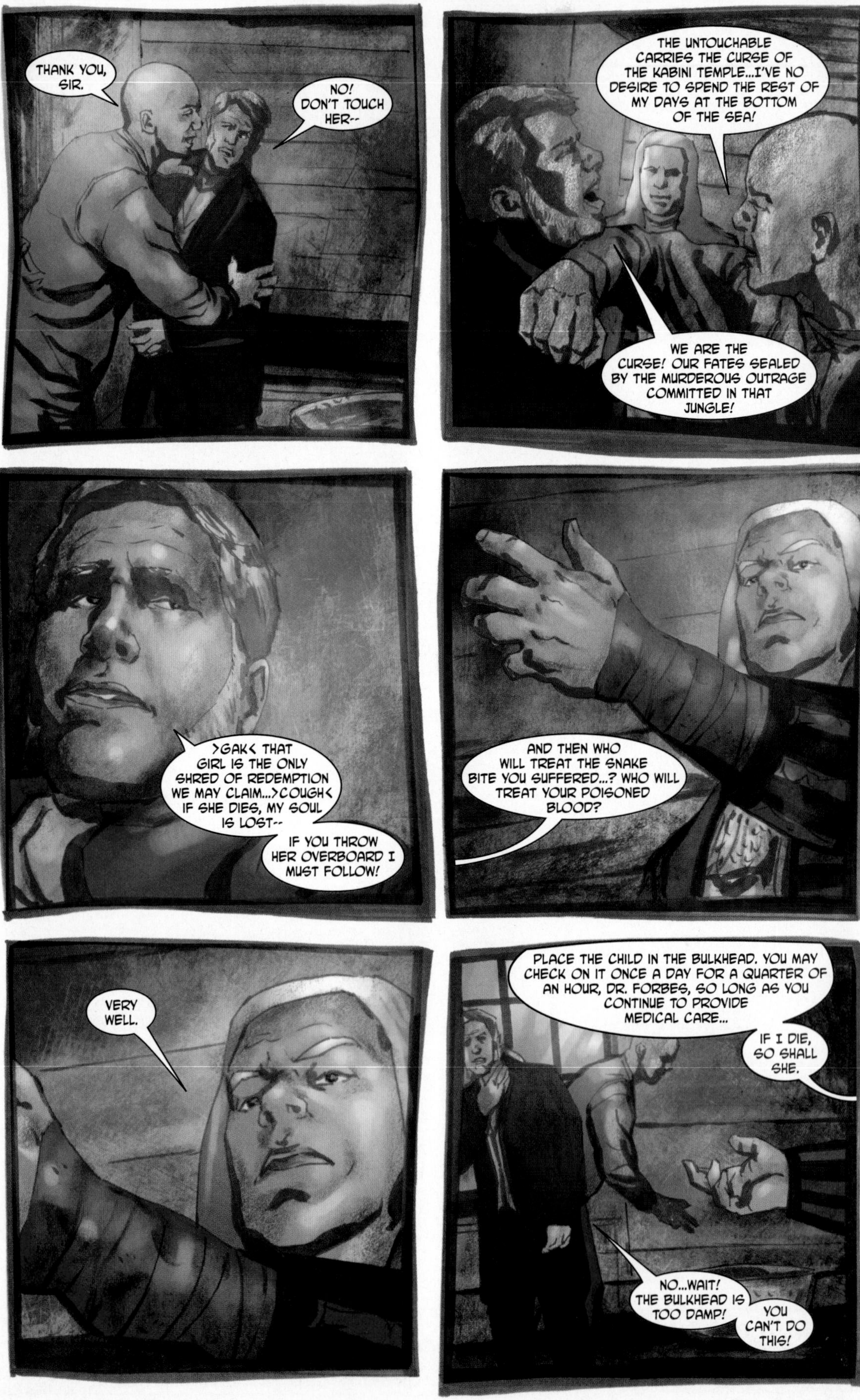
THANK YOU, SIR.
NO! DON'T TOUCH HER--
THE UNTOUCHABLE CARRIES THE CURSE OF THE KABINI TEMPLE...I'VE NO DESIRE TO SPEND THE REST OF MY DAYS AT THE BOTTOM OF THE SEA!
WE ARE THE CURSE! OUR FATES SEALED BY THE MURDEROUS OUTRAGE COMMITTED IN THAT JUNGLE!
>GAK< THAT GIRL IS THE ONLY SHRED OF REDEMPTION WE MAY CLAIM...>COUGH< IF SHE DIES, MY SOUL IS LOST--
IF YOU THROW HER OVERBOARD I MUST FOLLOW!
AND THEN WHO WILL TREAT THE SNAKE BITE YOU SUFFERED...? WHO WILL TREAT YOUR POISONED BLOOD?
VERY WELL.
PLACE THE CHILD IN THE BULKHEAD. YOU MAY CHECK ON IT ONCE A DAY FOR A QUARTER OF AN HOUR, DR. FORBES, SO LONG AS YOU CONTINUE TO PROVIDE MEDICAL CARE...
IF I DIE, SO SHALL SHE.
NO...WAIT! THE BULKHEAD IS TOO DAMP!
YOU CAN'T DO THIS!

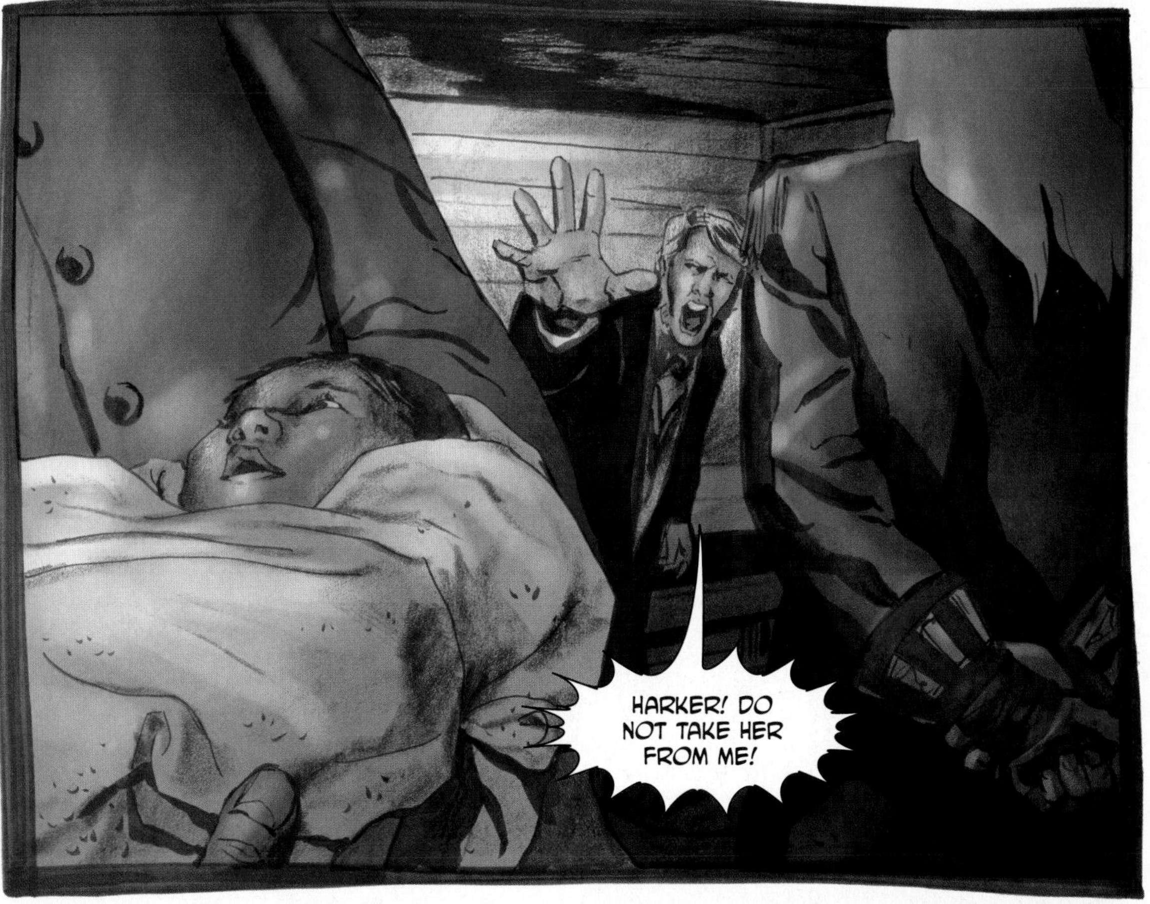
HARKER! DO NOT TAKE HER FROM ME!

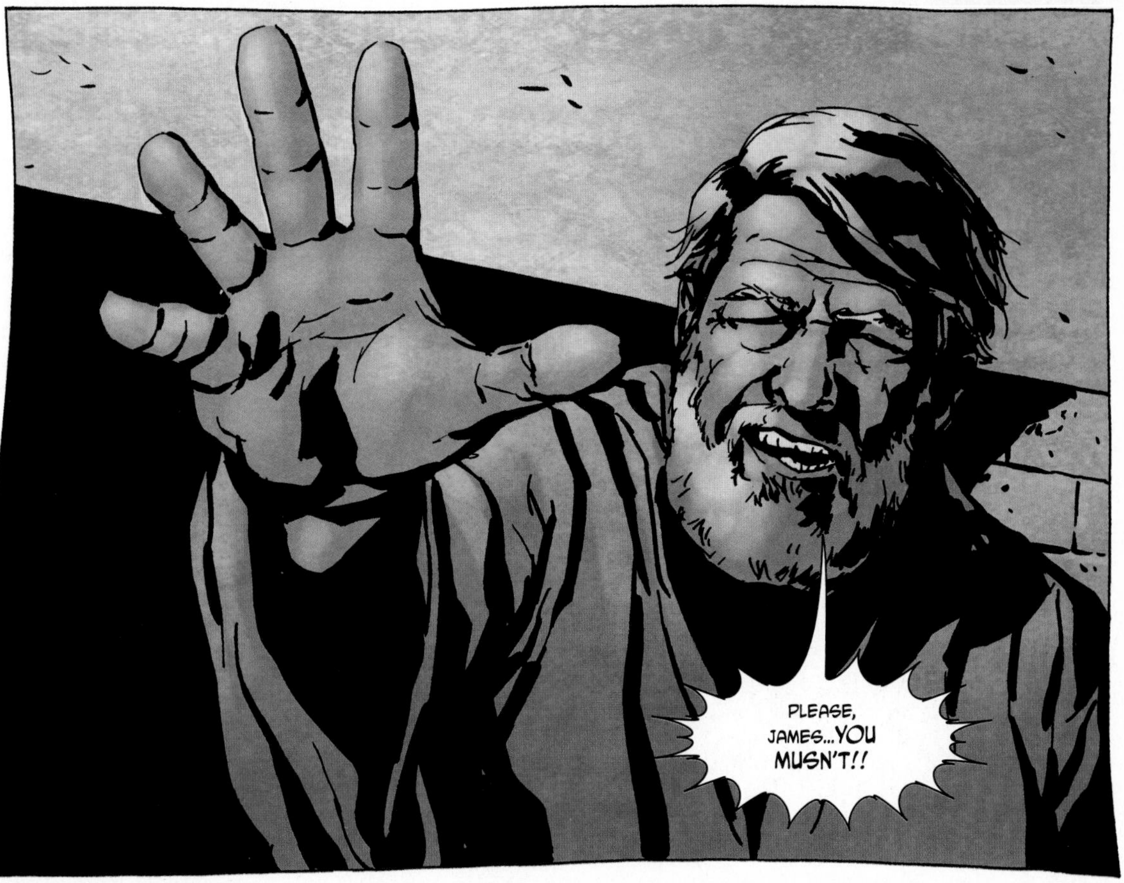
PLEASE, JAMES...YOU MUSN'T!!

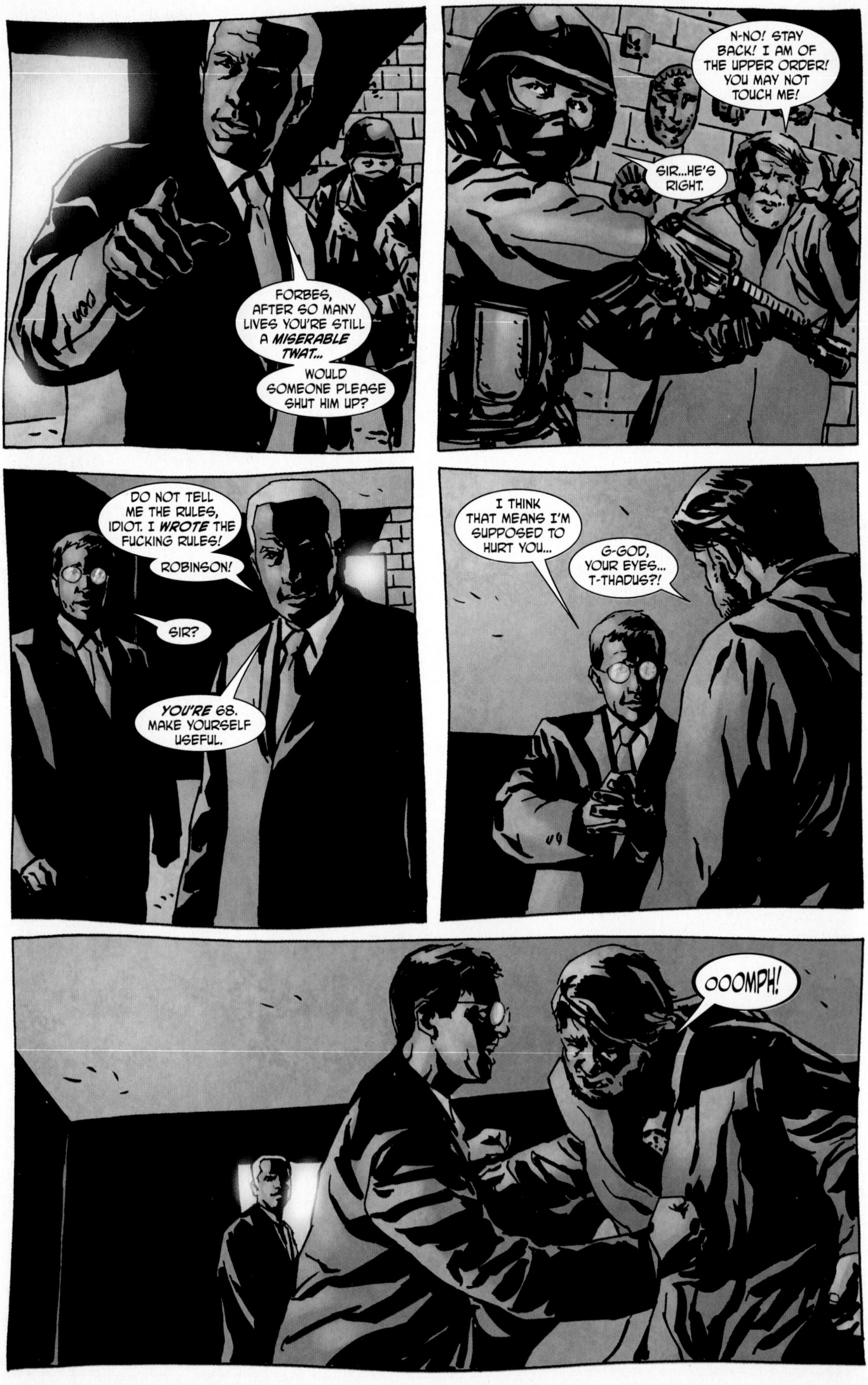
FORBES, AFTER SO MANY LIVES YOU'RE STILL A *MISERABLE TWAT...*
WOULD SOMEONE PLEASE SHUT HIM UP?
N-NO! STAY BACK! I AM OF THE UPPER ORDER! YOU MAY NOT TOUCH ME!
SIR...HE'S RIGHT.
DO NOT TELL ME THE RULES, IDIOT. I *WROTE* THE FUCKING RULES!
ROBINSON!
SIR?
YOU'RE 68. MAKE YOURSELF USEFUL.
I THINK THAT MEANS I'M SUPPOSED TO HURT YOU...
G-GOD, YOUR EYES... T-THADUS?!
OOOMPH!

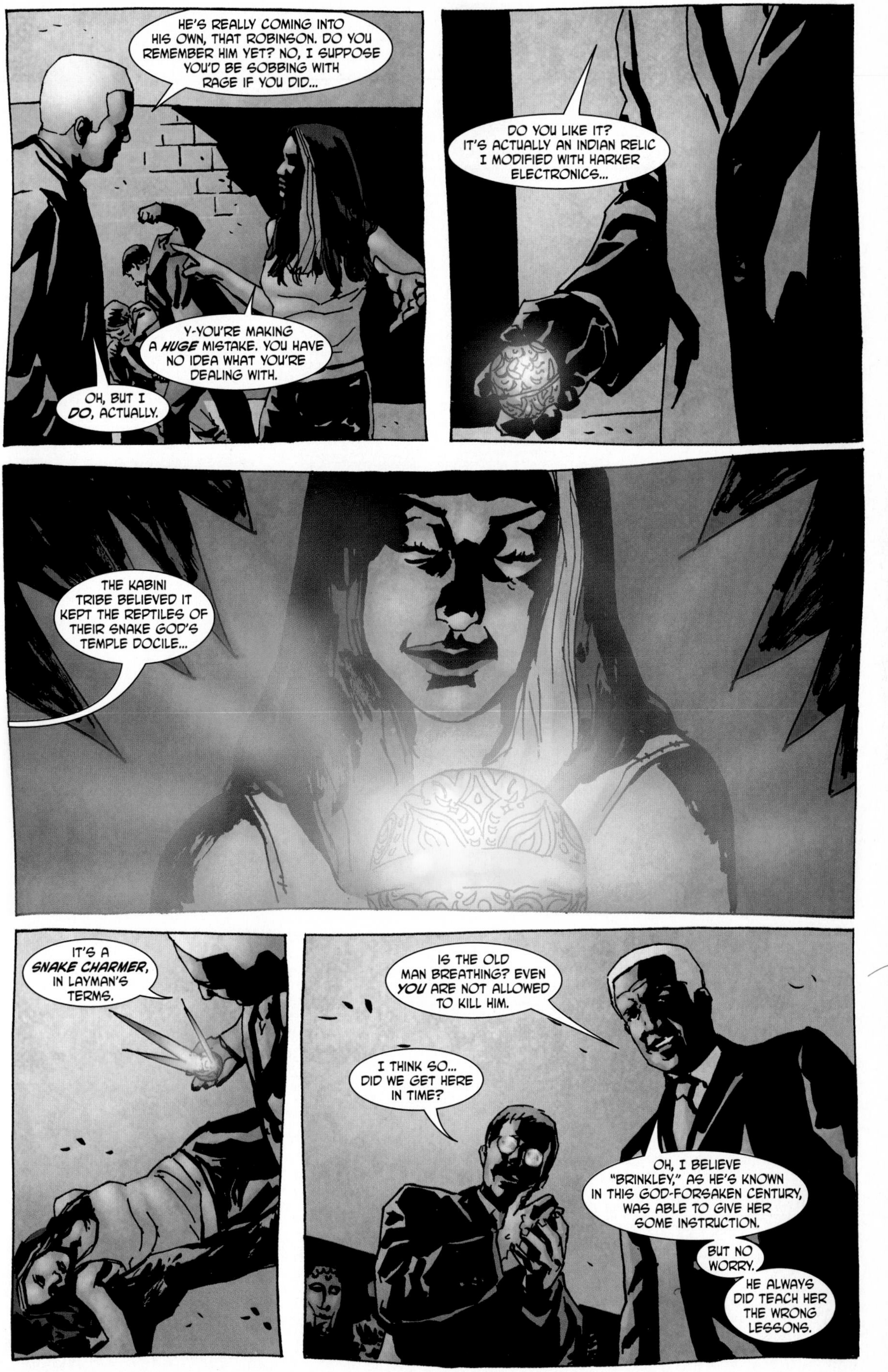
HE'S REALLY COMING INTO HIS OWN, THAT ROBINSON. DO YOU REMEMBER HIM YET? NO, I SUPPOSE YOU'D BE SOBBING WITH RAGE IF YOU DID...
Y-YOU'RE MAKING A *HUGE* MISTAKE. YOU HAVE NO IDEA WHAT YOU'RE DEALING WITH.
OH, BUT I *DO*, ACTUALLY.
DO YOU LIKE IT? IT'S ACTUALLY AN INDIAN RELIC I MODIFIED WITH HARKER ELECTRONICS...
THE KABINI TRIBE BELIEVED IT KEPT THE REPTILES OF THEIR SNAKE GOD'S TEMPLE DOCILE...
IT'S A *SNAKE CHARMER*, IN LAYMAN'S TERMS.
IS THE OLD MAN BREATHING? EVEN *YOU* ARE NOT ALLOWED TO KILL HIM.
I THINK SO... DID WE GET HERE IN TIME?
OH, I BELIEVE "BRINKLEY," AS HE'S KNOWN IN THIS GOD-FORSAKEN CENTURY, WAS ABLE TO GIVE HER SOME INSTRUCTION.
BUT NO WORRY.
HE ALWAYS DID TEACH HER THE WRONG LESSONS.

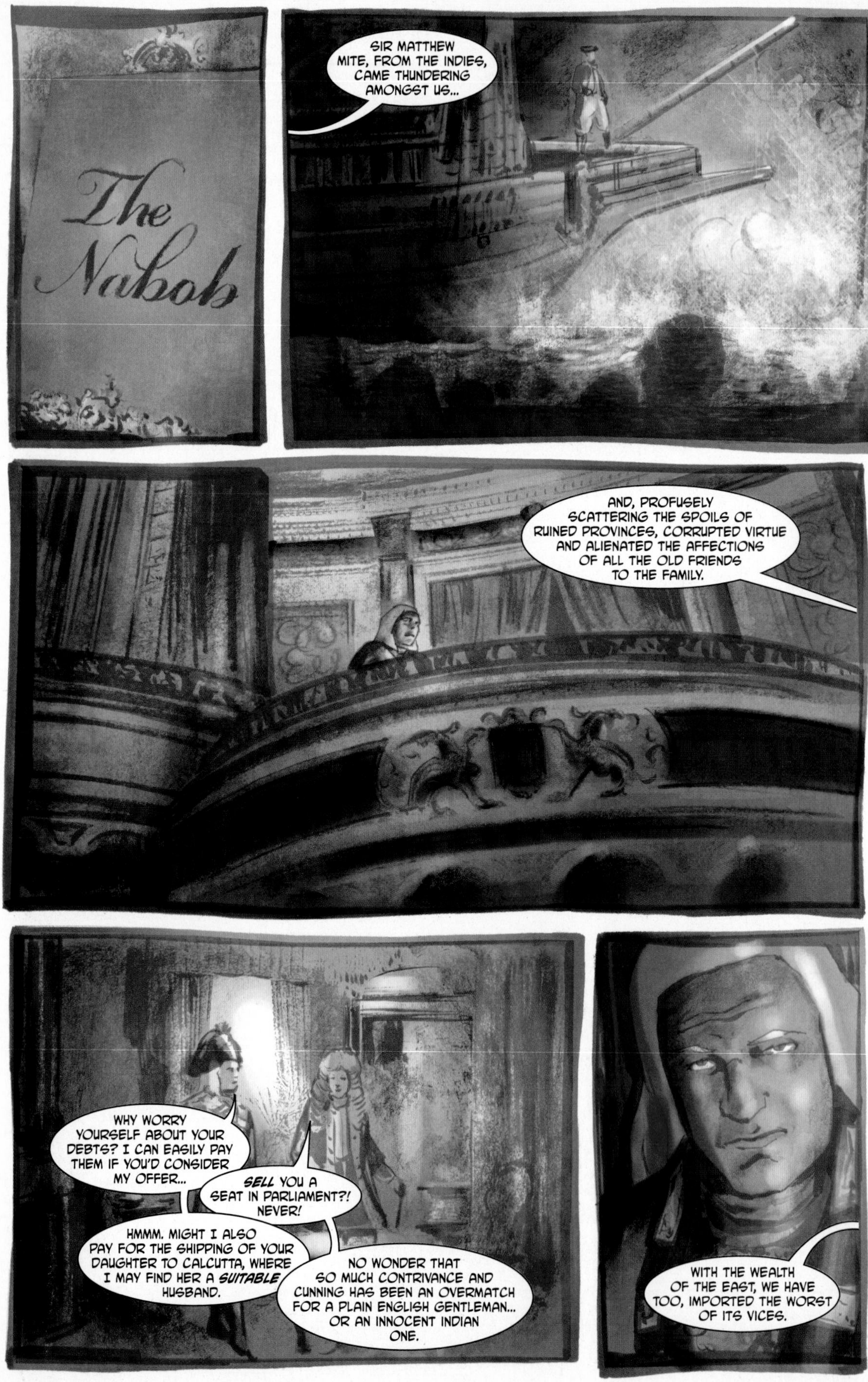
The Nabob
SIR MATTHEW MITE, FROM THE INDIES, CAME THUNDERING AMONGST US...
AND, PROFUSELY SCATTERING THE SPOILS OF RUINED PROVINCES, CORRUPTED VIRTUE AND ALIENATED THE AFFECTIONS OF ALL THE OLD FRIENDS TO THE FAMILY.
WHY WORRY YOURSELF ABOUT YOUR DEBTS? I CAN EASILY PAY THEM IF YOU'D CONSIDER MY OFFER...
SELL YOU A SEAT IN PARLIAMENT?! NEVER!
HMMM. MIGHT I ALSO PAY FOR THE SHIPPING OF YOUR DAUGHTER TO CALCUTTA, WHERE I MAY FIND HER A SUITABLE HUSBAND.
NO WONDER THAT SO MUCH CONTRIVANCE AND CUNNING HAS BEEN AN OVERMATCH FOR A PLAIN ENGLISH GENTLEMAN... OR AN INNOCENT INDIAN ONE.
WITH THE WEALTH OF THE EAST, WE HAVE TOO, IMPORTED THE WORST OF ITS VICES.

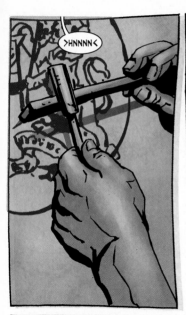

>HNNNN<

HOW OLD IS THAT NEEDLE?

THE PAST IS NOT EPHEMERAL, MR. ROBINSON. IT IS REAL...IT MARKS US.

FOR THE 68, THESE MARKS ARE SOMETIMES PAINFUL...BUT THE PAST IS PAINFUL...

THAT IS WHY SO FEW PEOPLE FACE IT.

HELLO, JESSICA PETERSON. ARE YOU READY TO FACE YOUR PAST?

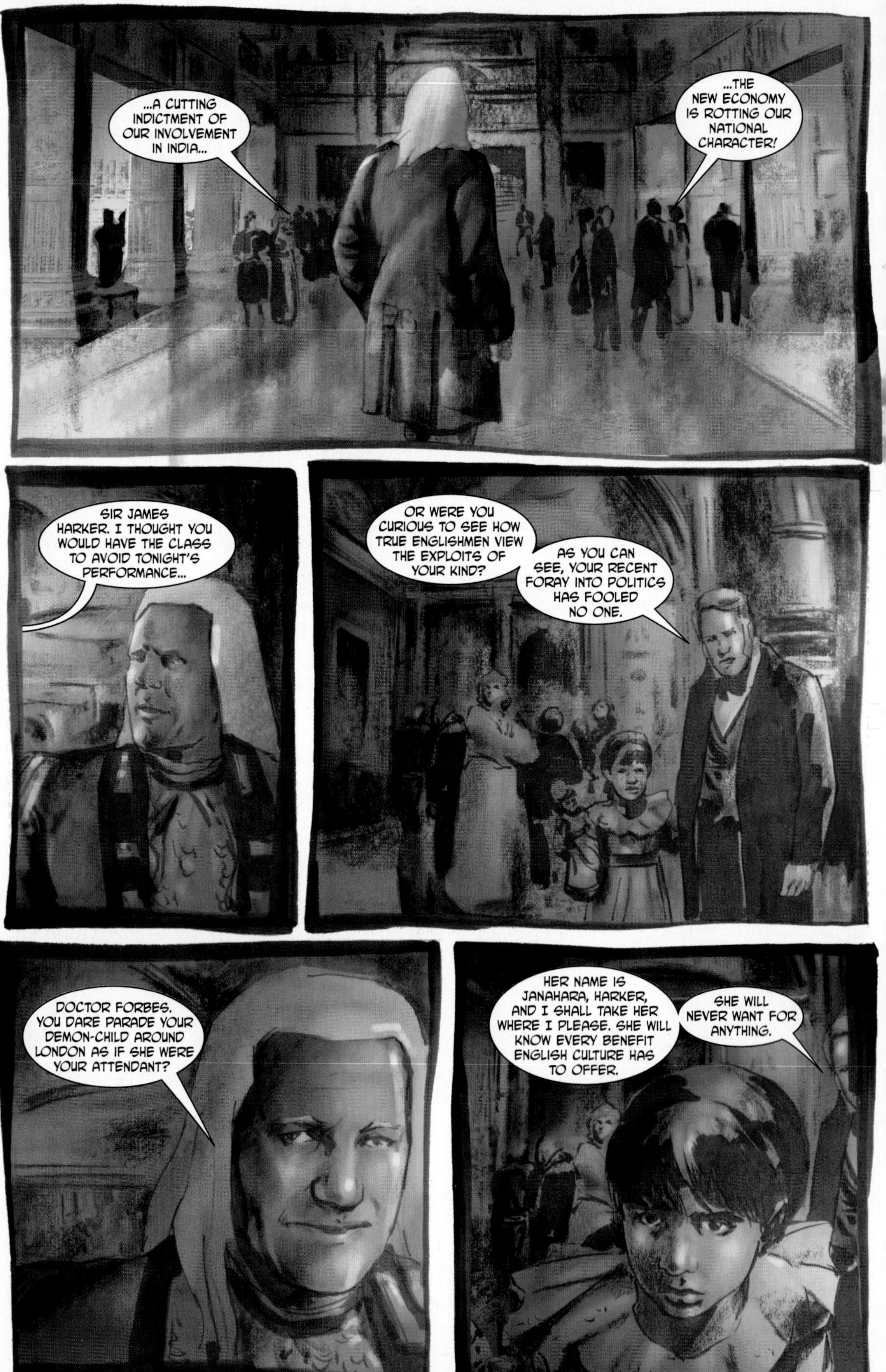
...A CUTTING INDICTMENT OF OUR INVOLVEMENT IN INDIA...
...THE NEW ECONOMY IS ROTTING OUR NATIONAL CHARACTER!
SIR JAMES HARKER. I THOUGHT YOU WOULD HAVE THE CLASS TO AVOID TONIGHT'S PERFORMANCE...
OR WERE YOU CURIOUS TO SEE HOW TRUE ENGLISHMEN VIEW THE EXPLOITS OF YOUR KIND?
AS YOU CAN SEE, YOUR RECENT FORAY INTO POLITICS HAS FOOLED NO ONE.
DOCTOR FORBES. YOU DARE PARADE YOUR DEMON-CHILD AROUND LONDON AS IF SHE WERE YOUR ATTENDANT?
HER NAME IS JANAHARA, HARKER, AND I SHALL TAKE HER WHERE I PLEASE. SHE WILL KNOW EVERY BENEFIT ENGLISH CULTURE HAS TO OFFER.
SHE WILL NEVER WANT FOR ANYTHING.

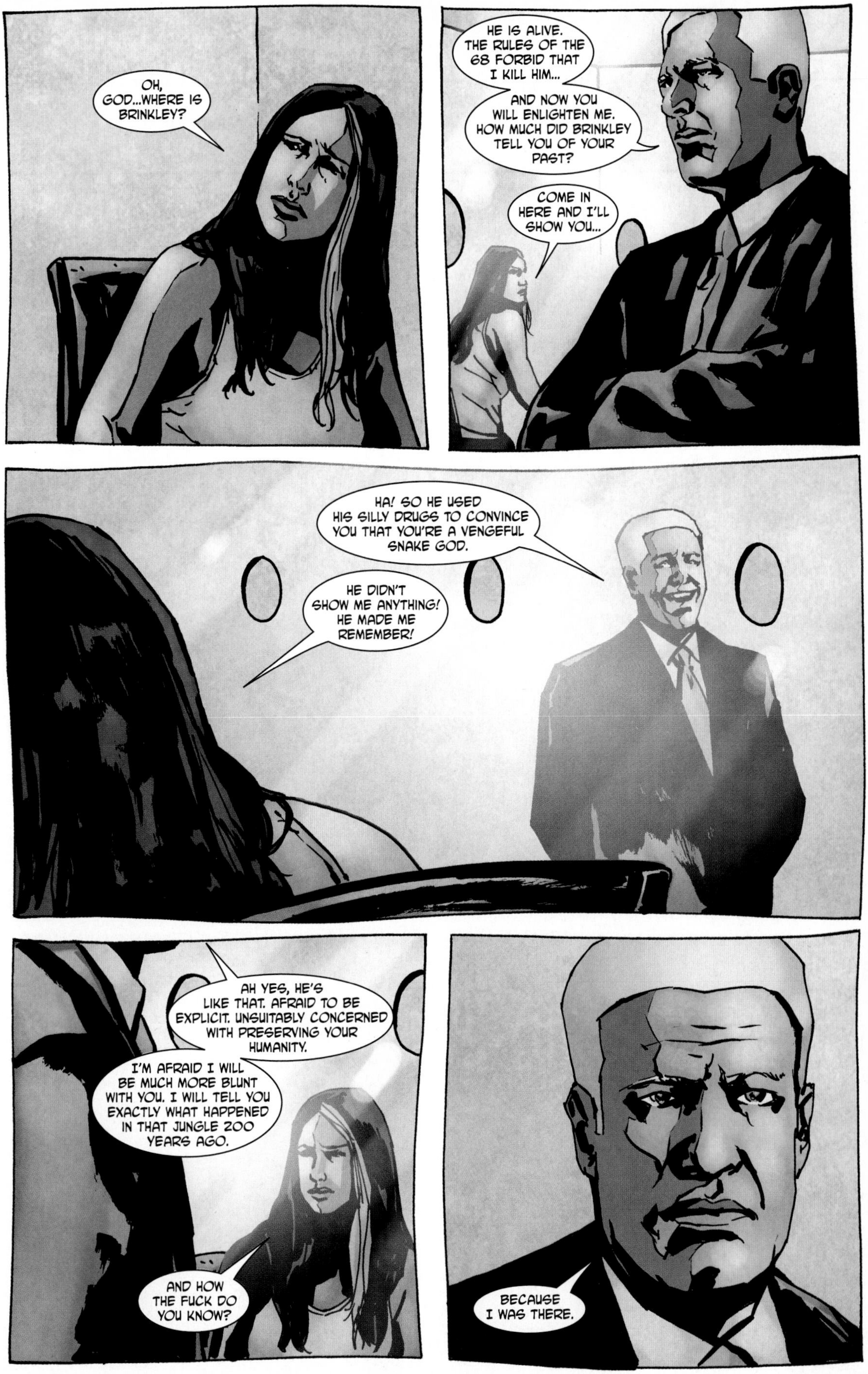
OH, GOD...WHERE IS BRINKLEY?
HE IS ALIVE. THE RULES OF THE 68 FORBID THAT I KILL HIM...
AND NOW YOU WILL ENLIGHTEN ME. HOW MUCH DID BRINKLEY TELL YOU OF YOUR PAST?
COME IN HERE AND I'LL SHOW YOU...
HA! SO HE USED HIS SILLY DRUGS TO CONVINCE YOU THAT YOU'RE A VENGEFUL SNAKE GOD.
HE DIDN'T SHOW ME ANYTHING! HE MADE ME REMEMBER!
AH YES, HE'S LIKE THAT. AFRAID TO BE EXPLICIT. UNSUITABLY CONCERNED WITH PRESERVING YOUR HUMANITY.
I'M AFRAID I WILL BE MUCH MORE BLUNT WITH YOU. I WILL TELL YOU EXACTLY WHAT HAPPENED IN THAT JUNGLE 200 YEARS AGO.
AND HOW THE FUCK DO YOU KNOW?
BECAUSE I WAS THERE.

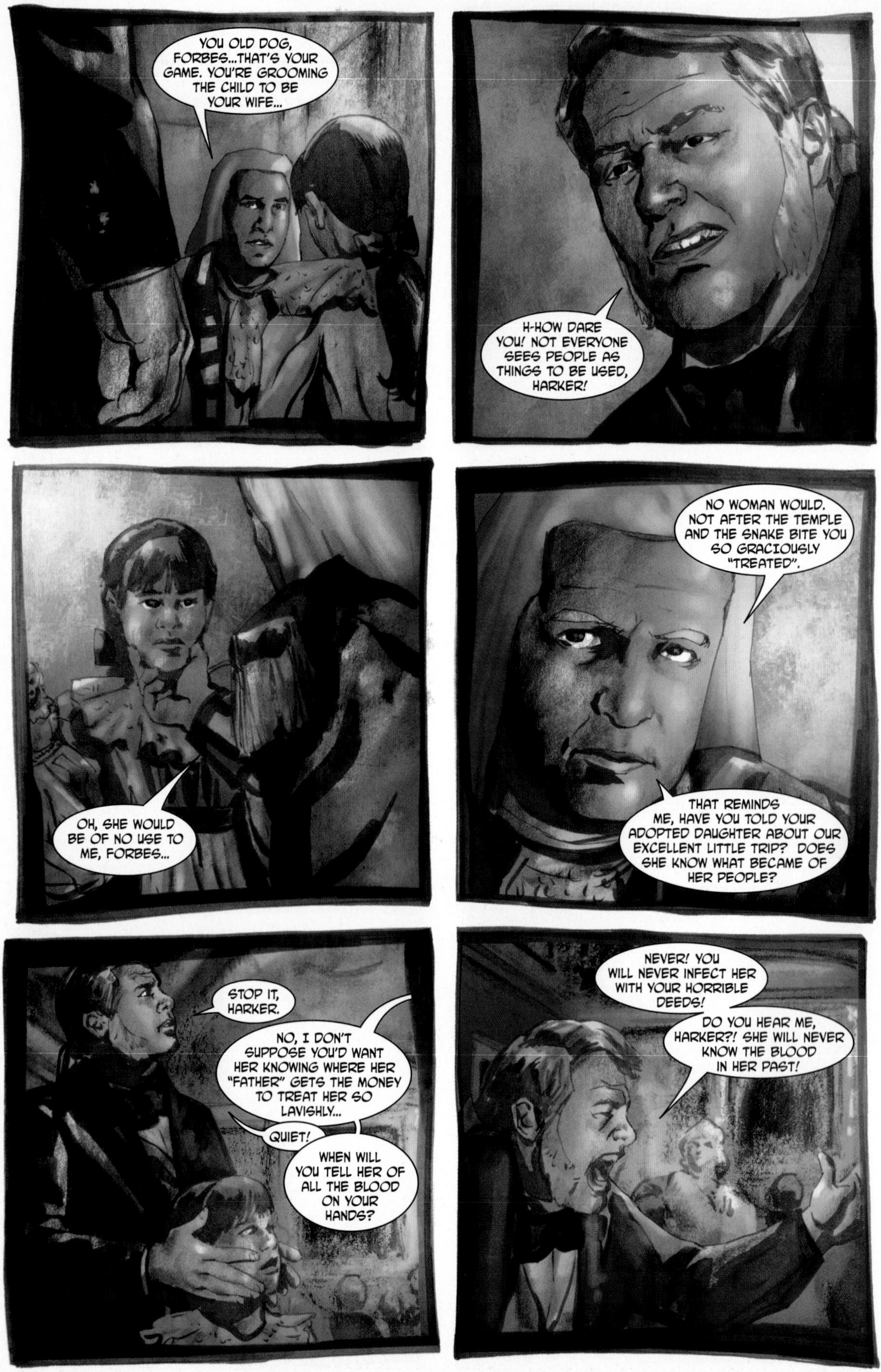
YOU OLD DOG, FORBES...THAT'S YOUR GAME. YOU'RE GROOMING THE CHILD TO BE YOUR WIFE...
H-HOW DARE YOU! NOT EVERYONE SEES PEOPLE AS THINGS TO BE USED, HARKER!
OH, SHE WOULD BE OF NO USE TO ME, FORBES...
NO WOMAN WOULD. NOT AFTER THE TEMPLE AND THE SNAKE BITE YOU SO GRACIOUSLY "TREATED".
THAT REMINDS ME, HAVE YOU TOLD YOUR ADOPTED DAUGHTER ABOUT OUR EXCELLENT LITTLE TRIP? DOES SHE KNOW WHAT BECAME OF HER PEOPLE?
STOP IT, HARKER.
NO, I DON'T SUPPOSE YOU'D WANT HER KNOWING WHERE HER "FATHER" GETS THE MONEY TO TREAT HER SO LAVISHLY...
QUIET!
WHEN WILL YOU TELL HER OF ALL THE BLOOD ON YOUR HANDS?
NEVER! YOU WILL NEVER INFECT HER WITH YOUR HORRIBLE DEEDS!
DO YOU HEAR ME, HARKER?! SHE WILL NEVER KNOW THE BLOOD IN HER PAST!

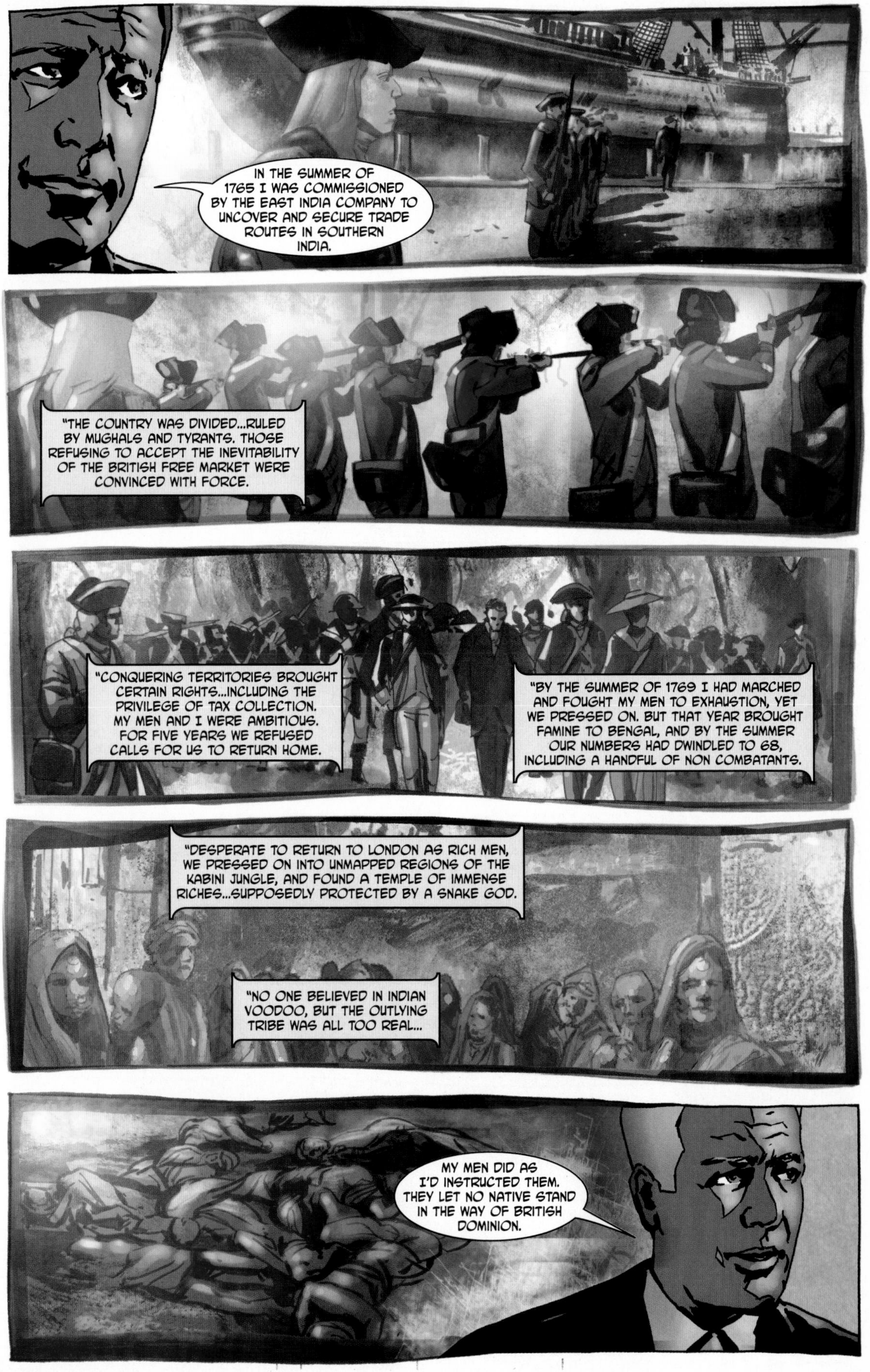
IN THE SUMMER OF 1765 I WAS COMMISSIONED BY THE EAST INDIA COMPANY TO UNCOVER AND SECURE TRADE ROUTES IN SOUTHERN INDIA.
"THE COUNTRY WAS DIVIDED...RULED BY MUGHALS AND TYRANTS. THOSE REFUSING TO ACCEPT THE INEVITABILITY OF THE BRITISH FREE MARKET WERE CONVINCED WITH FORCE.
"CONQUERING TERRITORIES BROUGHT CERTAIN RIGHTS...INCLUDING THE PRIVILEGE OF TAX COLLECTION. MY MEN AND I WERE AMBITIOUS. FOR FIVE YEARS WE REFUSED CALLS FOR US TO RETURN HOME.
"BY THE SUMMER OF 1769 I HAD MARCHED AND FOUGHT MY MEN TO EXHAUSTION, YET WE PRESSED ON. BUT THAT YEAR BROUGHT FAMINE TO BENGAL, AND BY THE SUMMER OUR NUMBERS HAD DWINDLED TO 68, INCLUDING A HANDFUL OF NON COMBATANTS.
"DESPERATE TO RETURN TO LONDON AS RICH MEN, WE PRESSED ON INTO UNMAPPED REGIONS OF THE KABINI JUNGLE, AND FOUND A TEMPLE OF IMMENSE RICHES...SUPPOSEDLY PROTECTED BY A SNAKE GOD.
"NO ONE BELIEVED IN INDIAN VOODOO, BUT THE OUTLYING TRIBE WAS ALL TOO REAL...
MY MEN DID AS I'D INSTRUCTED THEM. THEY LET NO NATIVE STAND IN THE WAY OF BRITISH DOMINION.

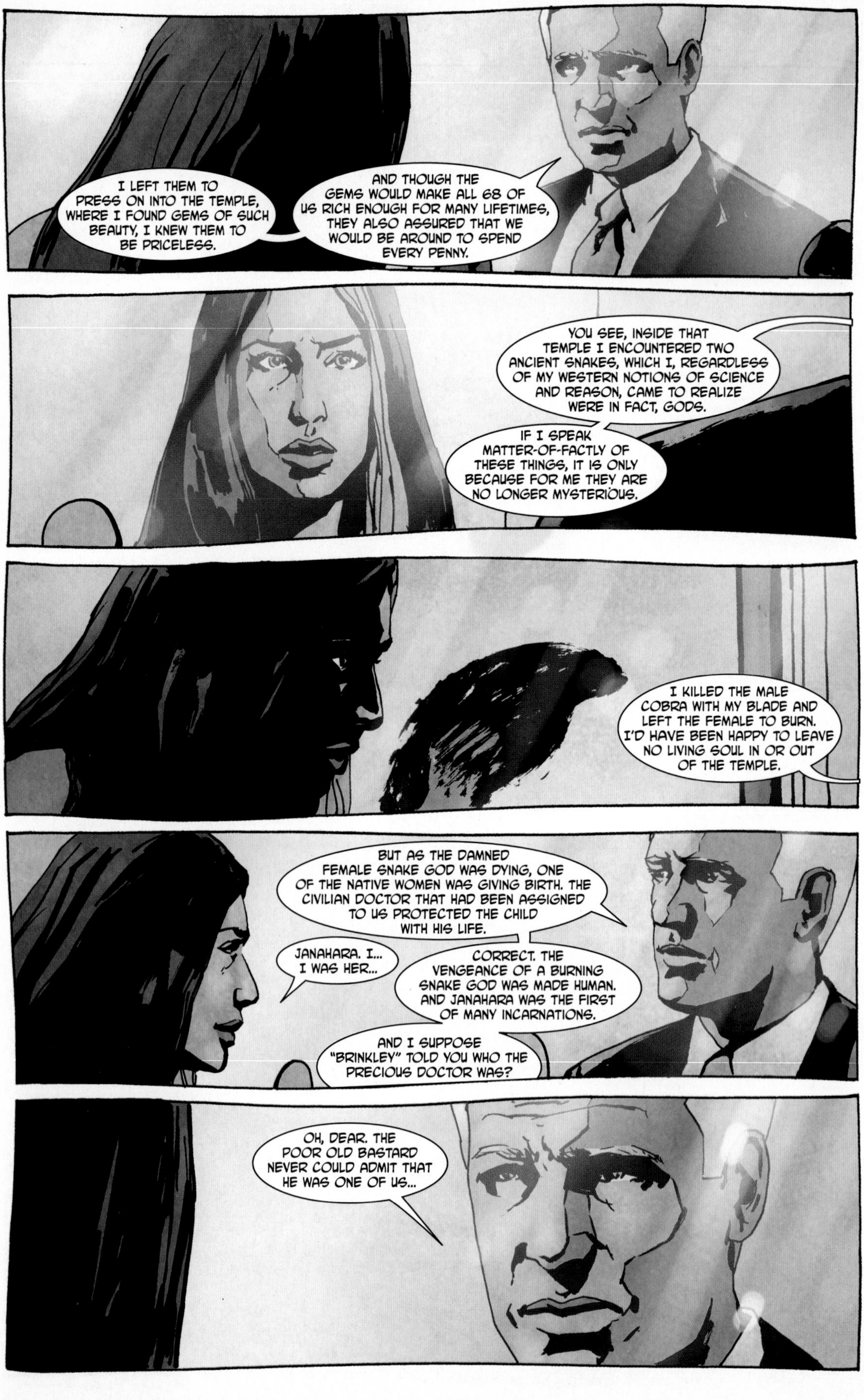
I LEFT THEM TO PRESS ON INTO THE TEMPLE, WHERE I FOUND GEMS OF SUCH BEAUTY, I KNEW THEM TO BE PRICELESS.
AND THOUGH THE GEMS WOULD MAKE ALL 68 OF US RICH ENOUGH FOR MANY LIFETIMES, THEY ALSO ASSURED THAT WE WOULD BE AROUND TO SPEND EVERY PENNY.
YOU SEE, INSIDE THAT TEMPLE I ENCOUNTERED TWO ANCIENT SNAKES, WHICH I, REGARDLESS OF MY WESTERN NOTIONS OF SCIENCE AND REASON, CAME TO REALIZE WERE IN FACT, GODS.
IF I SPEAK MATTER-OF-FACTLY OF THESE THINGS, IT IS ONLY BECAUSE FOR ME THEY ARE NO LONGER MYSTERIOUS.
I KILLED THE MALE COBRA WITH MY BLADE AND LEFT THE FEMALE TO BURN. I'D HAVE BEEN HAPPY TO LEAVE NO LIVING SOUL IN OR OUT OF THE TEMPLE.
BUT AS THE DAMNED FEMALE SNAKE GOD WAS DYING, ONE OF THE NATIVE WOMEN WAS GIVING BIRTH. THE CIVILIAN DOCTOR THAT HAD BEEN ASSIGNED TO US PROTECTED THE CHILD WITH HIS LIFE.
JANAHARA. I... I WAS HER...
CORRECT. THE VENGEANCE OF A BURNING SNAKE GOD WAS MADE HUMAN. AND JANAHARA WAS THE FIRST OF MANY INCARNATIONS.
AND I SUPPOSE "BRINKLEY" TOLD YOU WHO THE PRECIOUS DOCTOR WAS?
OH, DEAR. THE POOR OLD BASTARD NEVER COULD ADMIT THAT HE WAS ONE OF US...

FROM THE LAND OF HINDI, AND OUR SECRET PAST...THE SPOILS OF DEATH, THAT MUST SURELY LAST...

TO SHOW YOU LOVE, THOUGH BORN OF HATE... "TWENTY-FIVE, THIRTY-FIVE, SIXTY-EIGHT."

WHAT ARE YOU DOING, FATHER?

JANAHARA! I-I WAS JUST GATHERING SOME SPECIAL GEMS FROM THE SAFE, DARLING.

WHERE DO THE GEMS COME FROM?

I'VE TOLD YOU THAT. THEY COME FROM A SPECIAL PLACE, LIKE YOU. A PLACE THAT WE NEED NOT TALK ABOUT.

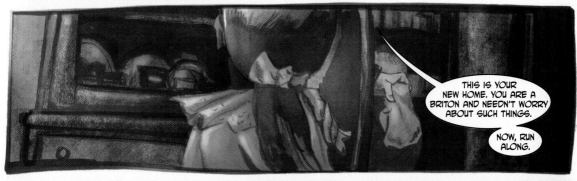
THIS IS YOUR NEW HOME. YOU ARE A BRITON AND NEEDN'T WORRY ABOUT SUCH THINGS.

NOW, RUN ALONG.

FROM THE LAND OF HINDI, AND OUR SECRET PAST...

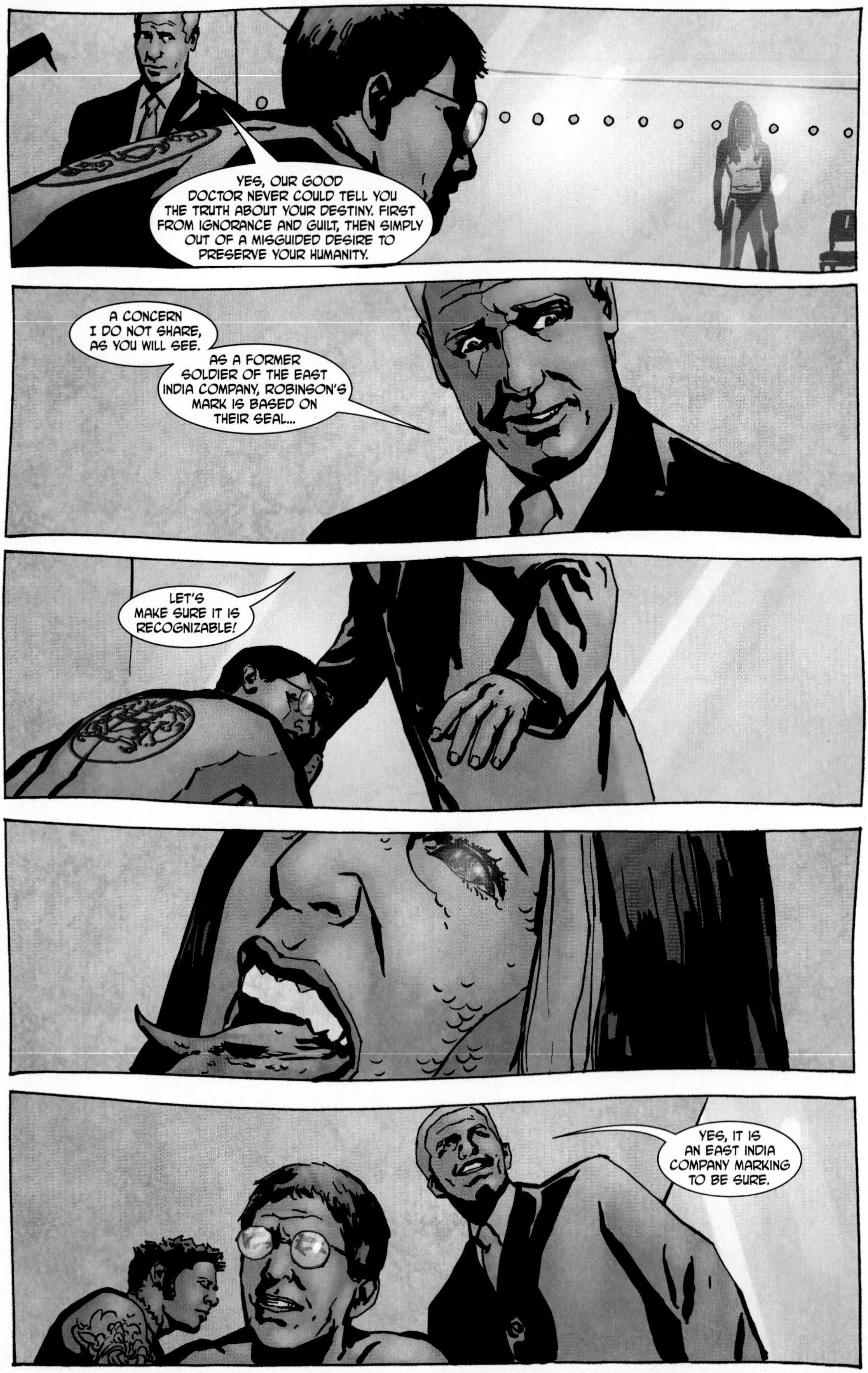
YES, OUR GOOD DOCTOR NEVER COULD TELL YOU THE TRUTH ABOUT YOUR DESTINY. FIRST FROM IGNORANCE AND GUILT, THEN SIMPLY OUT OF A MISGUIDED DESIRE TO PRESERVE YOUR HUMANITY.
A CONCERN I DO NOT SHARE, AS YOU WILL SEE.
AS A FORMER SOLDIER OF THE EAST INDIA COMPANY, ROBINSON'S MARK IS BASED ON THEIR SEAL...
LET'S MAKE SURE IT IS RECOGNIZABLE!
YES, IT IS AN EAST INDIA COMPANY MARKING TO BE SURE.

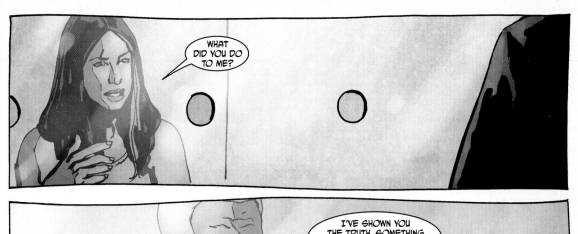

WHAT DID YOU DO TO ME?

I'VE SHOWN YOU THE TRUTH. SOMETHING YOUR PRECIOUS "BRINKLEY" COULDN'T DO.

DID HE TELL YOU THAT YOU WERE STRONG INSIDE? THAT YOU CONTAINED AN INSTINCT THAT COULD PROTECT YOU?

YOU ARE A MURDERER. THE BEAST INSIDE YOU WANTS NOTHING MORE THAN TO KILL.

TO KILL THE 68, WHO DESECRATED ITS TEMPLE AND SLAUGHTERED ITS PEOPLE. THAT IS ALL YOU LIVE FOR. BELIEVE ME, JESS, I KNOW WHAT I'M DEALING WITH.

WHAT ARE YOU TALKING ABOUT?! THIS ALL HAPPENED 200 YEARS AGO!

DID YOU BELIEVE YOU WERE THE ONLY BEING TRAPPED IN A CYCLE OF REINCARNATION? DESPITE WHAT "DADDY" MAY HAVE TOLD YOU, YOU'RE NOT THAT SPECIAL.

ALL 68 OF US ARE REBORN EVERY GENERATION. WE ARE HUNTED BY THE SNAKE GODDESS. SHE SEEKS TO KILL US ALL WITHIN A SINGLE LIFETIME SO THAT SHE MAY REST FOR GOOD.

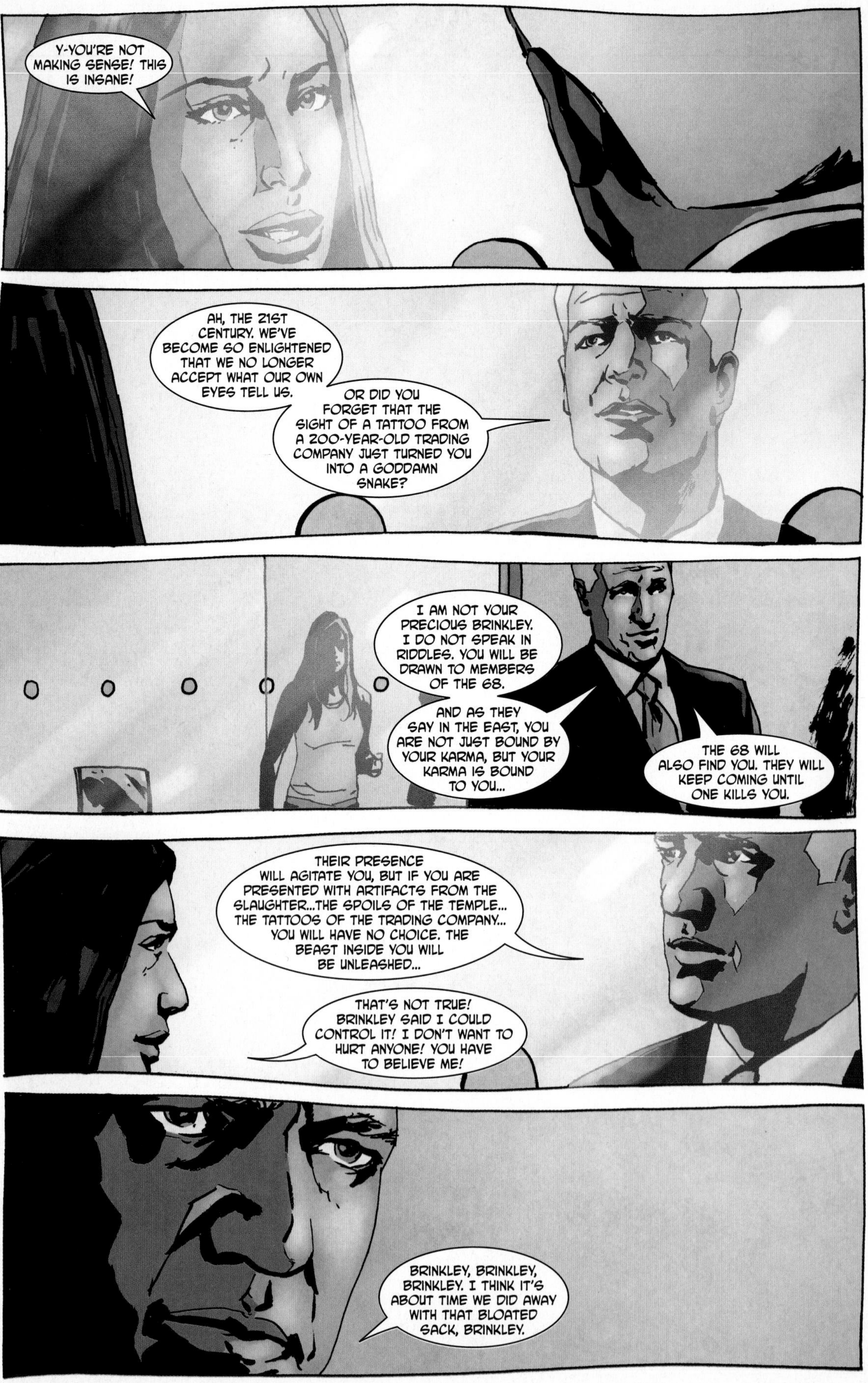
Y-YOU'RE NOT MAKING SENSE! THIS IS INSANE!
AH, THE 21ST CENTURY. WE'VE BECOME SO ENLIGHTENED THAT WE NO LONGER ACCEPT WHAT OUR OWN EYES TELL US.
OR DID YOU FORGET THAT THE SIGHT OF A TATTOO FROM A 200-YEAR-OLD TRADING COMPANY JUST TURNED YOU INTO A GODDAMN SNAKE?
I AM NOT YOUR PRECIOUS BRINKLEY. I DO NOT SPEAK IN RIDDLES. YOU WILL BE DRAWN TO MEMBERS OF THE 68.
AND AS THEY SAY IN THE EAST, YOU ARE NOT JUST BOUND BY YOUR KARMA, BUT YOUR KARMA IS BOUND TO YOU...
THE 68 WILL ALSO FIND YOU. THEY WILL KEEP COMING UNTIL ONE KILLS YOU.
THEIR PRESENCE WILL AGITATE YOU, BUT IF YOU ARE PRESENTED WITH ARTIFACTS FROM THE SLAUGHTER...THE SPOILS OF THE TEMPLE... THE TATTOOS OF THE TRADING COMPANY... YOU WILL HAVE NO CHOICE. THE BEAST INSIDE YOU WILL BE UNLEASHED...
THAT'S NOT TRUE! BRINKLEY SAID I COULD CONTROL IT! I DON'T WANT TO HURT ANYONE! YOU HAVE TO BELIEVE ME!
BRINKLEY, BRINKLEY, BRINKLEY. I THINK IT'S ABOUT TIME WE DID AWAY WITH THAT BLOATED SACK, BRINKLEY.

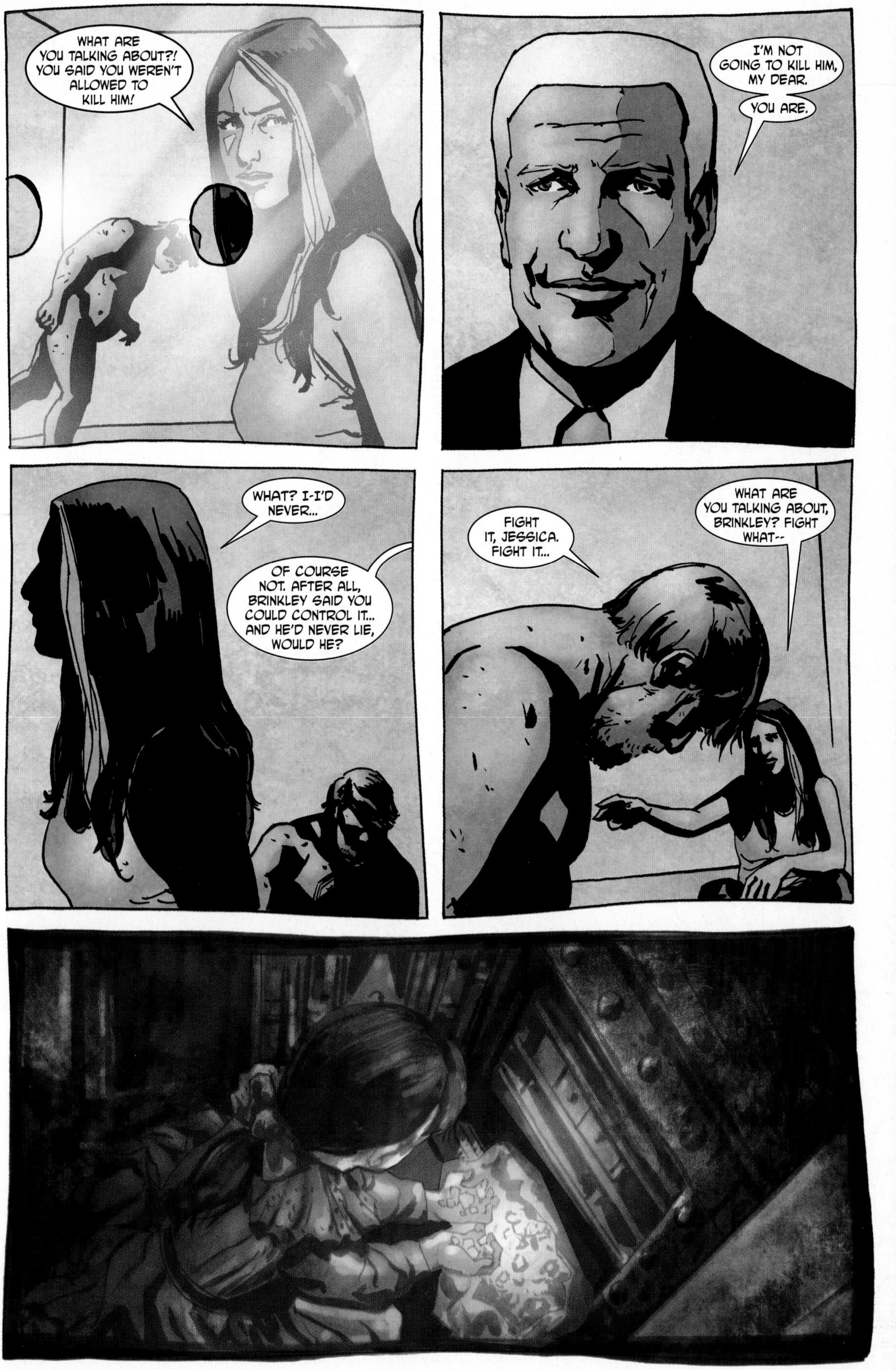
WHAT ARE YOU TALKING ABOUT?! YOU SAID YOU WEREN'T ALLOWED TO KILL HIM!
I'M NOT GOING TO KILL HIM, MY DEAR.
YOU ARE.
WHAT? I-I'D NEVER...
OF COURSE NOT. AFTER ALL, BRINKLEY SAID YOU COULD CONTROL IT... AND HE'D NEVER LIE, WOULD HE?
FIGHT IT, JESSICA. FIGHT IT...
WHAT ARE YOU TALKING ABOUT, BRINKLEY? FIGHT WHAT--

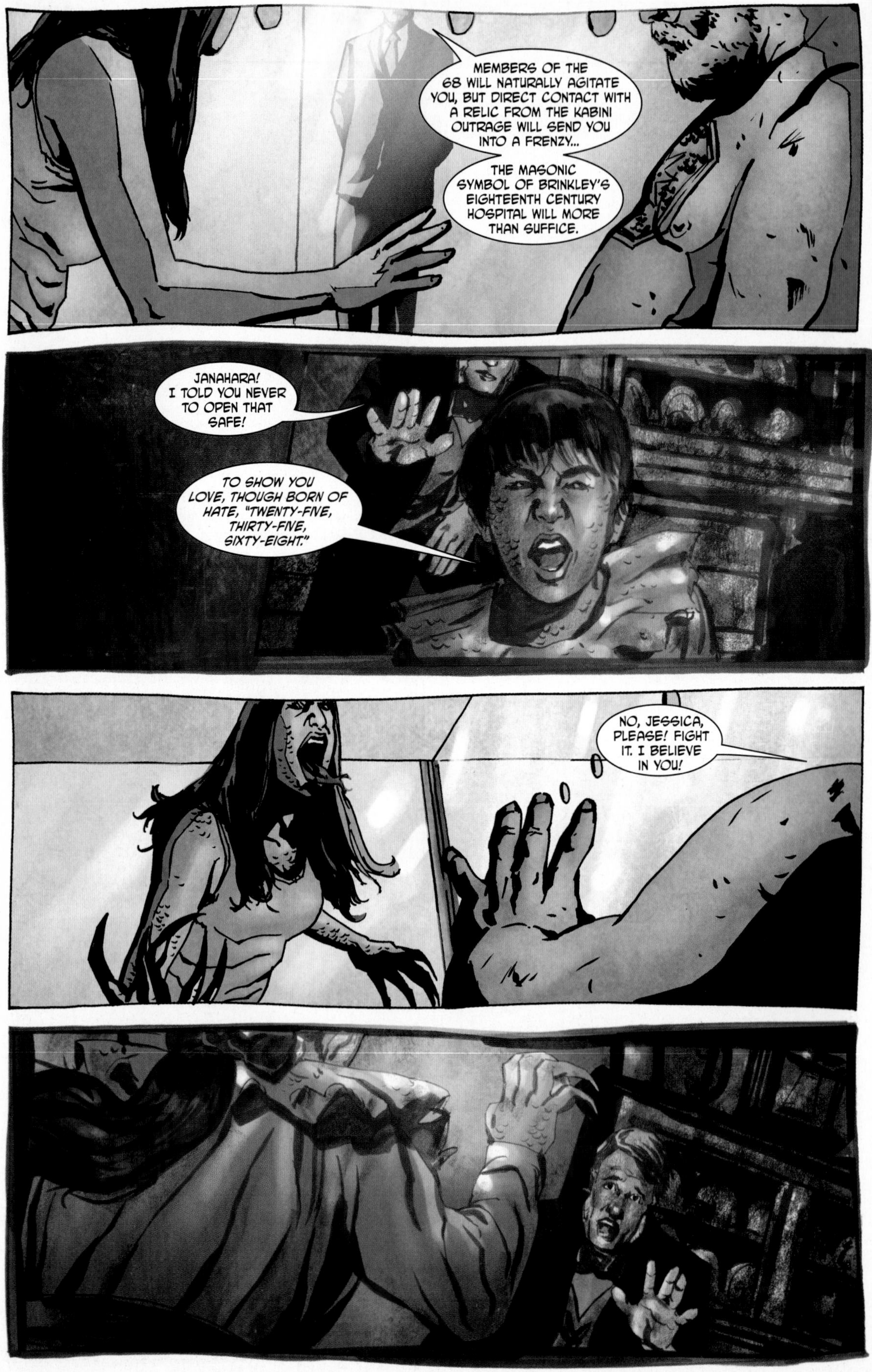
MEMBERS OF THE 68 WILL NATURALLY AGITATE YOU, BUT DIRECT CONTACT WITH A RELIC FROM THE KABINI OUTRAGE WILL SEND YOU INTO A FRENZY...
THE MASONIC SYMBOL OF BRINKLEY'S EIGHTEENTH CENTURY HOSPITAL WILL MORE THAN SUFFICE.
JANAHARA! I TOLD YOU NEVER TO OPEN THAT SAFE!
TO SHOW YOU LOVE, THOUGH BORN OF HATE, "TWENTY-FIVE, THIRTY-FIVE, SIXTY-EIGHT."
NO, JESSICA, PLEASE! FIGHT IT. I BELIEVE IN YOU!

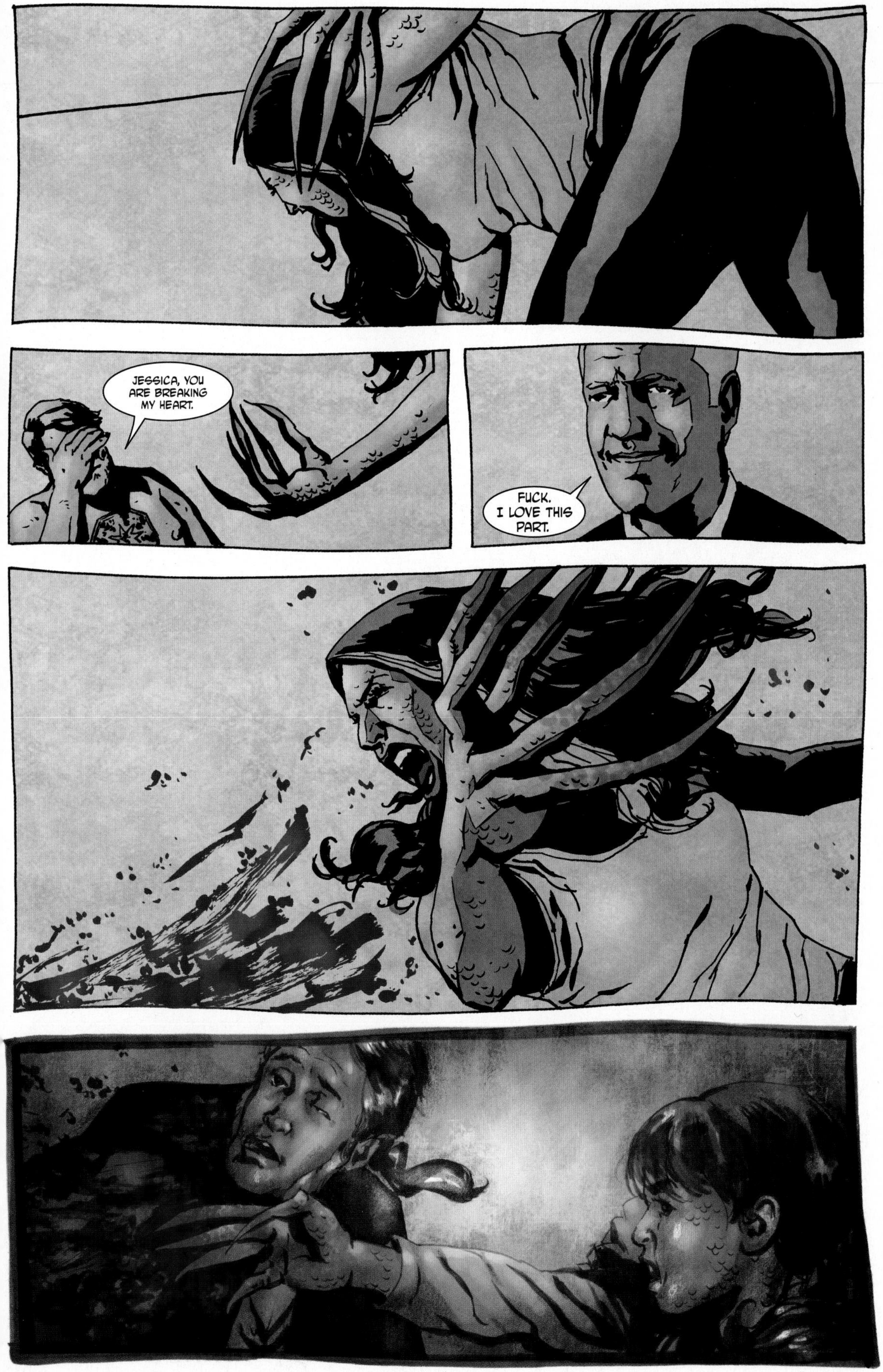
JESSICA, YOU ARE BREAKING MY HEART.
FUCK. I LOVE THIS PART.

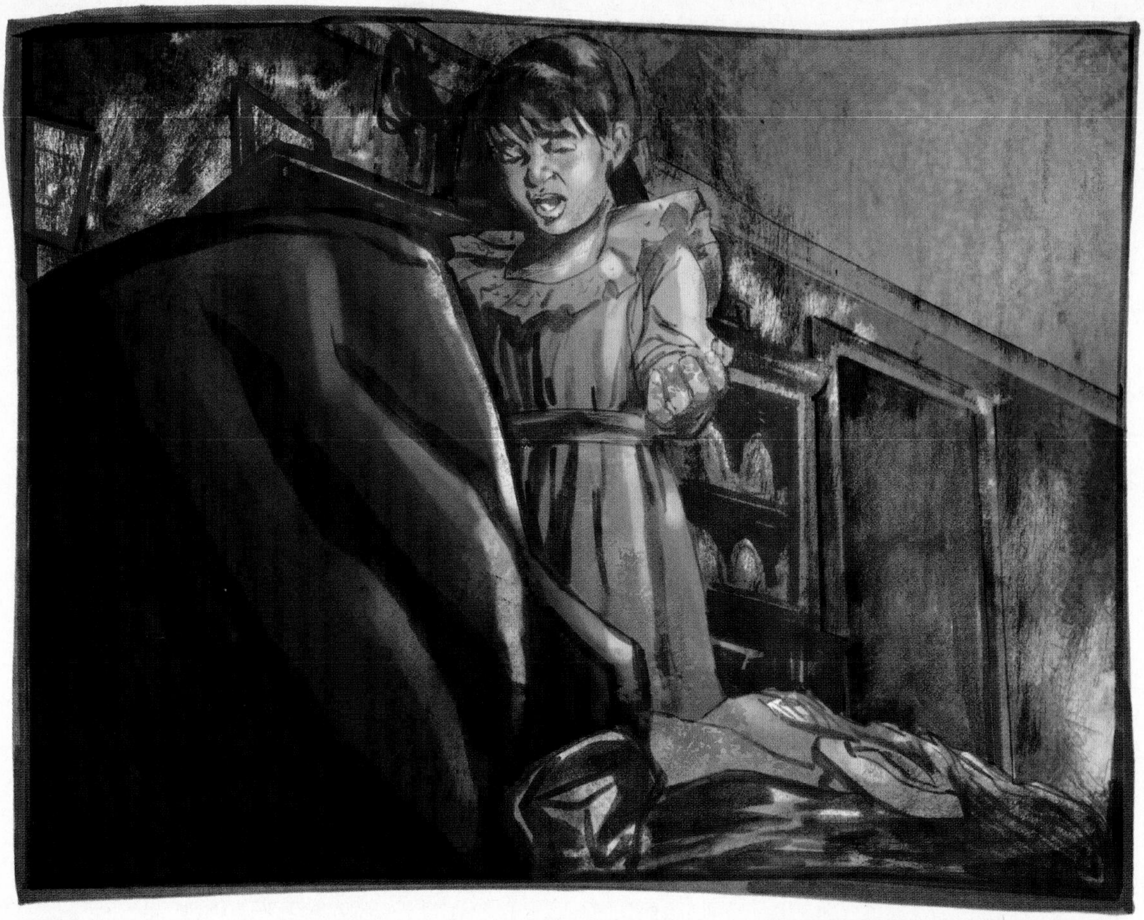

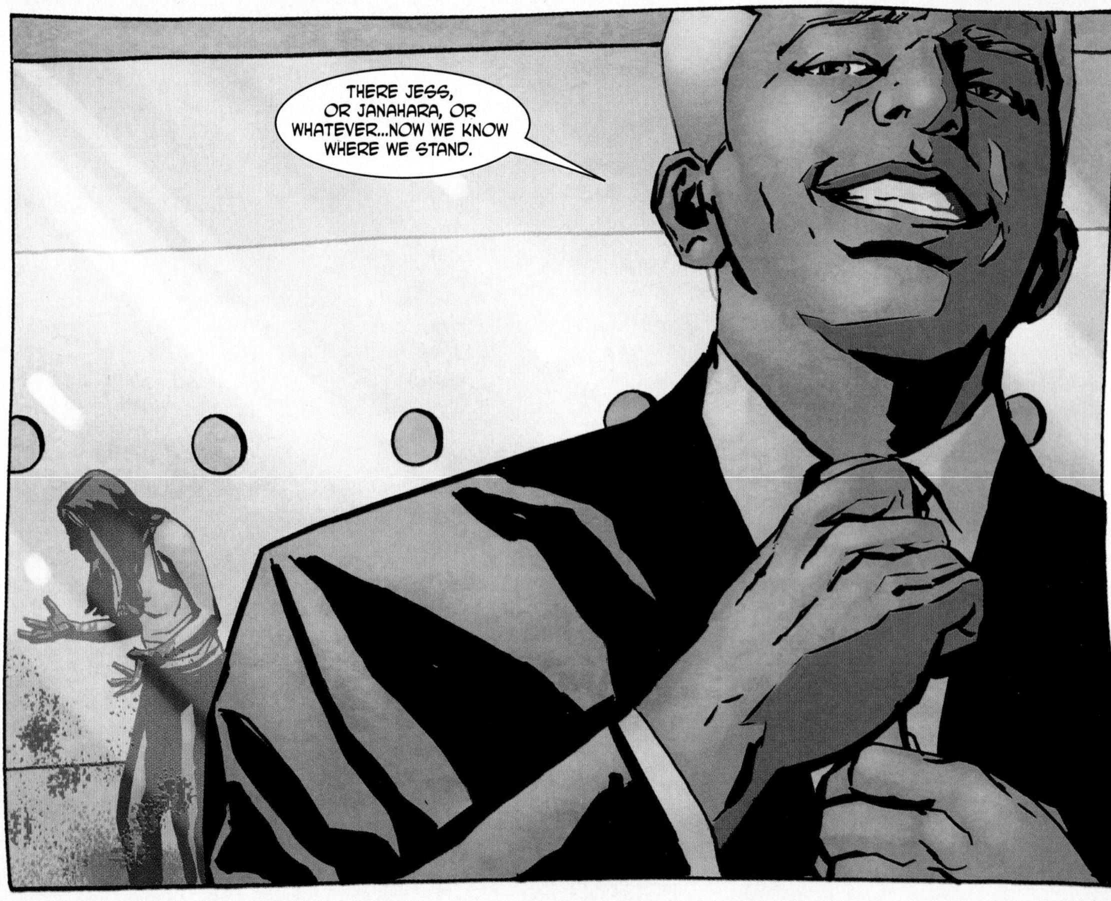
THERE JESS, OR JANAHARA, OR WHATEVER...NOW WE KNOW WHERE WE STAND.

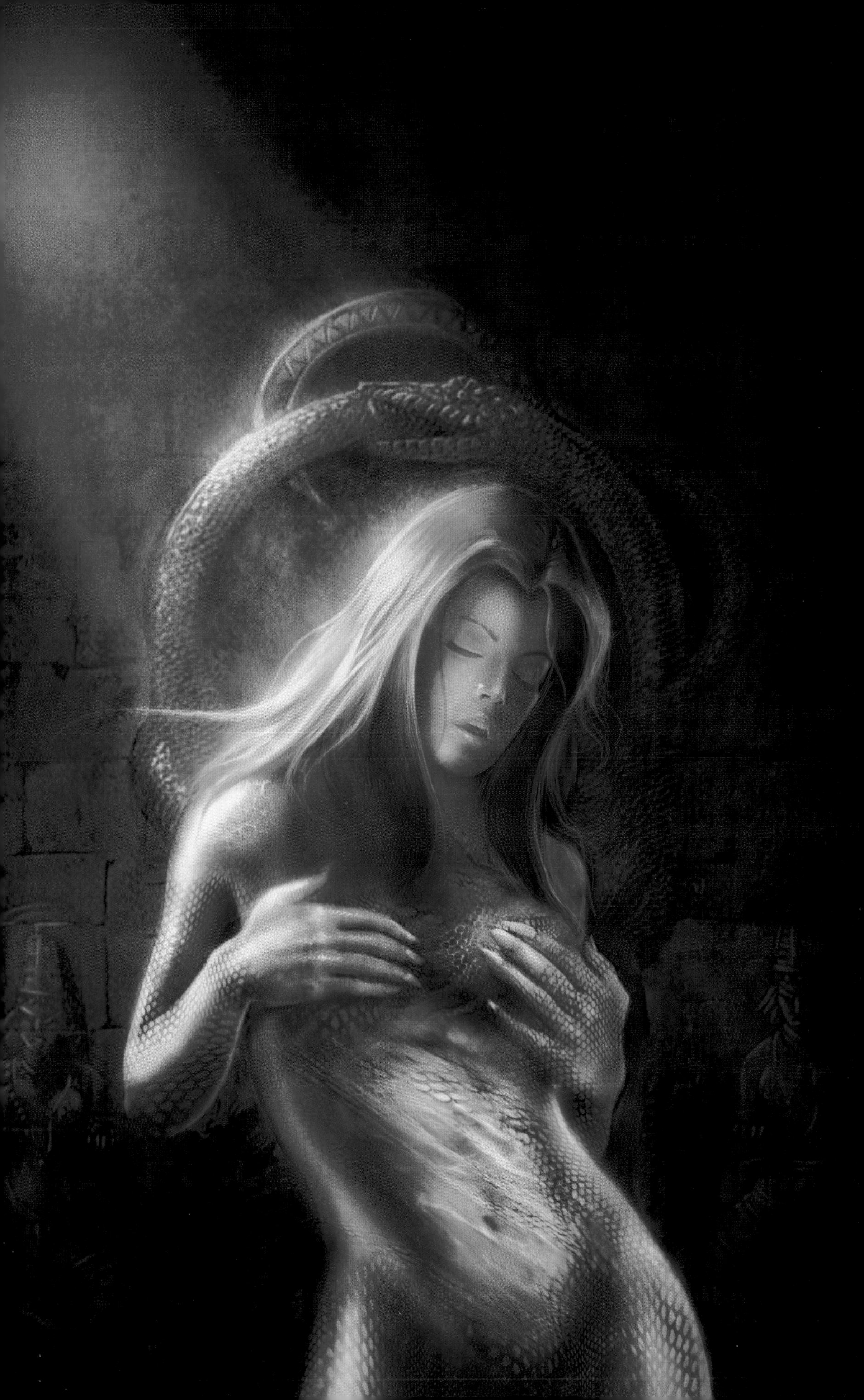

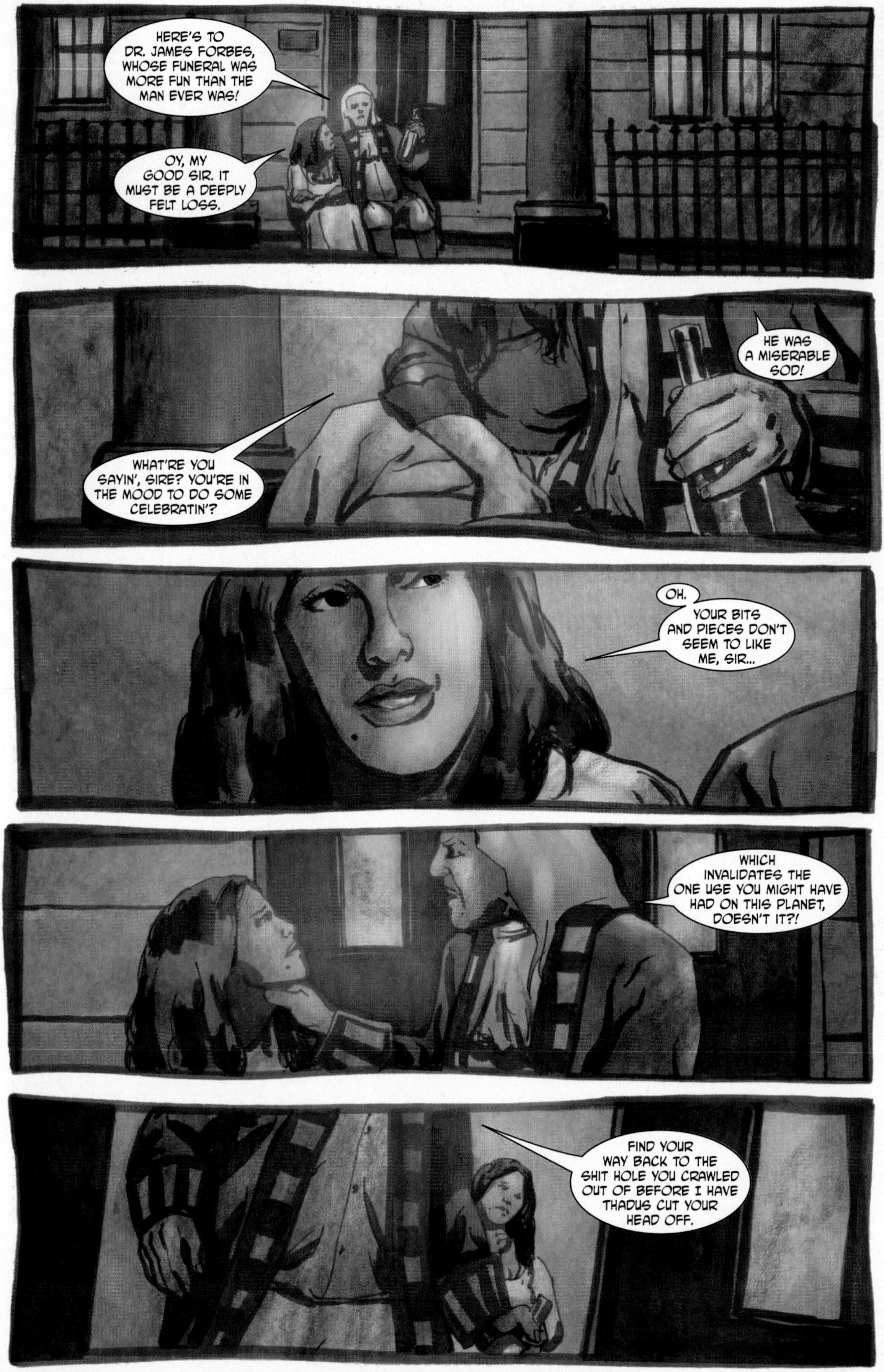
HERE'S TO DR. JAMES FORBES, WHOSE FUNERAL WAS MORE FUN THAN THE MAN EVER WAS!
OY, MY GOOD SIR. IT MUST BE A DEEPLY FELT LOSS.
HE WAS A MISERABLE SOD!
WHAT'RE YOU SAYIN', SIRE? YOU'RE IN THE MOOD TO DO SOME CELEBRATIN'?
OH.
YOUR BITS AND PIECES DON'T SEEM TO LIKE ME, SIR...
WHICH INVALIDATES THE ONE USE YOU MIGHT HAVE HAD ON THIS PLANET, DOESN'T IT?!
FIND YOUR WAY BACK TO THE SHIT HOLE YOU CRAWLED OUT OF BEFORE I HAVE THADUS CUT YOUR HEAD OFF.

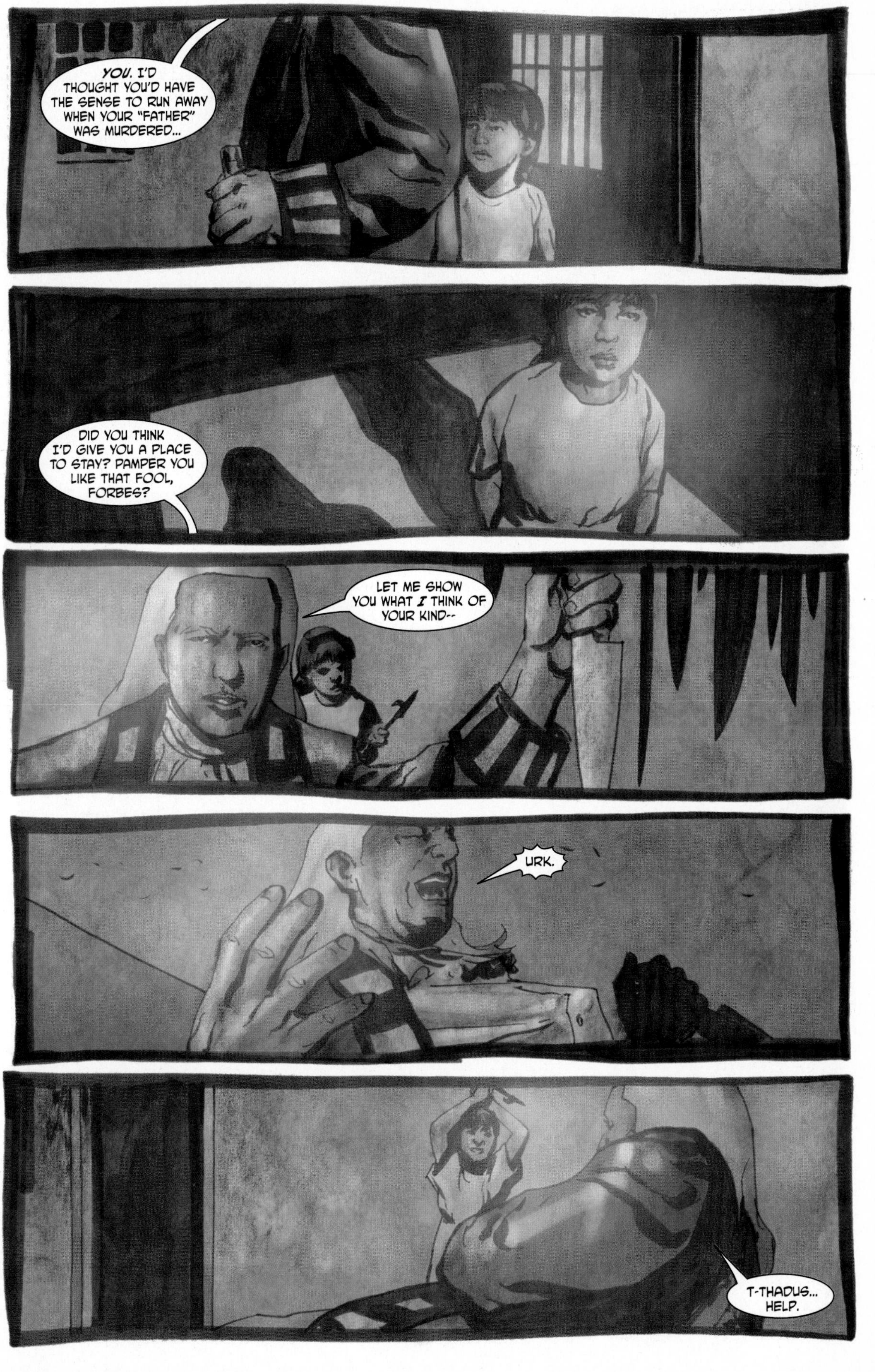
YOU. I'D THOUGHT YOU'D HAVE THE SENSE TO RUN AWAY WHEN YOUR "FATHER" WAS MURDERED...
DID YOU THINK I'D GIVE YOU A PLACE TO STAY? PAMPER YOU LIKE THAT FOOL, FORBES?
LET ME SHOW YOU WHAT I THINK OF YOUR KIND--
URK.
T-THADUS... HELP.

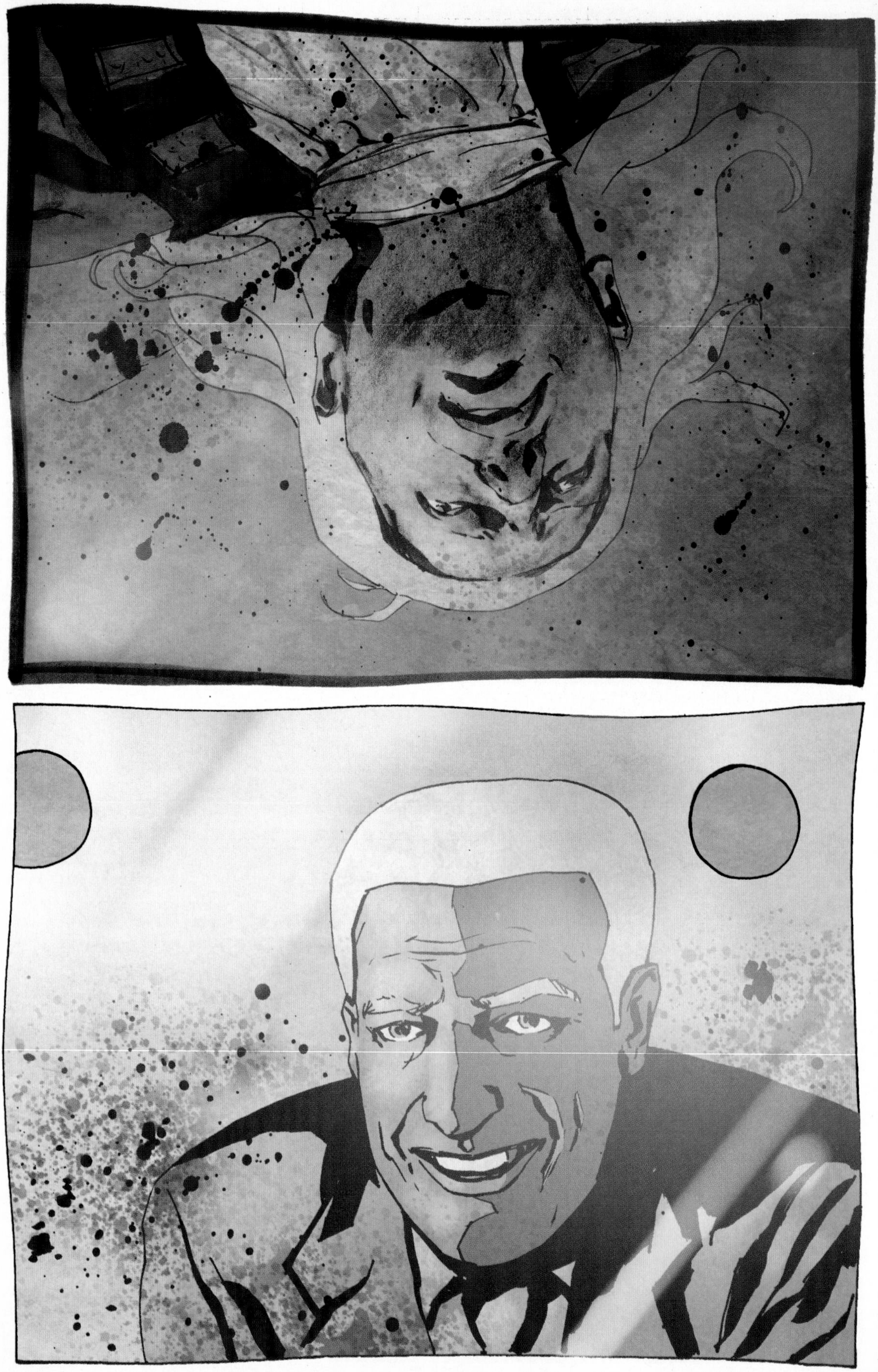

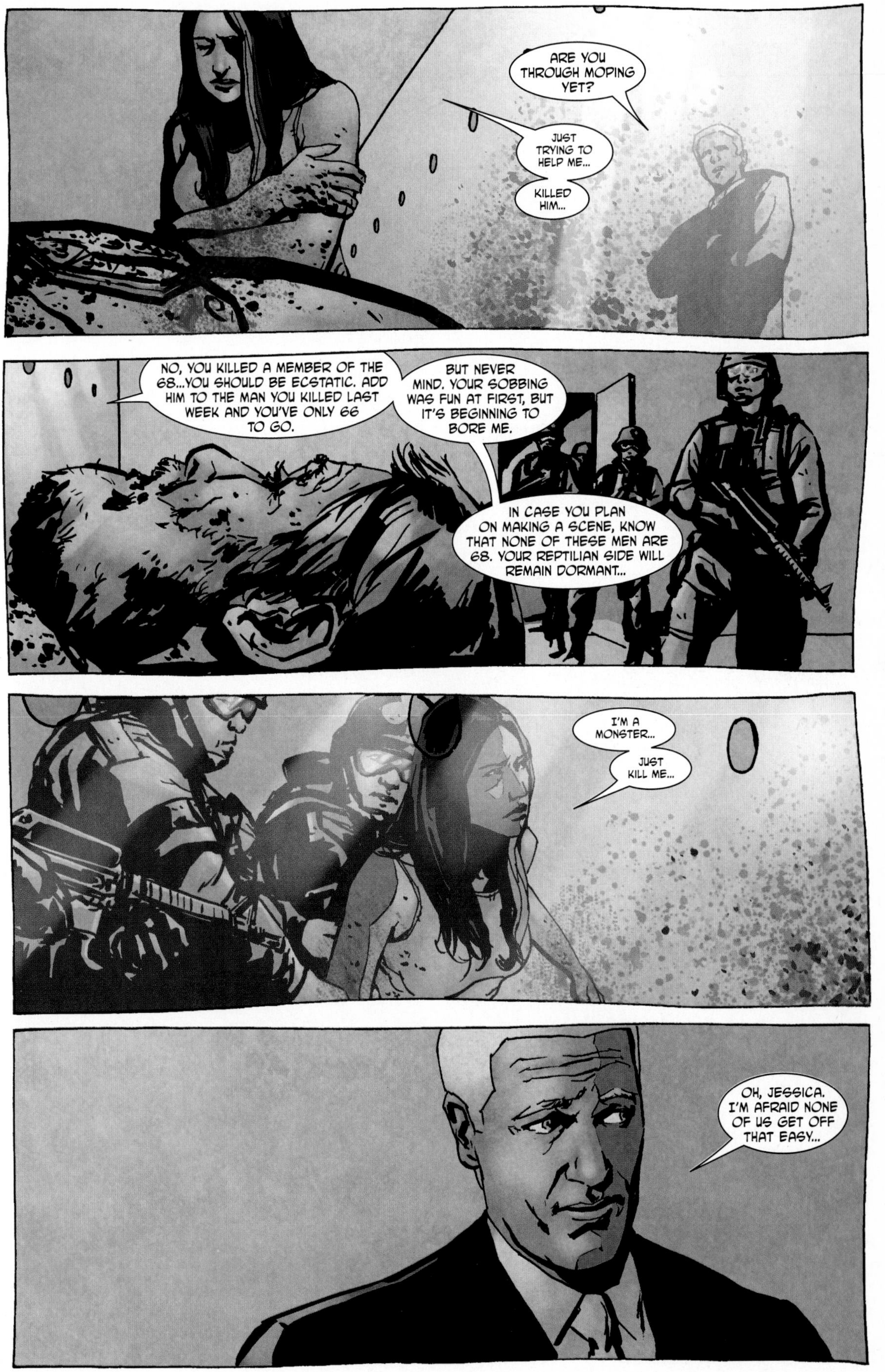
ARE YOU THROUGH MOPING YET?
JUST TRYING TO HELP ME...
KILLED HIM...
NO, YOU KILLED A MEMBER OF THE 68...YOU SHOULD BE ECSTATIC. ADD HIM TO THE MAN YOU KILLED LAST WEEK AND YOU'VE ONLY 66 TO GO.
BUT NEVER MIND. YOUR SOBBING WAS FUN AT FIRST, BUT IT'S BEGINNING TO BORE ME.
IN CASE YOU PLAN ON MAKING A SCENE, KNOW THAT NONE OF THESE MEN ARE 68. YOUR REPTILIAN SIDE WILL REMAIN DORMANT...
I'M A MONSTER...
JUST KILL ME...
OH, JESSICA. I'M AFRAID NONE OF US GET OFF THAT EASY...

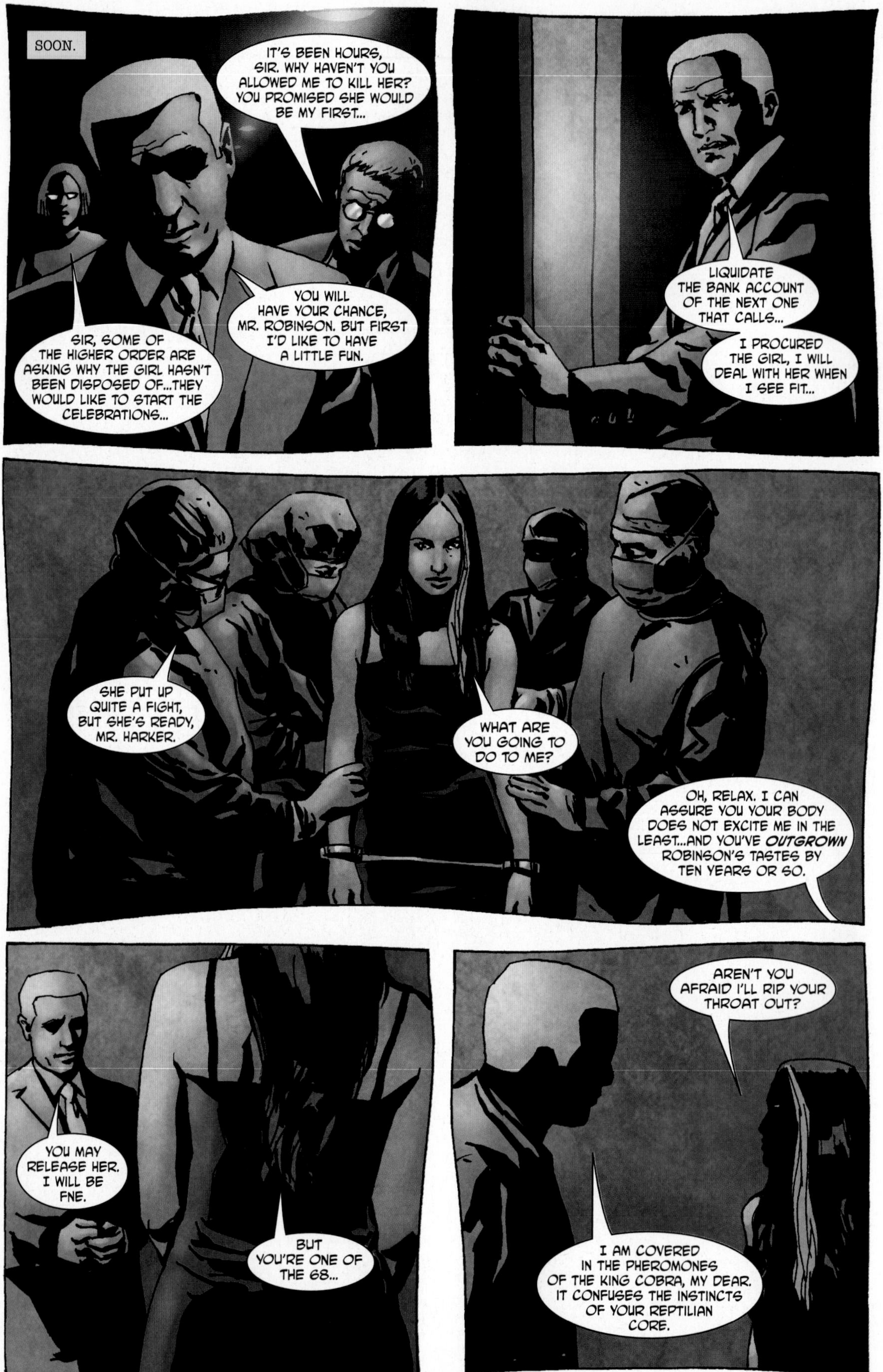
SOON.
IT'S BEEN HOURS, SIR. WHY HAVEN'T YOU ALLOWED ME TO KILL HER? YOU PROMISED SHE WOULD BE MY FIRST...
SIR, SOME OF THE HIGHER ORDER ARE ASKING WHY THE GIRL HASN'T BEEN DISPOSED OF...THEY WOULD LIKE TO START THE CELEBRATIONS...
YOU WILL HAVE YOUR CHANCE, MR. ROBINSON. BUT FIRST I'D LIKE TO HAVE A LITTLE FUN.
LIQUIDATE THE BANK ACCOUNT OF THE NEXT ONE THAT CALLS...
I PROCURED THE GIRL, I WILL DEAL WITH HER WHEN I SEE FIT...
SHE PUT UP QUITE A FIGHT, BUT SHE'S READY, MR. HARKER.
WHAT ARE YOU GOING TO DO TO ME?
OH, RELAX. I CAN ASSURE YOU YOUR BODY DOES NOT EXCITE ME IN THE LEAST...AND YOU'VE *OUTGROWN* ROBINSON'S TASTES BY TEN YEARS OR SO.
YOU MAY RELEASE HER. I WILL BE FNE.
BUT YOU'RE ONE OF THE 68...
AREN'T YOU AFRAID I'LL RIP YOUR THROAT OUT?
I AM COVERED IN THE PHEROMONES OF THE KING COBRA, MY DEAR. IT CONFUSES THE INSTINCTS OF YOUR REPTILIAN CORE.

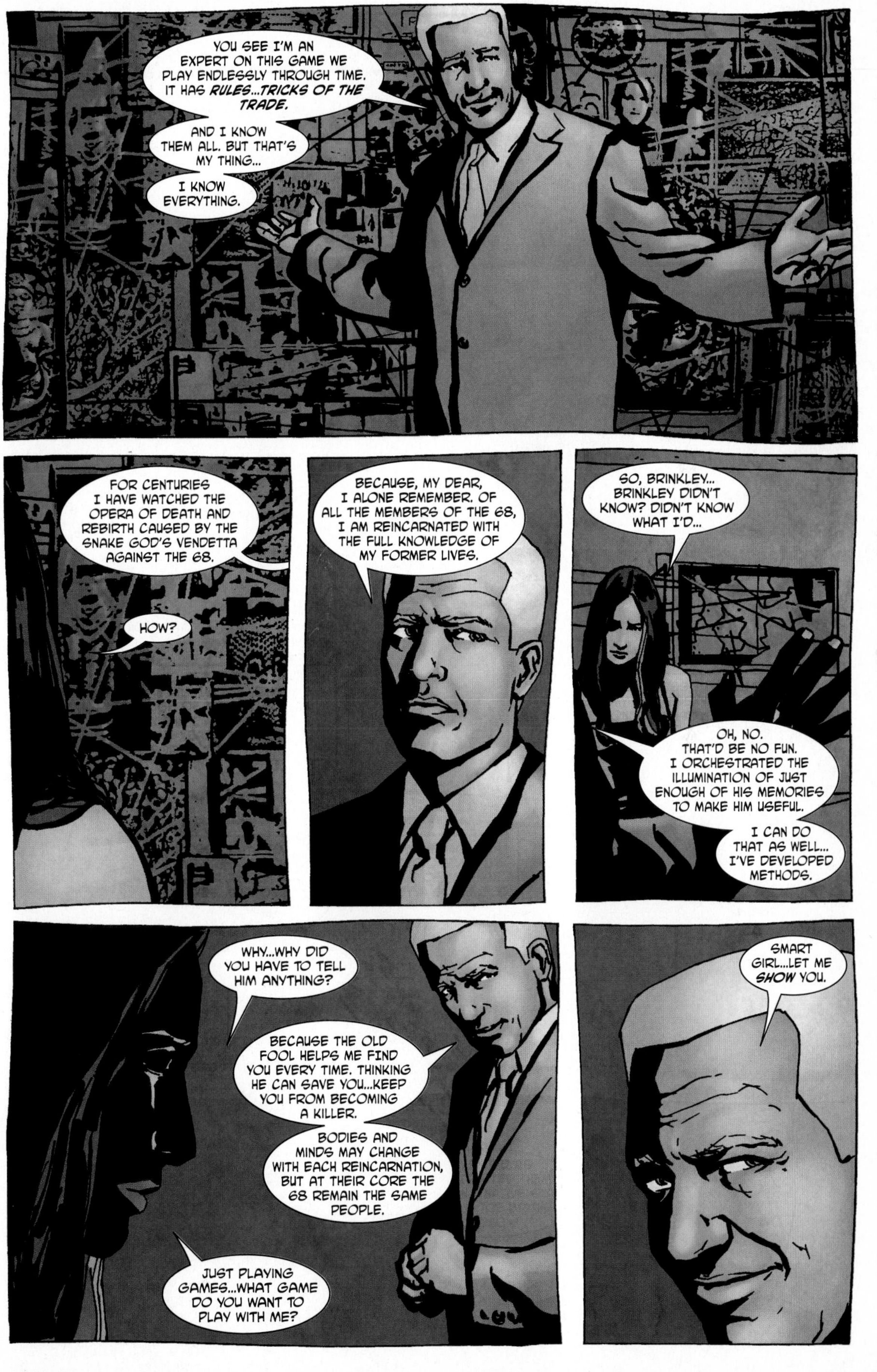
YOU SEE I'M AN EXPERT ON THIS GAME WE PLAY ENDLESSLY THROUGH TIME. IT HAS *RULES...TRICKS OF THE TRADE.*
AND I KNOW THEM ALL. BUT THAT'S MY THING...
I KNOW EVERYTHING.
FOR CENTURIES I HAVE WATCHED THE OPERA OF DEATH AND REBIRTH CAUSED BY THE SNAKE GOD'S VENDETTA AGAINST THE 68.
HOW?
BECAUSE, MY DEAR, I ALONE REMEMBER. OF ALL THE MEMBERS OF THE 68, I AM REINCARNATED WITH THE FULL KNOWLEDGE OF MY FORMER LIVES.
SO, BRINKLEY... BRINKLEY DIDN'T KNOW? DIDN'T KNOW WHAT I'D...
OH, NO. THAT'D BE NO FUN. I ORCHESTRATED THE ILLUMINATION OF JUST ENOUGH OF HIS MEMORIES TO MAKE HIM USEFUL.
I CAN DO THAT AS WELL... I'VE DEVELOPED METHODS.
WHY...WHY DID YOU HAVE TO TELL HIM ANYTHING?
BECAUSE THE OLD FOOL HELPS ME FIND YOU EVERY TIME. THINKING HE CAN SAVE YOU...KEEP YOU FROM BECOMING A KILLER.
BODIES AND MINDS MAY CHANGE WITH EACH REINCARNATION, BUT AT THEIR CORE THE 68 REMAIN THE SAME PEOPLE.
JUST PLAYING GAMES...WHAT GAME DO YOU WANT TO PLAY WITH ME?
SMART GIRL...LET ME *SHOW* YOU.

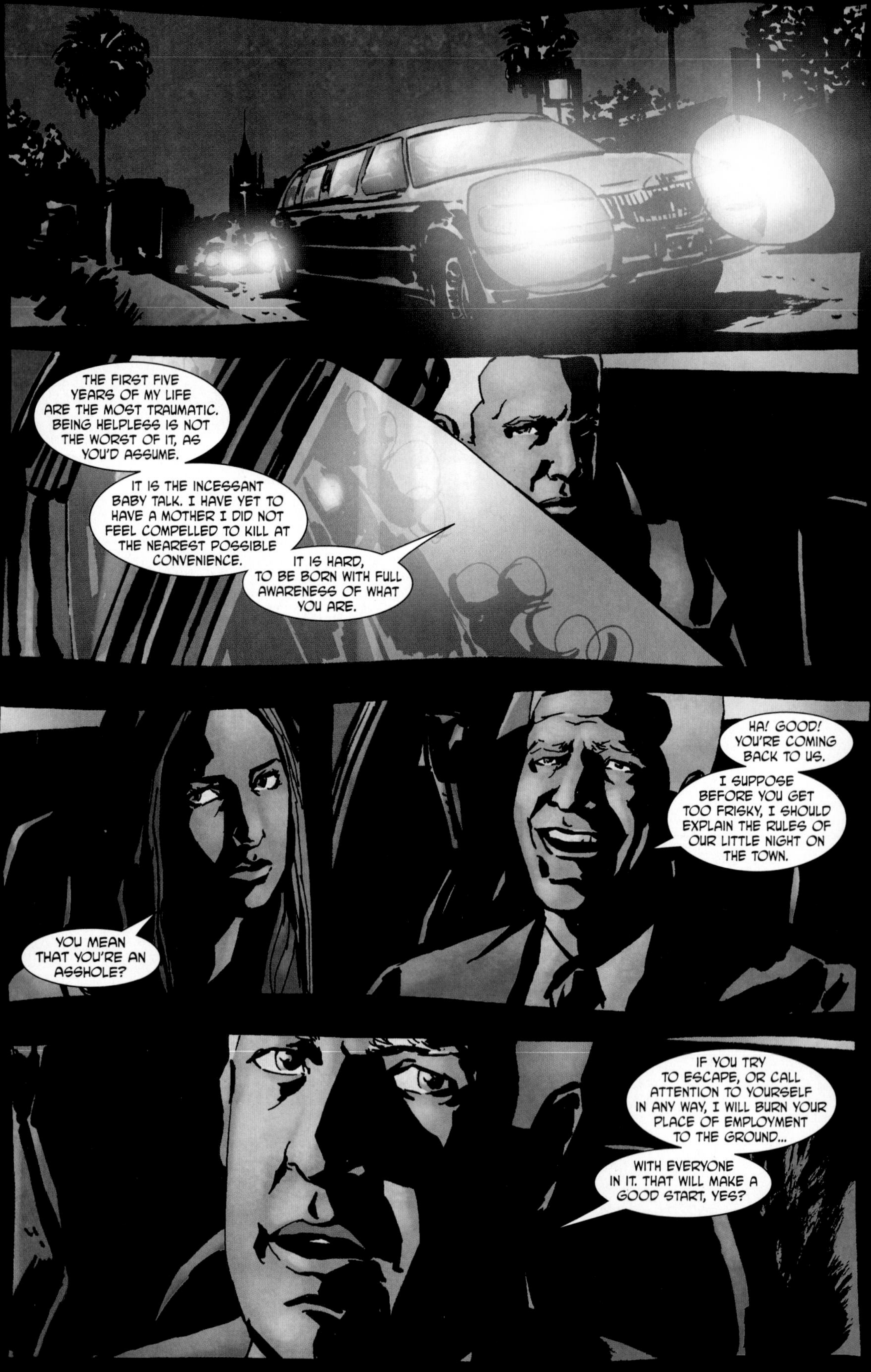
THE FIRST FIVE YEARS OF MY LIFE ARE THE MOST TRAUMATIC. BEING HELPLESS IS NOT THE WORST OF IT, AS YOU'D ASSUME.
IT IS THE INCESSANT BABY TALK. I HAVE YET TO HAVE A MOTHER I DID NOT FEEL COMPELLED TO KILL AT THE NEAREST POSSIBLE CONVENIENCE.
IT IS HARD, TO BE BORN WITH FULL AWARENESS OF WHAT YOU ARE.
YOU MEAN THAT YOU'RE AN ASSHOLE?
HA! GOOD! YOU'RE COMING BACK TO US.
I SUPPOSE BEFORE YOU GET TOO FRISKY, I SHOULD EXPLAIN THE RULES OF OUR LITTLE NIGHT ON THE TOWN.
IF YOU TRY TO ESCAPE, OR CALL ATTENTION TO YOURSELF IN ANY WAY, I WILL BURN YOUR PLACE OF EMPLOYMENT TO THE GROUND...
WITH EVERYONE IN IT. THAT WILL MAKE A GOOD START, YES?

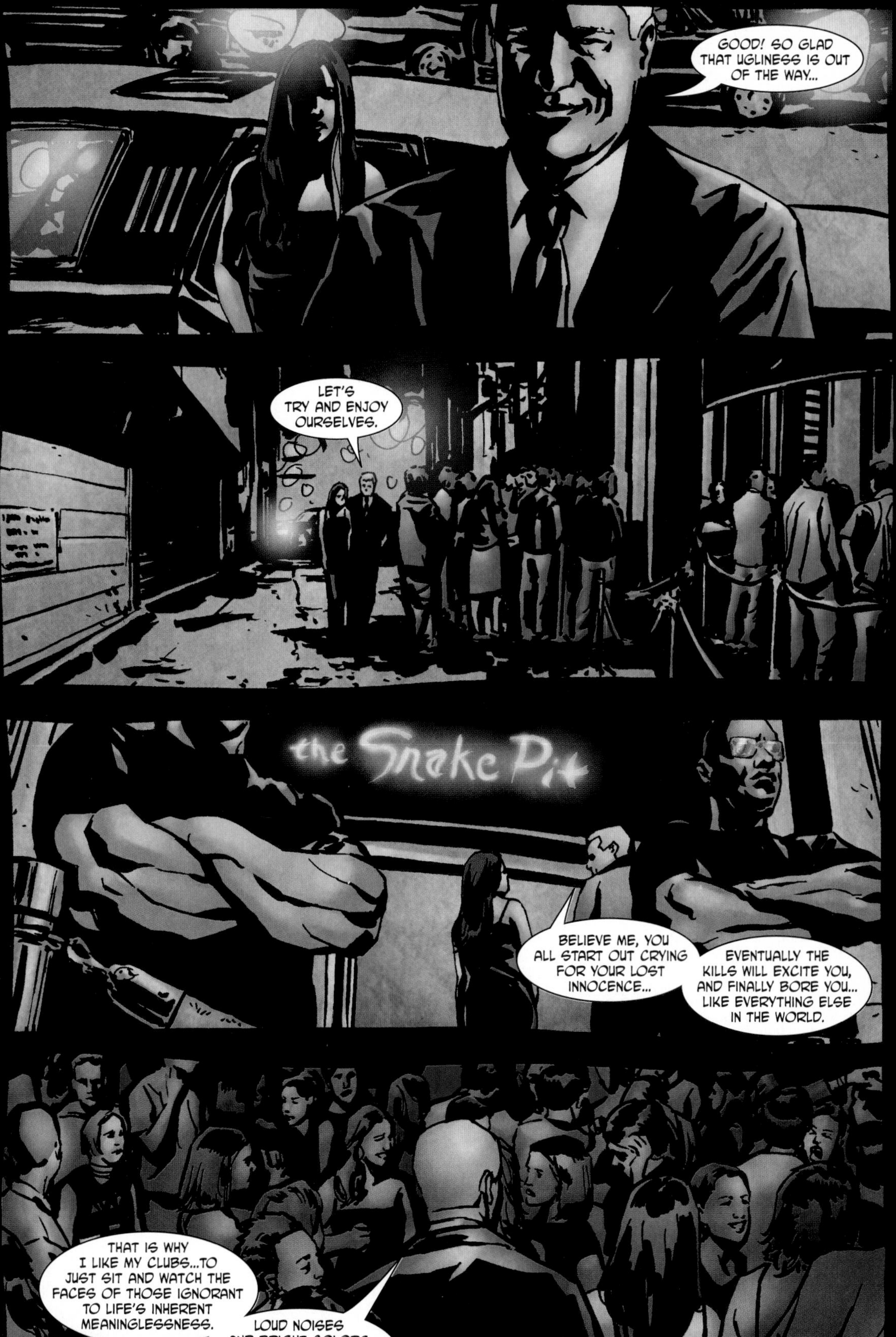
GOOD! SO GLAD THAT UGLINESS IS OUT OF THE WAY...
LET'S TRY AND ENJOY OURSELVES.
the Snake Pit
BELIEVE ME, YOU ALL START OUT CRYING FOR YOUR LOST INNOCENCE...
EVENTUALLY THE KILLS WILL EXCITE YOU, AND FINALLY BORE YOU... LIKE EVERYTHING ELSE IN THE WORLD.
THAT IS WHY I LIKE MY CLUBS...TO JUST SIT AND WATCH THE FACES OF THOSE IGNORANT TO LIFE'S INHERENT MEANINGLESSNESS.
LOUD NOISES AND BRIGHT COLORS ARE ENOUGH TO ENTERTAIN THE MAJORITY OF PEOPLE...

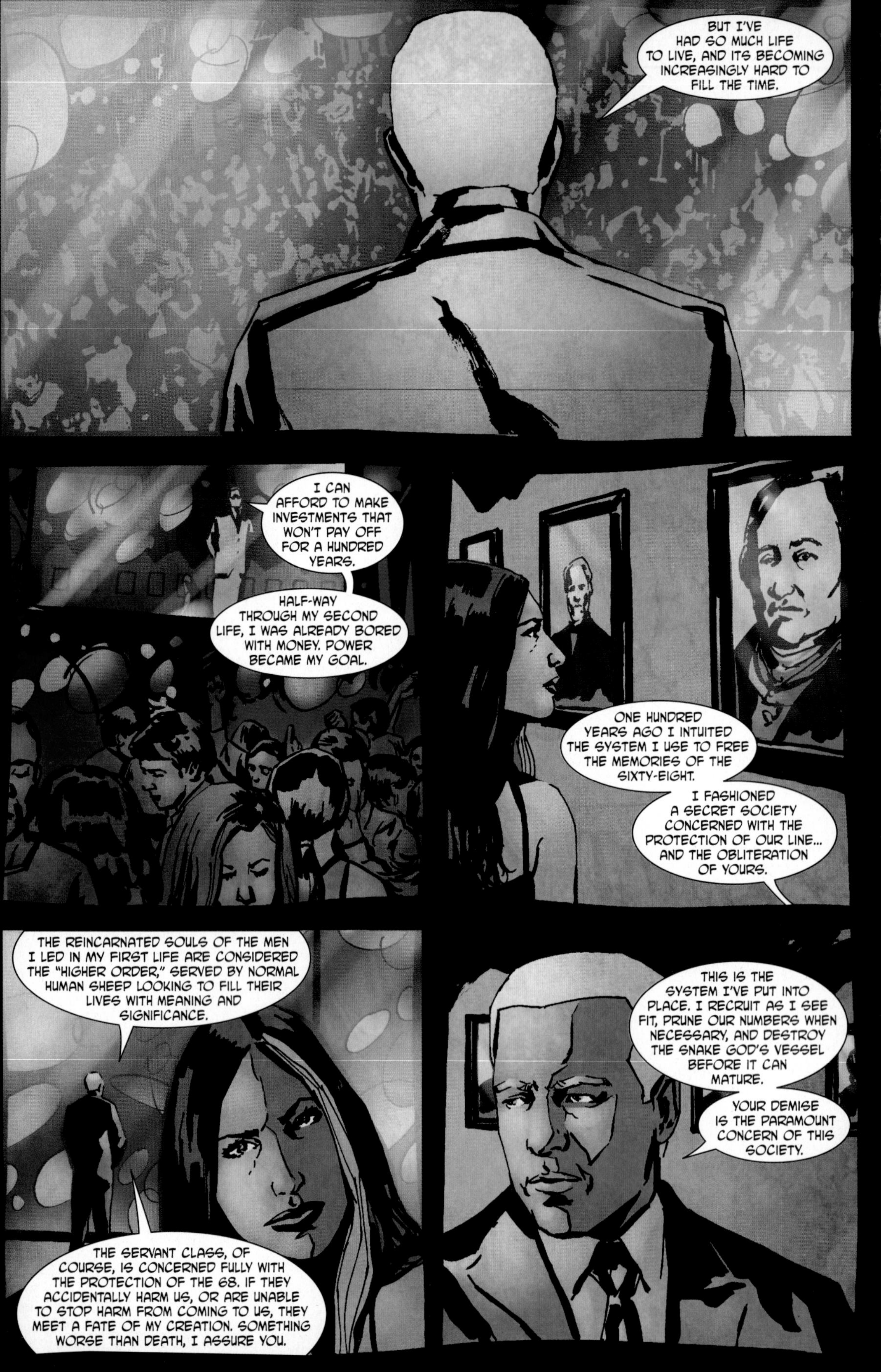
BUT I'VE HAD SO MUCH LIFE TO LIVE, AND ITS BECOMING INCREASINGLY HARD TO FILL THE TIME.
I CAN AFFORD TO MAKE INVESTMENTS THAT WON'T PAY OFF FOR A HUNDRED YEARS.
HALF-WAY THROUGH MY SECOND LIFE, I WAS ALREADY BORED WITH MONEY. POWER BECAME MY GOAL.
ONE HUNDRED YEARS AGO I INTUITED THE SYSTEM I USE TO FREE THE MEMORIES OF THE SIXTY-EIGHT.
I FASHIONED A SECRET SOCIETY CONCERNED WITH THE PROTECTION OF OUR LINE... AND THE OBLITERATION OF YOURS.
THE REINCARNATED SOULS OF THE MEN I LED IN MY FIRST LIFE ARE CONSIDERED THE "HIGHER ORDER," SERVED BY NORMAL HUMAN SHEEP LOOKING TO FILL THEIR LIVES WITH MEANING AND SIGNIFICANCE.
THE SERVANT CLASS, OF COURSE, IS CONCERNED FULLY WITH THE PROTECTION OF THE 68. IF THEY ACCIDENTALLY HARM US, OR ARE UNABLE TO STOP HARM FROM COMING TO US, THEY MEET A FATE OF MY CREATION. SOMETHING WORSE THAN DEATH, I ASSURE YOU.
THIS IS THE SYSTEM I'VE PUT INTO PLACE. I RECRUIT AS I SEE FIT, PRUNE OUR NUMBERS WHEN NECESSARY, AND DESTROY THE SNAKE GOD'S VESSEL BEFORE IT CAN MATURE.
YOUR DEMISE IS THE PARAMOUNT CONCERN OF THIS SOCIETY.

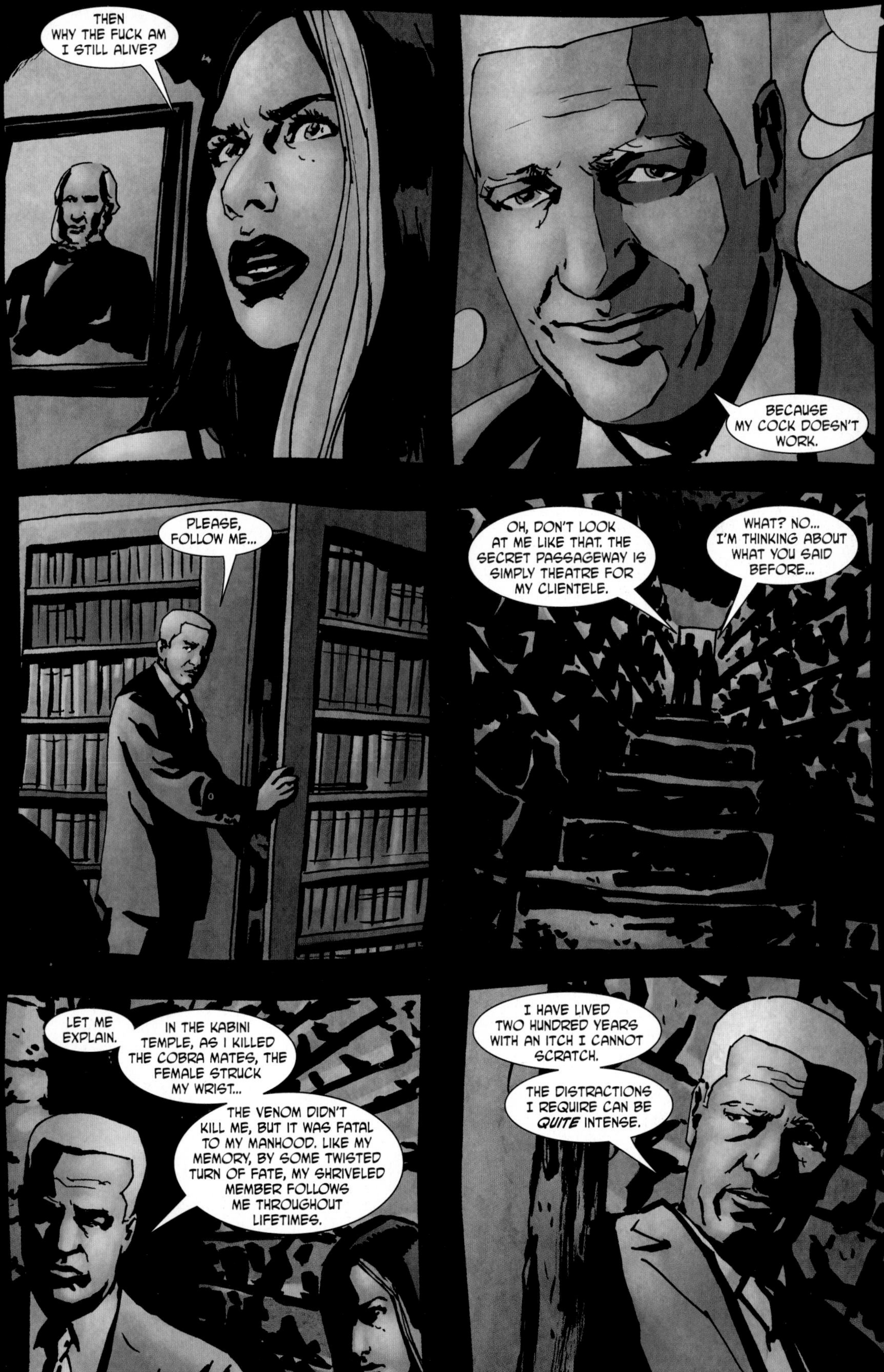
THEN WHY THE FUCK AM I STILL ALIVE?
BECAUSE MY COCK DOESN'T WORK.
PLEASE, FOLLOW ME...
OH, DON'T LOOK AT ME LIKE THAT. THE SECRET PASSAGEWAY IS SIMPLY THEATRE FOR MY CLIENTELE.
WHAT? NO... I'M THINKING ABOUT WHAT YOU SAID BEFORE...
LET ME EXPLAIN.
IN THE KABINI TEMPLE, AS I KILLED THE COBRA MATES, THE FEMALE STRUCK MY WRIST...
THE VENOM DIDN'T KILL ME, BUT IT WAS FATAL TO MY MANHOOD. LIKE MY MEMORY, BY SOME TWISTED TURN OF FATE, MY SHRIVELED MEMBER FOLLOWS ME THROUGHOUT LIFETIMES.
I HAVE LIVED TWO HUNDRED YEARS WITH AN ITCH I CANNOT SCRATCH.
THE DISTRACTIONS I REQUIRE CAN BE *QUITE* INTENSE.

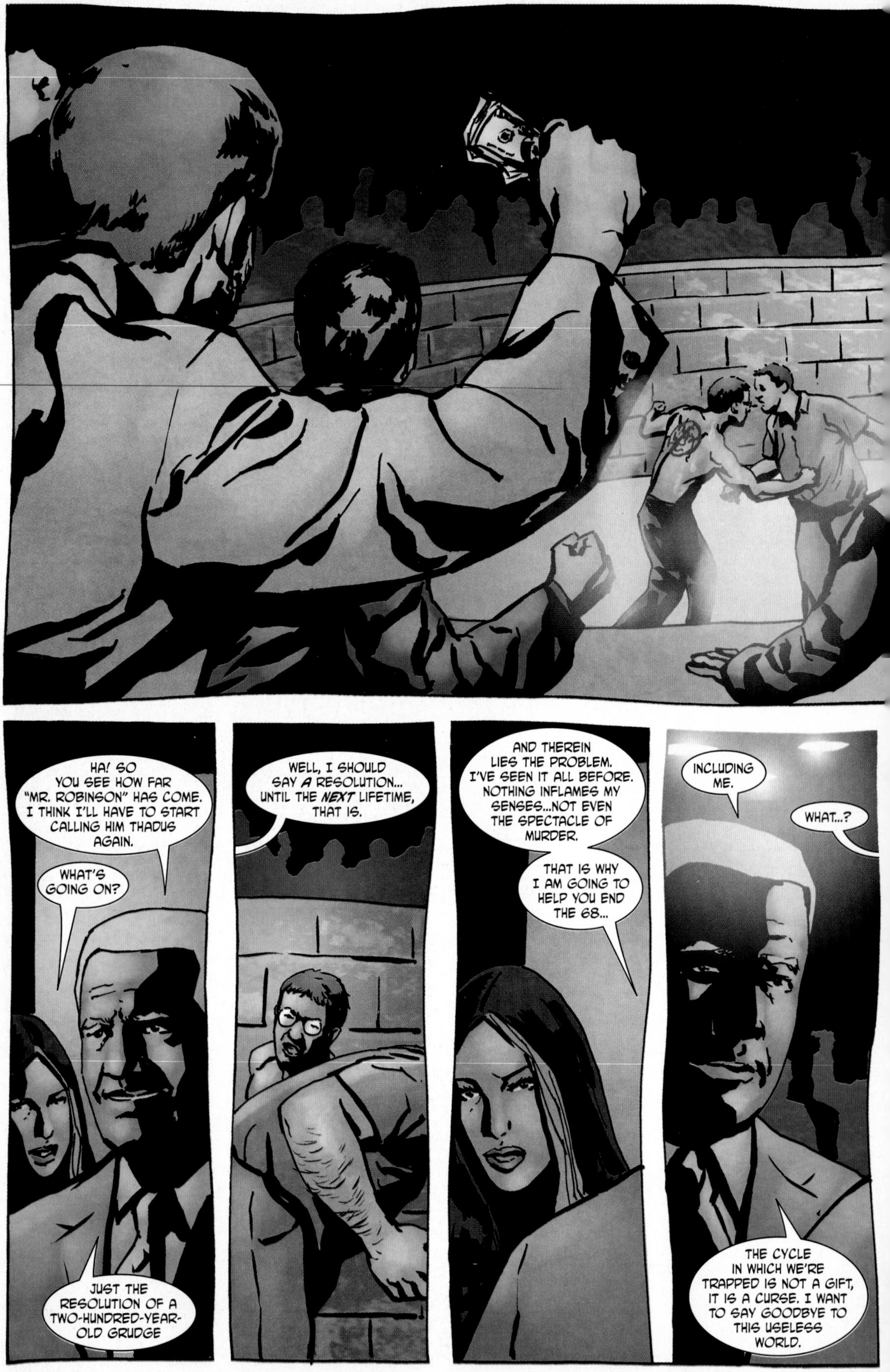
HA! SO YOU SEE HOW FAR "MR. ROBINSON" HAS COME. I THINK I'LL HAVE TO START CALLING HIM THADUS AGAIN.
WHAT'S GOING ON?
JUST THE RESOLUTION OF A TWO-HUNDRED-YEAR-OLD GRUDGE
WELL, I SHOULD SAY *A* RESOLUTION... UNTIL THE *NEXT* LIFETIME, THAT IS.
AND THEREIN LIES THE PROBLEM. I'VE SEEN IT ALL BEFORE. NOTHING INFLAMES MY SENSES...NOT EVEN THE SPECTACLE OF MURDER.
THAT IS WHY I AM GOING TO HELP YOU END THE 68...
INCLUDING ME.
WHAT...?
THE CYCLE IN WHICH WE'RE TRAPPED IS NOT A GIFT, IT IS A CURSE. I WANT TO SAY GOODBYE TO THIS USELESS WORLD.

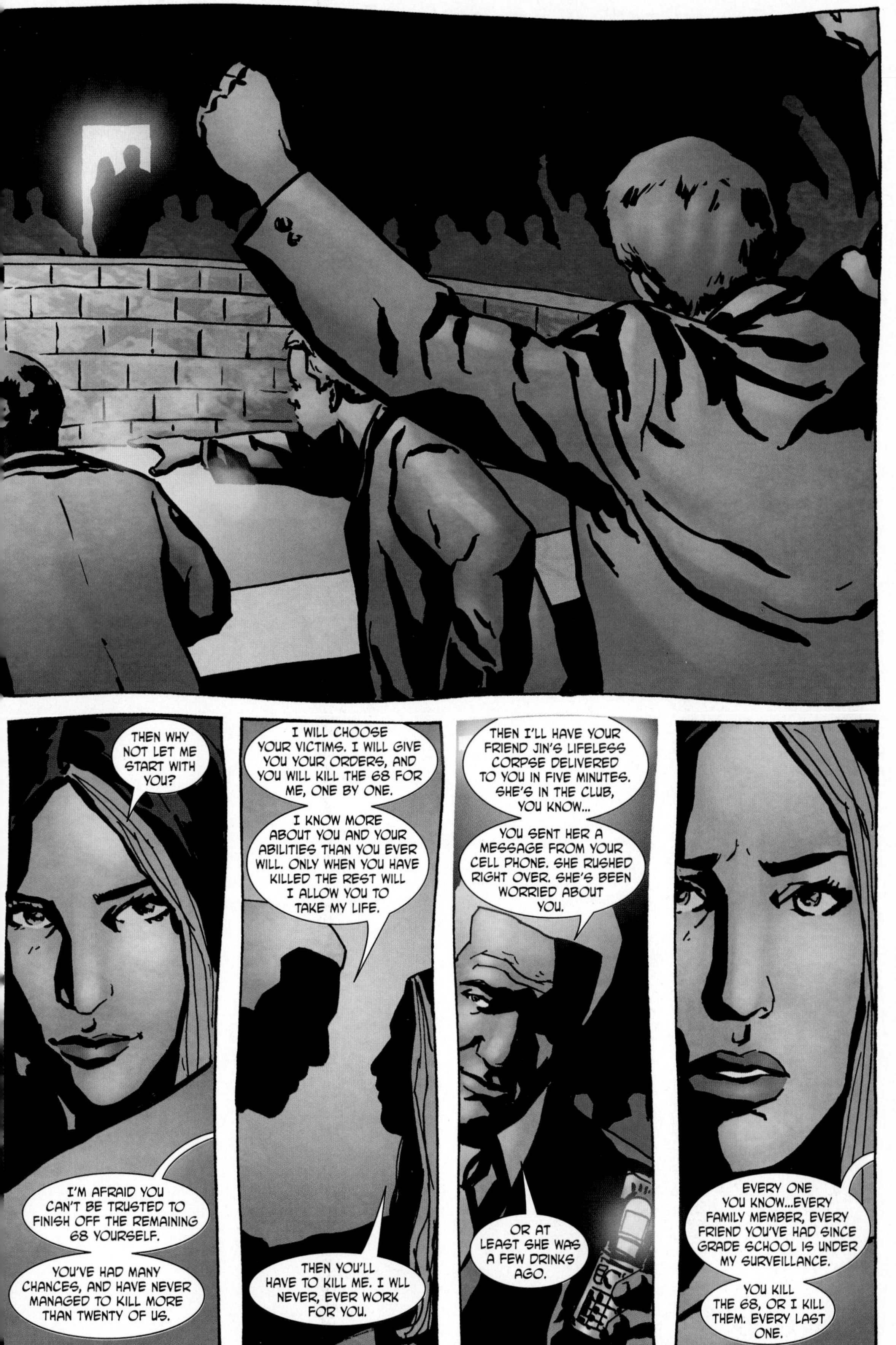
THEN WHY NOT LET ME START WITH YOU?
I'M AFRAID YOU CAN'T BE TRUSTED TO FINISH OFF THE REMAINING 68 YOURSELF.
YOU'VE HAD MANY CHANCES, AND HAVE NEVER MANAGED TO KILL MORE THAN TWENTY OF US.
I WILL CHOOSE YOUR VICTIMS. I WILL GIVE YOU YOUR ORDERS, AND YOU WILL KILL THE 68 FOR ME, ONE BY ONE.
I KNOW MORE ABOUT YOU AND YOUR ABILITIES THAN YOU EVER WILL. ONLY WHEN YOU HAVE KILLED THE REST WILL I ALLOW YOU TO TAKE MY LIFE.
THEN YOU'LL HAVE TO KILL ME. I WLL NEVER, EVER WORK FOR YOU.
THEN I'LL HAVE YOUR FRIEND JIN'S LIFELESS CORPSE DELIVERED TO YOU IN FIVE MINUTES. SHE'S IN THE CLUB, YOU KNOW...
YOU SENT HER A MESSAGE FROM YOUR CELL PHONE. SHE RUSHED RIGHT OVER. SHE'S BEEN WORRIED ABOUT YOU.
OR AT LEAST SHE WAS A FEW DRINKS AGO.
EVERY ONE YOU KNOW...EVERY FAMILY MEMBER, EVERY FRIEND YOU'VE HAD SINCE GRADE SCHOOL IS UNDER MY SURVEILLANCE.
YOU KILL THE 68, OR I KILL THEM. EVERY LAST ONE.

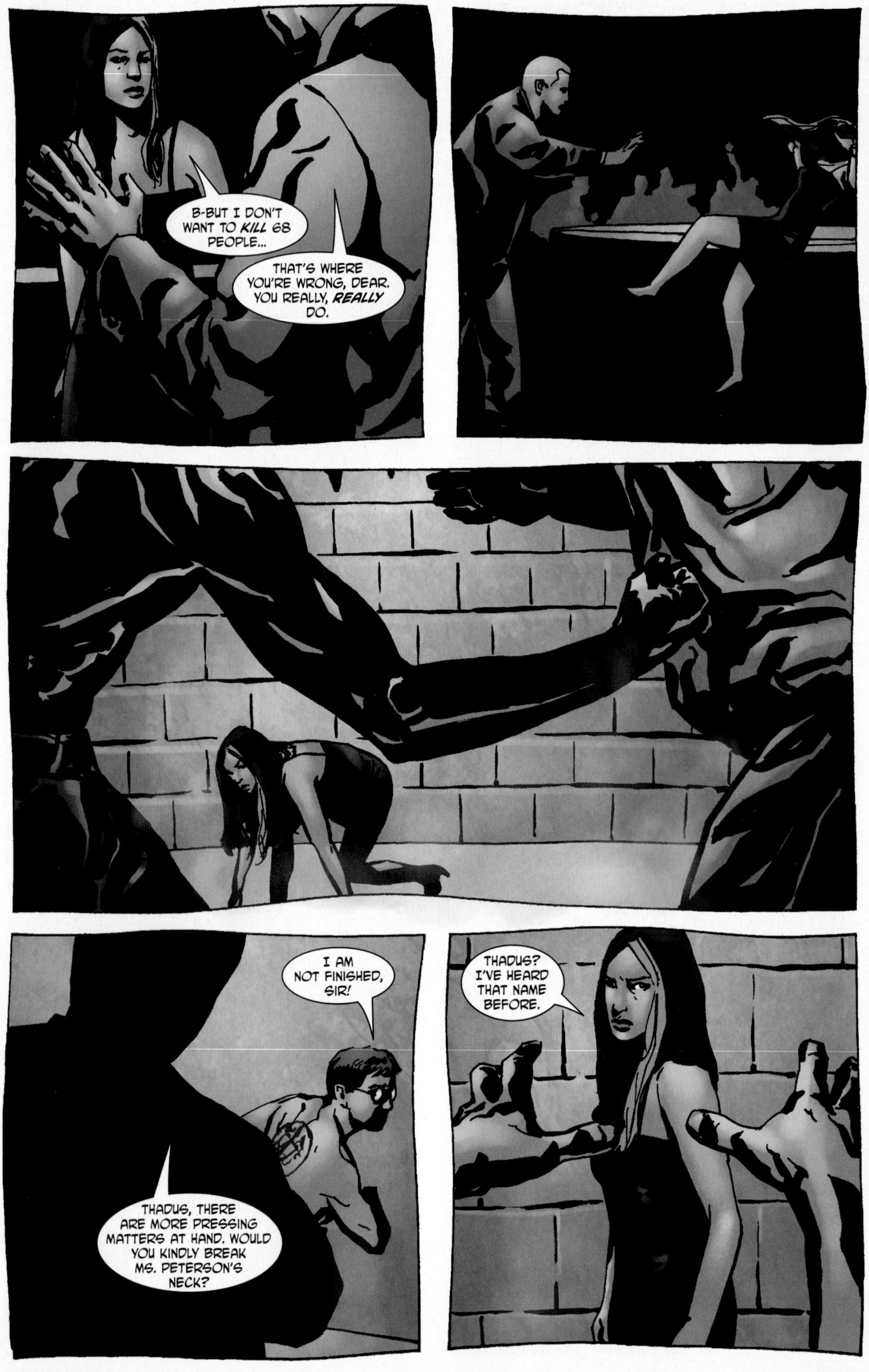
B-BUT I DON'T WANT TO KILL 68 PEOPLE...
THAT'S WHERE YOU'RE WRONG, DEAR. YOU REALLY, REALLY DO.
I AM NOT FINISHED, SIR!
THADUS, THERE ARE MORE PRESSING MATTERS AT HAND. WOULD YOU KINDLY BREAK MS. PETERSON'S NECK?
THADUS? I'VE HEARD THAT NAME BEFORE.

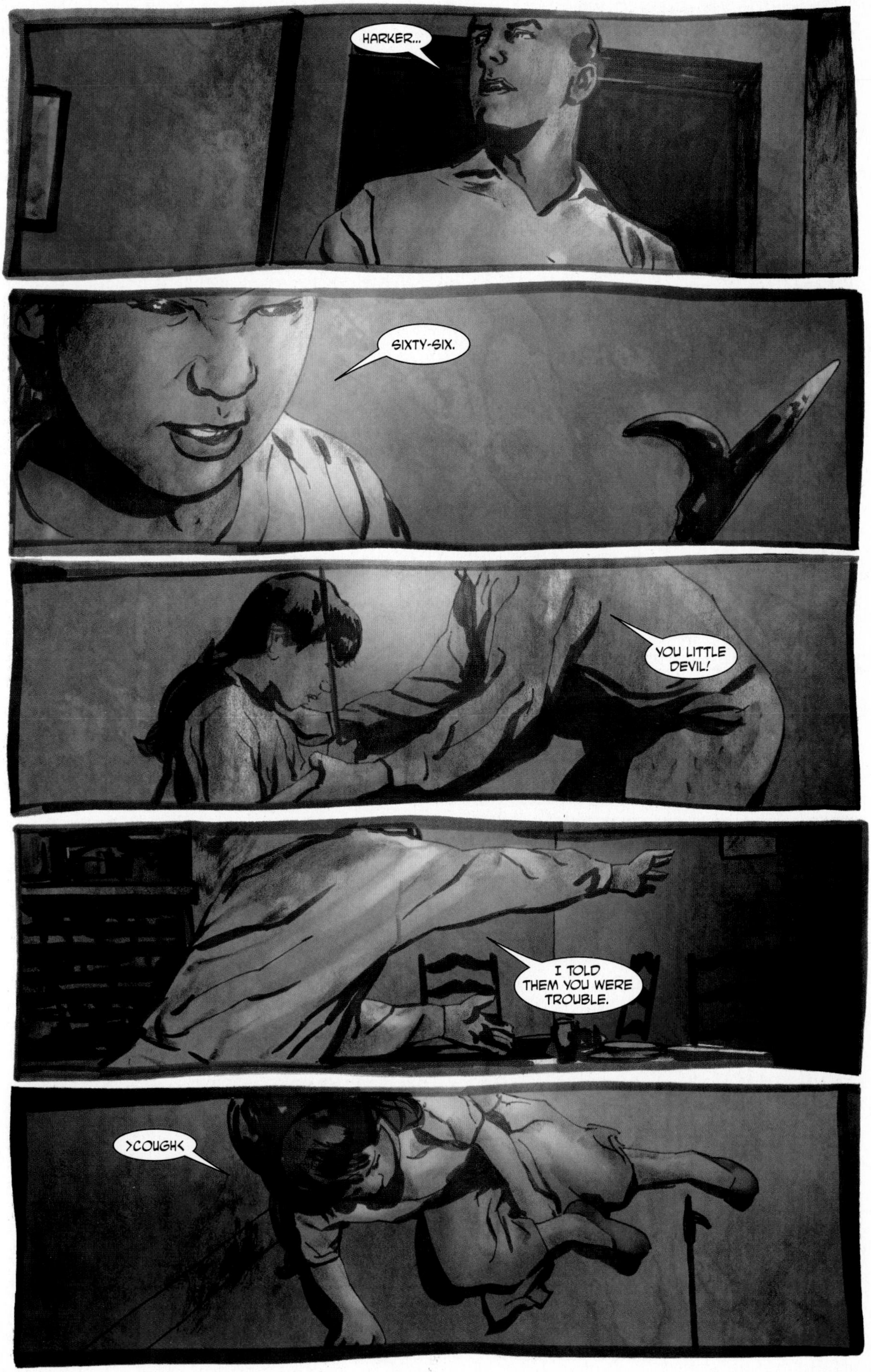
HARKER...
SIXTY-SIX.
YOU LITTLE DEVIL!
I TOLD THEM YOU WERE TROUBLE.
>COUGH<

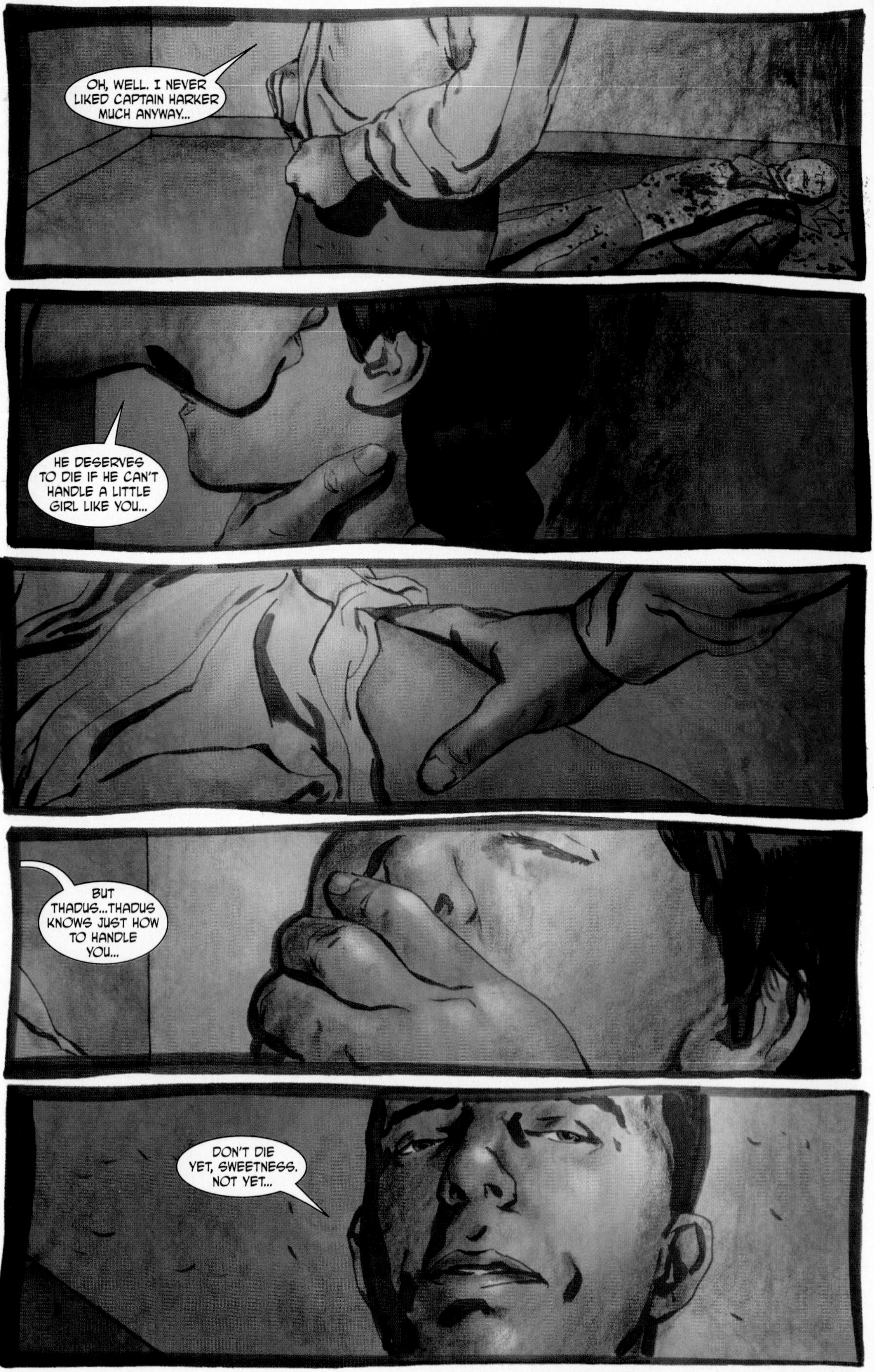
OH, WELL. I NEVER LIKED CAPTAIN HARKER MUCH ANYWAY...
HE DESERVES TO DIE IF HE CAN'T HANDLE A LITTLE GIRL LIKE YOU...
BUT THADUS...THADUS KNOWS JUST HOW TO HANDLE YOU...
DON'T DIE YET, SWEETNESS. NOT YET...

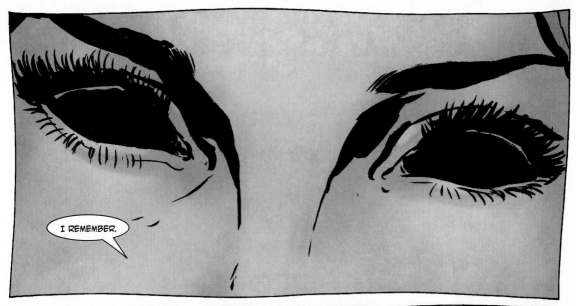

I REMEMBER.

DON'T DIE YET. NOT YET...

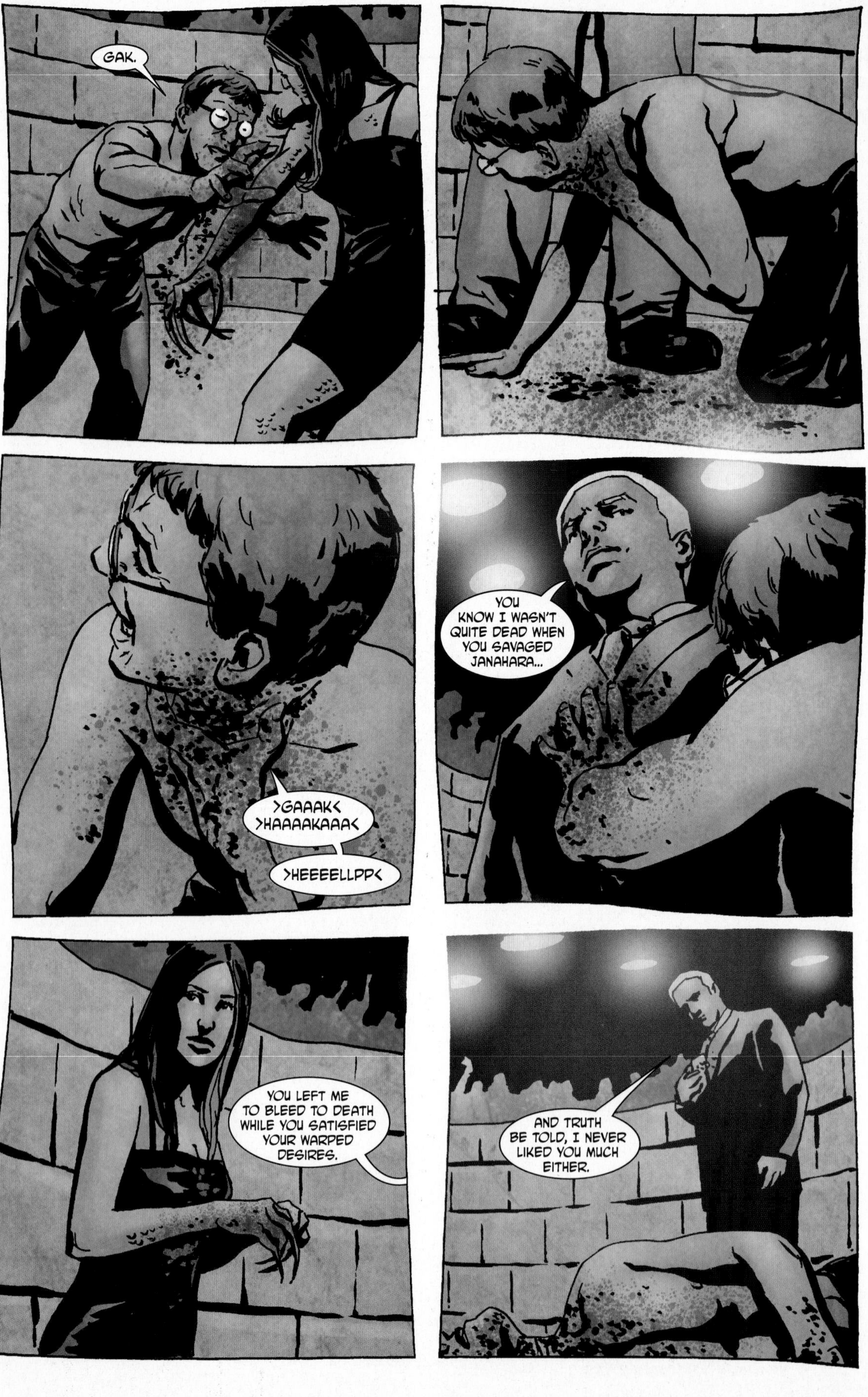
GAK.
>GAAAK<
>HAAAAKAAA<
>HEEEELLPP<
YOU KNOW I WASN'T QUITE DEAD WHEN YOU SAVAGED JANAHARA...
YOU LEFT ME TO BLEED TO DEATH WHILE YOU SATISFIED YOUR WARPED DESIRES.
AND TRUTH BE TOLD, I NEVER LIKED YOU MUCH EITHER.

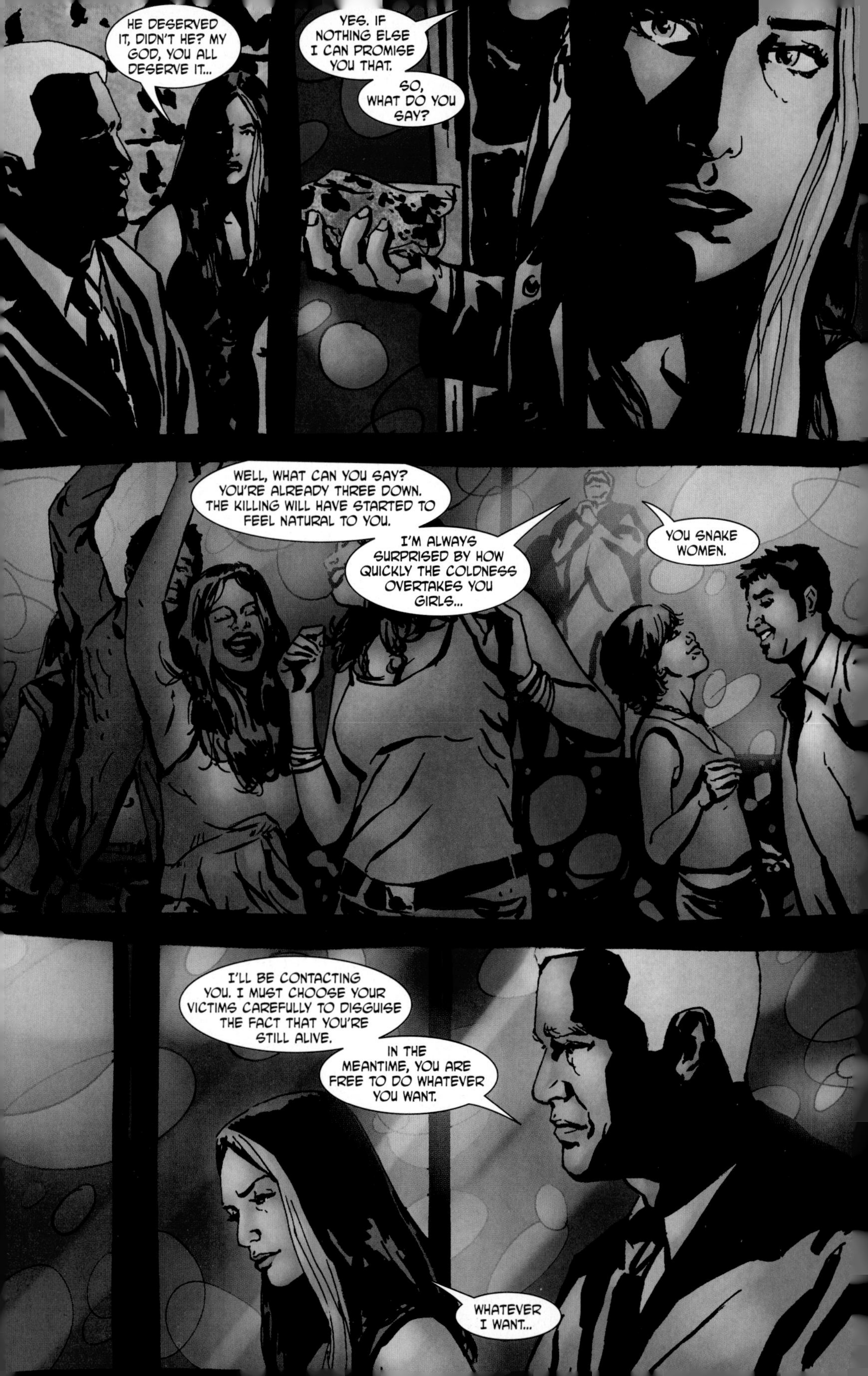
HE DESERVED IT, DIDN'T HE? MY GOD, YOU ALL DESERVE IT...
YES. IF NOTHING ELSE I CAN PROMISE YOU THAT.
SO, WHAT DO YOU SAY?
WELL, WHAT CAN YOU SAY? YOU'RE ALREADY THREE DOWN. THE KILLING WILL HAVE STARTED TO FEEL NATURAL TO YOU.
I'M ALWAYS SURPRISED BY HOW QUICKLY THE COLDNESS OVERTAKES YOU GIRLS...
YOU SNAKE WOMEN.
I'LL BE CONTACTING YOU. I MUST CHOOSE YOUR VICTIMS CAREFULLY TO DISGUISE THE FACT THAT YOU'RE STILL ALIVE.
IN THE MEANTIME, YOU ARE FREE TO DO WHATEVER YOU WANT.
WHATEVER I WANT...

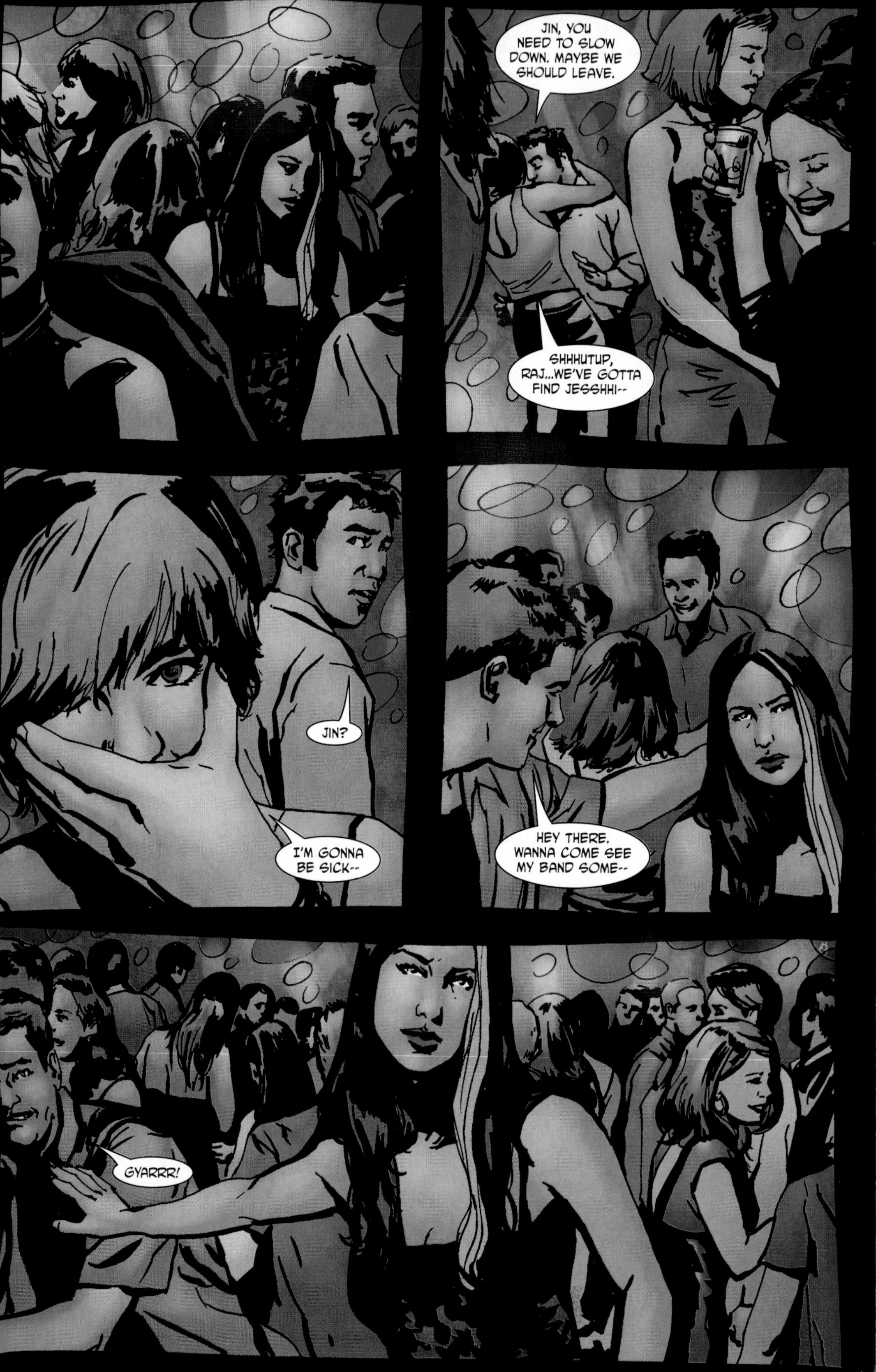
JIN, YOU NEED TO SLOW DOWN. MAYBE WE SHOULD LEAVE.
SHHHUTUP, RAJ...WE'VE GOTTA FIND JESSHHI--
JIN?
I'M GONNA BE SICK--
HEY THERE. WANNA COME SEE MY BAND SOME--
GYARRR!

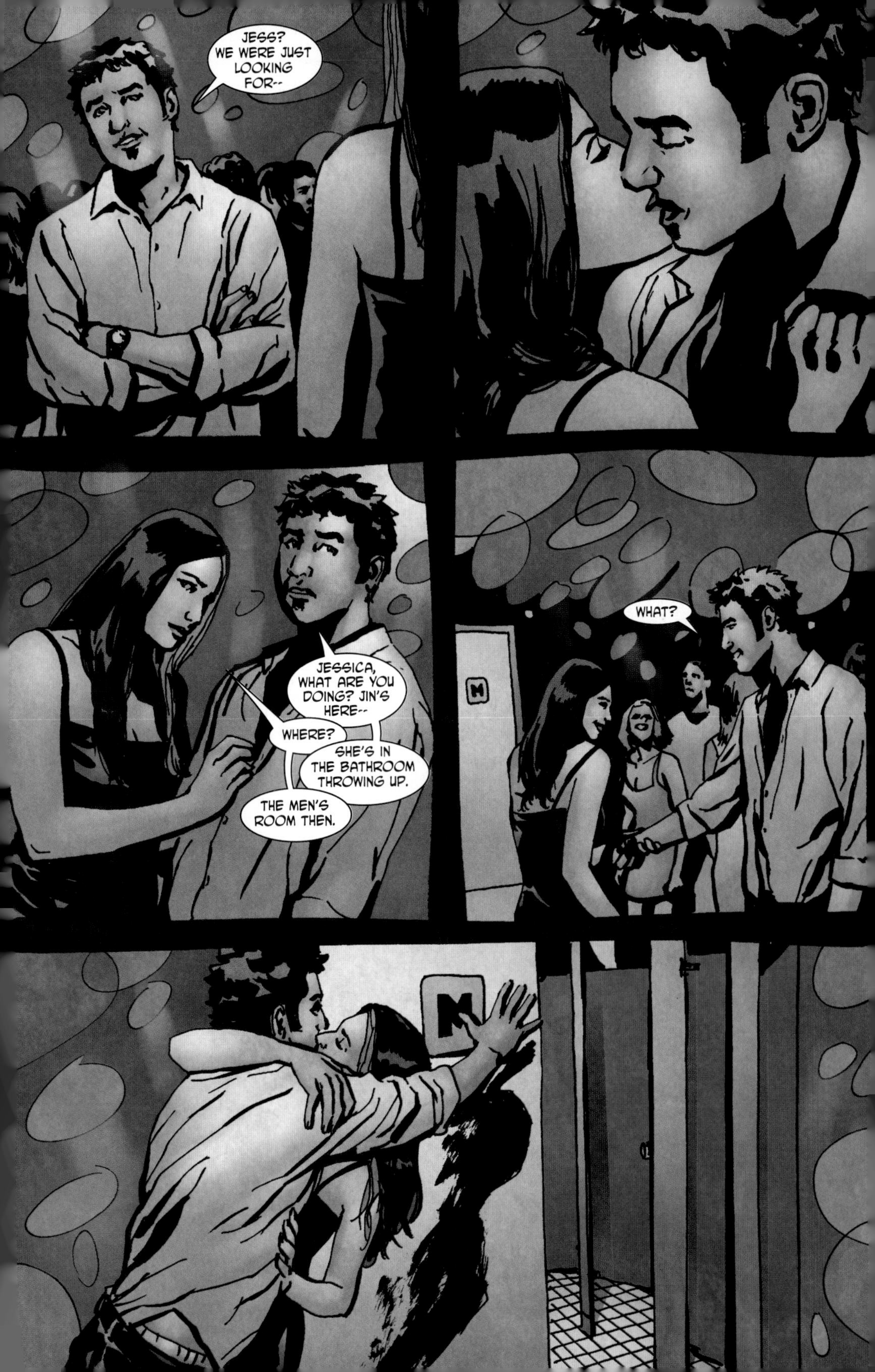
JESS? WE WERE JUST LOOKING FOR--
JESSICA, WHAT ARE YOU DOING? JIN'S HERE--
WHERE?
SHE'S IN THE BATHROOM THROWING UP.
THE MEN'S ROOM THEN.
WHAT?

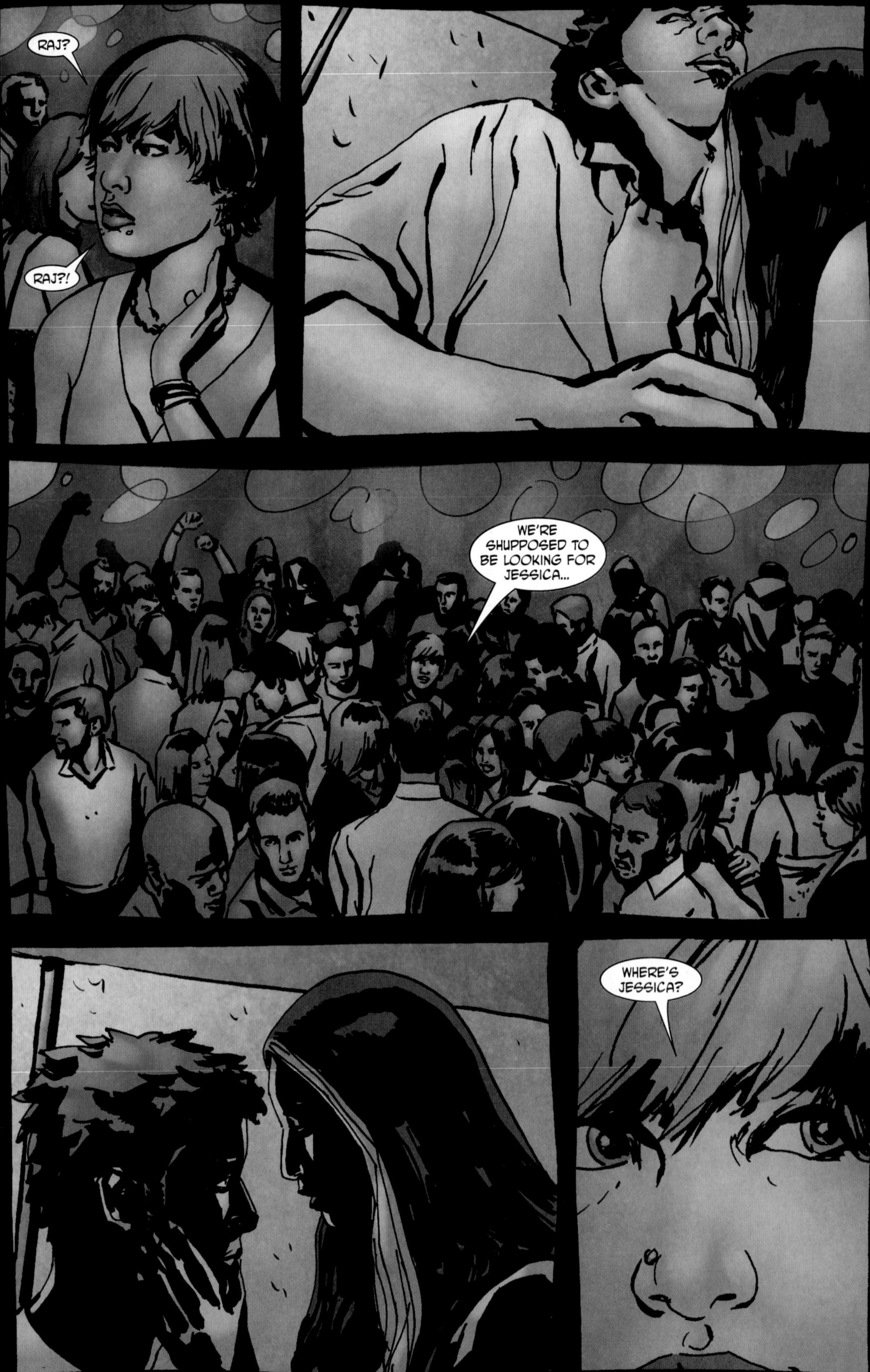
RAJ?
RAJ?!
WE'RE SHUPPOSED TO BE LOOKING FOR JESSICA...
WHERE'S JESSICA?

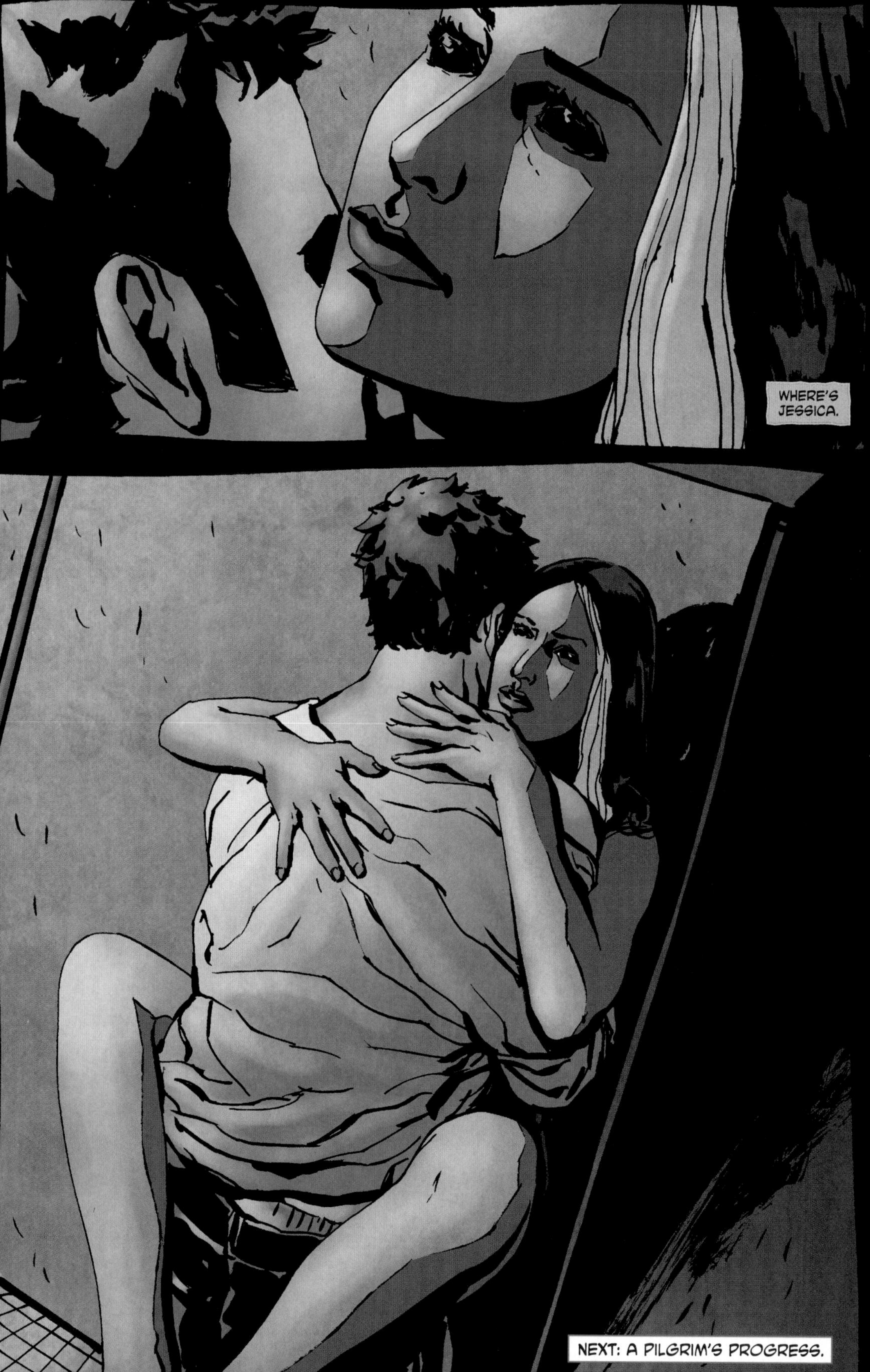
WHERE'S JESSICA.
NEXT: A PILGRIM'S PROGRESS.

CREATORS COMMENTARY

WRITER, ZEB WELLS AND ARTIST, MICHAEL GAYDOS CHAT ABOUT CREATING THE SNAKE WOMAN SAGA.

HI, THIS IS ZEB WELLS, WRITER OF ***SNAKE WOMAN***...

...AND THIS IS MICHAEL GAYDOS, ARTIST FOR ***SNAKE WOMAN*** TO VOLUME 1.

AND FOR THE NEXT SIX PAGES, WE'LL BE LETTING YOU IN ON WHAT WENT INTO CREATING THESE PAGES FROM ***SNAKE WOMAN*** #5.

YOU KNOW, ZEB AND I DIDN'T REALLY HAVE MUCH CONTACT THROUGH A LOT OF THE BOOK. I GOT THE SCRIPT, I DID MY THING, AND EVERY ONCE IN A WHILE, I'D GET SOME COMMENT ON THINGS THAT NEEDED TO BE CHANGED.

YEAH, [SERIES EDITOR] MACKENZIE CADENHEAD WAS OUR IN-BETWEEN, SHE MADE SURE EVERYTHING RAN SMOOTHLY. ACTUALLY, I THINK THIS IS THE FIRST TIME WE'VE EVER REALLY SPOKEN AT LENGTH.

YEAH. NICE TO MEET YOU, ZEB

YEAH, MICHAEL, NICE TO MEET YOU.

THE FIRST SETTING OF THIS SCENE, WITH HARKER'S OFFICES OVERLOOKING THE NIGHTCLUB AND BUILT OVER A SECRET FIGHTING RING, I WAS TRYING TO SHOW THE DIFFERENT WAYS THAT HARKER WAS TRYING TO FILL HIS TIME. REALLY, HE'S JUST WAITING UNTIL THE END. EVEN WITH ALL THIS STIMULATION GOING ON ALL AROUND HIM, HE JUST REMAINS CALM. IT DOESN'T REALLY AFFECT HIM AT ALL.

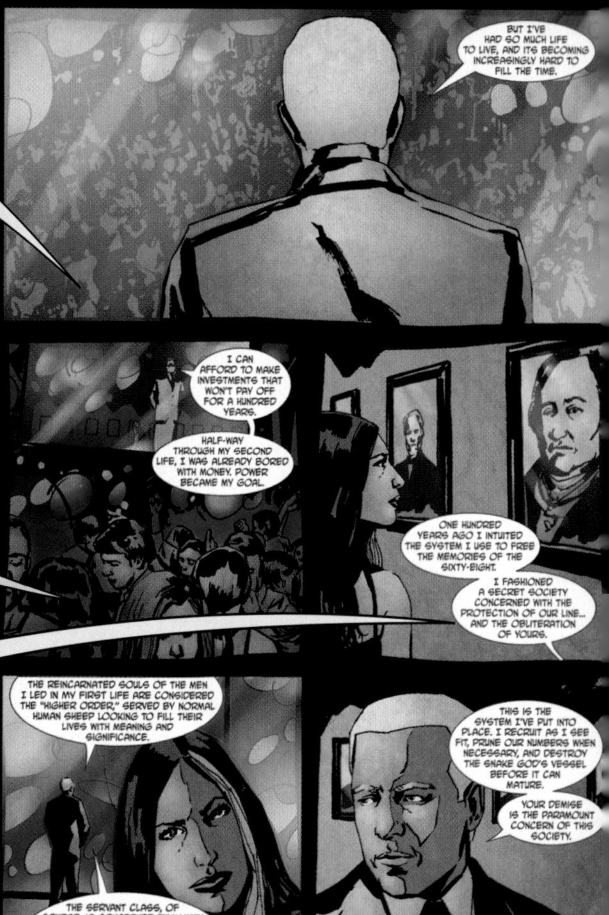
BUT I'VE HAD SO MUCH LIFE TO LIVE, AND ITS BECOMING INCREASINGLY HARD TO FILL THE TIME.
I CAN AFFORD TO MAKE INVESTMENTS THAT WON'T PAY OFF FOR A HUNDRED YEARS.
HALF-WAY THROUGH MY SECOND LIFE, I WAS ALREADY BORED WITH MONEY. POWER BECAME MY GOAL.
ONE HUNDRED YEARS AGO I INTUITED THE SYSTEM I USE TO FREE THE MEMORIES OF THE SIXTY-EIGHT.
I FASHIONED A SECRET SOCIETY CONCERNED WITH THE PROTECTION OF OUR LINE... AND THE OBLITERATION OF YOURS.
THE REINCARNATED SOULS OF THE MEN I LED IN MY FIRST LIFE ARE CONSIDERED THE "HIGHER ORDER," SERVED BY NORMAL HUMAN SHEEP LOOKING TO FILL THEIR LIVES WITH MEANING AND SIGNIFICANCE.
THE SERVANT CLASS, OF COURSE, IS CONCERNED FULLY WITH THE PROTECTION OF THE 68. IF THEY ACCIDENTALLY HARM US, OR ARE UNABLE TO STOP HARM FROM COMING TO US, THEY MEET A FATE OF MY CREATION. SOMETHING WORSE THAN DEATH I ASSURE YOU.
THIS IS THE SYSTEM I'VE PUT INTO PLACE. I RECRUIT AS I SEE FIT, PRUNE OUR NUMBERS WHEN NECESSARY, AND DESTROY THE SNAKE GOD'S VESSEL BEFORE IT CAN MATURE.
YOUR DEMISE IS THE PARAMOUNT CONCERN OF THIS SOCIETY.

YEAH, THOUGH FOR AN ARTIST, A BIG CLUB SCENE ISN'T SOMETHING THAT WE GET TOO EXCITED ABOUT. THE CHALLENGE FOR ME WAS TRYING TO FIND A WAY TO CONVEY IT THAT WASN'T NECESSARILY THE EASIEST WAY POSSIBLE, BUT A WAY THAT WASN'T TOO CONFUSING. I DIDN'T WANT IT TO BE STATIC, BUT ALSO, I DIDN'T WANT IMAGES THAT ARE JUMBLED TOGETHER, AND YOU CAN'T DECIPHER ANYTHING OUT OF THEM. I'M USED TO DOING MORE INTIMATE FACIAL EXPRESSIONS, LOOKING AT THE PERSON AND DECIPHERING WHAT THEY'RE THINKING--THE THRONGS OF PEOPLE ISN'T WHAT I USUALLY DO. IT WAS INTERESTING, THOUGH, AND I THINK IT TURNED OUT PRETTY WELL HERE.

I REALLY LIKE THIS MOMENT, WITH HARKER LOOKING OUT OVER THE CROWD, RIGHT NEXT TO THE SCENE WITH ALL THESE PICTURES OF GUYS FROM THE 18TH CENTURY. WHERE DID THESE GUYS COME FROM?

I CAN'T REMEMBER WHAT YOU WROTE IN THE SCRIPT, BUT IT WAS SOMETHING LIKE "PICTURES OF EAST INDIA COMPANY TRADE OFFICIALS." I THINK I JUST USED SOME RANDOM 18TH CENTURY PORTRAITS AS INSPIRATION.

YEAH, THAT WAS ONE OF THOSE THINGS WHERE 99% OF THE READERS WOULDN'T HAVE KNOWN WHAT AN EAST INDIA COMPANY TRADE OFFICIAL WOULD HAVE LOOKED LIKE.

ONE OF THE THINGS THAT I FOUND INTERESTING THROUGHOUT THE WHOLE STORY WAS THAT, EVEN THOUGH HARKER WAS DIFFERENT PEOPLE THROUGH THE DIFFERENT TIME PERIODS, HE WAS STILL THE SAME GUY [DUE TO HIS RETAINED MEMORY FROM LIFETIME TO LIFETIME], SO I TRIED TO CHANGE UP HIS LOOK A LITTLE BIT WHILE STILL MAKING HIM RECOGNIZABLY HARKER.

YEAH, AT THE BEGINNING, IT WAS A LITTLE HARDER TO FIND OUT WHO HARKER WAS. BUT THEN I STARTED SEEING MICHAEL'S CHARACTER DESIGNS, WHICH WERE GREAT. AFTER SEEING THE FIRST ISSUE, IT WAS EASIER TO WRITE THE BOOKS. ONCE I SAW HOW THE CHARACTERS WERE "ACTING" IN THE BOOKS IT WAS MUCH EASIER TO WRITE THEM. HARKER ESPECIALLY, THAT CALM MENACE HE HAD. MICHAEL WAS ABLE TO CAPTURE THAT, AND IT HELPED ME FIND THE CHARACTER'S VOICE.

THIS WHOLE PLOT ELEMENT OF HARKER NEEDING ALL THIS VISCERAL STIMULATION AROUND HIM STARTED WITH WANTING HIM TO BE BORED. WE WANTED HIM TO BE BORED WITH HIS LIFE. THIS PANEL WAS PROBABLY JUST AN EASY WAY TO MAKE THAT EXPLICIT. I DO FEEL LIKE I DON'T KNOW WHAT WAS GOING ON THERE, BUT I WANTED TO HAVE A CHARACTER THAT WAS REALLY, REALLY UPSET WITH THE MEANINGLESSNESS OF LIFE.

BUT AT THE SAME TIME I THOUGHT THAT HARKER'S CHARACTER WAS CARNAL AND HUNGRY FOR POWER, AND I WANTED TO ADD THAT AS AN EXTRA INCENTIVE AS TO WHY HE WAS READY TO THROW IT ALL IN.

THEN WHY THE FUCK AM I STILL ALIVE?

BECAUSE MY COCK DOESN'T WORK.

PLEASE, FOLLOW ME...

OH, DON'T LOOK AT ME LIKE THAT. THE SECRET PASSAGEWAY IS SIMPLY THEATRE FOR MY CLIENTELE.

WHAT? NO... I'M THINKING ABOUT WHAT YOU SAID BEFORE...

AS I WAS DRAWING THIS PARTICULAR PANEL, I JUST KEPT ADDING BLACK. I WANTED TO GET TO THE POINT WHERE YOU HAD THE LEAST AMOUNT OF WHITE SHOWING BUT YOU COULD STILL TELL WHAT WAS GOING ON. IT WAS IMPORTANT TO CONTRAST THIS PANEL WITH THE BRIGHTNESS AND COLORS OF THE NIGHTCLUB, SO I HAD ALL THE LIGHT IN THE PANEL COME FROM THE TOP STEP, WITH THE DARKNESS SWALLOWING EVERYTHING ELSE.

LET ME EXPLAIN.

IN THE KABINI TEMPLE, AS I KILLED THE COBRA MATES, THE FEMALE STRUCK MY WRIST...

THE VENOM DIDN'T KILL ME, BUT IT WAS FATAL TO MY MANHOOD. LIKE MY MEMORY, BY SOME TWISTED TURN OF FATE, MY SHRIVELED MEMBER FOLLOWS ME THROUGHOUT LIFETIMES.

I HAVE LIVED TWO HUNDRED YEARS WITH AN ITCH I CANNOT SCRATCH.

THE DISTRACTIONS I REQUIRE CAN BE QUITE INTENSE.

I REMEMBER MACKENZIE DIDN'T LIKE THE FACT THAT THERE WAS A BOOKSHELF SECRET PASSAGE. SHE MADE ME ADD IN THE LINE ABOUT THE PASSAGEWAY BEING "THEATRE FOR THE CLIENTELE" IN THE NEXT PANEL.

NOTE FROM THE EDITOR: REALLY?! I DON'T REMEMBER THAT. IT'S A GOOD LINE, THOUGH. NICE WORK, ZEB!
--MC

DID YOU DESIGN THE TATTOO?

I MADE THE TATTOO AFTER RESEARCHING THE EAST INDIA COMPANY. THIS WAS ONE OF THE SYMBOLS THEY USED. WE TALKED ABOUT PORTRAITS OF THE STODGY OLD BRITISH GUYS, NOBODY'S GOING TO KNOW WHO THEY ARE. BUT FOR OUR SAKE, WE'RE REALLY TRYING TO DO OUR PART AS WRITER AND ARTIST TO BE AUTHENTIC. THERE ARE THOSE FANS THAT GET INTO IT AND LOOK UP ALL THIS STUFF. IT'S REALLY FUN FOR ME, BECAUSE IT EXPANDS MY LEARNING OF NEW THINGS.

THAT'S THE FUN THING ABOUT DOING RESEARCH, YOU HAVE TO LEARN THINGS THAT YOU WOULDN'T HAVE TRACKED DOWN OR THOUGHT ABOUT BEFORE.

HA! SO YOU SEE HOW FAR "MR. ROBINSON" HAS COME. I THINK I'LL HAVE TO START CALLING HIM THADUS AGAIN.

WHAT'S GOING ON?

JUST THE RESOLUTION OF A TWO HUNDRED-YEAR OLD GRUDGE.

WELL, I SHOULD SAY A RESOLUTION... UNTIL THE NEXT LIFETIME, THAT IS.

AND THEREIN LIES THE PROBLEM. I'VE SEEN IT ALL BEFORE. NOTHING INFLAMES MY SENSES...NOT EVEN THE SPECTACLE OF MURDER.

THAT IS WHY I AM GOING TO HELP YOU END THE 68...

THE CYCLE IN WHICH WE'RE TRAPPED IS NOT A GIFT, IT IS A CURSE. I WANT TO SAY GOODBYE TO THIS USELESS WORLD.

INCLUDING ME.

WHAT..?

THEN WHY NOT LET ME START WITH YOU?

I'M AFRAID YOU CAN'T BE TRUSTED TO FINISH OFF THE REMAINING 68 YOURSELF.

YOU'VE HAD MANY CHANCES, AND HAVE NEVER MANAGED TO KILL MORE THAN TWENTY OF US.

I WILL CHOOSE YOUR VICTIMS. I WILL GIVE YOU YOUR ORDERS, AND YOU WILL KILL THE 68 FOR ME, ONE BY ONE.

I KNOW MORE ABOUT YOU AND YOUR ABILITIES THAN YOU EVER WILL. ONLY WHEN YOU HAVE KILLED THE REST WILL I ALLOW YOU TO TAKE MY LIFE.

THEN YOU'LL HAVE TO KILL ME. I WILL NEVER WORK FOR YOU.

THEN I'LL HAVE YOUR FRIEND JIN'S LIFELESS CORPSE DELIVERED TO YOU IN FIVE MINUTES. SHE'S IN THE CLUB, YOU KNOW...

YOU SENT HER A MESSAGE FROM YOUR CELL PHONE. SHE RUSHED RIGHT OVER. SHE'S BEEN WORRIED ABOUT YOU.

OR AT LEAST SHE WAS A FEW DRINKS AGO.

EVERY ONE YOU KNOW...EVERY FAMILY MEMBER, EVERY FRIEND YOU'VE HAD SINCE GRADE SCHOOL, IS UNDER MY SURVEILLANCE.

YOU KILL THE 68, OR I KILL THEM, EVERY LAST ONE.

I KNEW WE NEEDED THE STORY TO BE ABOUT JESSICA KILLING THESE PEOPLE. AND WE WANTED IT TO BE ABOUT A REGULAR GIRL WHO HAS TO KILL. WE FIGURED SHE NEEDED A LITTLE PRODDING TO MAKE HER AT LEAST A LITTLE SYMPATHETIC. WE WANTED HARKER THERE TO FORCE HER OR AT LEAST MAKE HER FEEL THAT SHE DOESN'T HAVE A CHOICE. WE NEEDED THAT CATALYST SO THAT SHE WOULDN'T JUST STOP DOING IT.

I WAS HAVING SOME PROBLEMS WITH HOW I WAS GOING TO FIT EVERYTHING INTO THIS SMALL PANEL. IN THE END, I DECIDED TO BREAK IT DOWN IN THE SIMPLEST WAY, BY SHOWING THE GESTURE OF HIM GRABBING HER AND THEIR FACES COMING TOGETHER. THROUGHOUT THE BOOK, I KEPT HARKER'S HAIR ALWAYS AS A WHITE MASS, EVEN WHEN HIS FACE WAS IN SHADOW, SO THAT WAS AN EASY THING HERE. THEN I JUST ADDED IN JESS' GREEN STREAK AS A NICE TOUCH.

THE COOL THING ABOUT HARKER IS THAT HE'S TRYING TO PROTECT JESS ON ONE LEVEL, BECAUSE HE NEEDS HER. BUT ON ANOTHER LEVEL, HE NEEDS TO FORCE HER TO DO WHAT HE NEEDS HER TO DO. IT'S LITERALLY HARKER PUSHING HER INTO THE POOL AND FORCING HER TO SWIM. I LOVE THIS PANEL, BECAUSE IT LITERALLY LOOKS LIKE HE'S PUSHING HER INTO THE POOL.

B-BUT I DON'T WANT TO *KILL* 68 PEOPLE...

THAT'S WHERE YOU'RE WRONG, DEAR. YOU REALLY, *REALLY* DO.

THIS GUY THAT ROBINSON IS FIGHTING IS ACTUALLY PAUL GILMORE, FROM SNAKE WOMAN #6. IN THE ORIGINAL VERSION OF THE SCRIPT FOR #5, HE WASN'T ANYONE IN PARTICULAR, BUT THEN, WHEN WE DECIDED TO INCORPORATE HIM INTO #6, WE TWEAKED THIS SCENE TO REFLECT PAUL'S APPEARANCE.

I AM NOT FINISHED, SIR!

THADUS? I'VE HEARD THAT NAME BEFORE.

THADUS, THERE ARE MORE PRESSING MATTERS AT HAND. WOULD YOU KINDLY BREAK MS. PETERSON'S NECK?

MICHAEL, THIS PANEL ENDED UP BECOMING THE PANEL THEY SHOWED UNDER THE RECAPS FOR ISSUES #7-#10.

REALLY? THIS PANEL WAS A LITTLE DIFFICULT TO FIGURE OUT, IN TERMS OF WHICH WAY I WAS GOING TO APPROACH IT. THE BEST WAY WAS DEFINITELY FROM ROBINSON'S POINT-OF-VIEW. THAT WAY THE FOCUS COULD BE ENTIRELY ON JESS, AND I COULD USE ROBINSON'S HANDS FOR HIS EXPRESSION. AND THEN ON HER FACE, I TRIED TO SHOW THAT IT WASN'T CLEAR WHAT WAS GOING ON OR WHAT SHE WAS FEELING. IT WAS KIND OF CONFUSION, I GUESS. COMING TO SOME SORT OF REALIZATION.

I DEFINITELY WANTED TO GIVE THE FLASHBACK PAGES A DIFFERENT LOOK. THE BORDERS ARE THICKER AND IRREGULAR. A LOT OF THEM WERE VERY WIDESCREEN, I WANTED TO GET THE CINEMATIC LOOK. I WANTED TO GET THE INTIMACY BETWEEN THE CHARACTERS. I THINK IN THE SCRIPT, THAT'S WHAT REALLY IS CALLED FOR, ESPECIALLY WITH THE YOUNG JANAHARA AND THADUS. A LOT OF WHAT GOES ON IN THESE TWO PAGES, WHAT'S BEST SEEN IS UNSEEN.

HAVING TO DO WITH THE COLOR, THE ORIGINAL PAGES I DID WITH A GRAYISH TONE TO IT, AND THE COLORISTS CAME BACK TO ME WITH A VERY ORANGISH PALETTE, SO I WENT BACK AND TWEAKED IT. I WENT BACK IN THERE WITH BLUE TONE TO MAKE CERTAIN THINGS POP. I GUESS IT CAME OUT AS A KIND OF WEIRD TONE.

WE REALLY COULDN'T SHOW WHAT IS GOING ON, OR THADUS' INTENTIONS TOWARDS JANAHARA, AND THESE LITTLE GLIMPSES SAY MORE, AND LEAVE MORE TO THE IMAGINATION.

WE WERE DEFINITELY ON THE SAME PAGE, THAT WE JUST NEEDED TO SUGGEST WHAT WAS GOING ON. I CAN'T REMEMBER HOW SPECIFIC THE DIRECTION WAS, THOUGH, BUT OBVIOUSLY I THINK THE CHOICES YOU MADE WERE REALLY, REALLY, REALLY EFFECTIVE. ESPECIALLY THIS SECOND PAGE IS SUCH AN EFFECTIVE PAGE FOR WHAT IT IS. JUST SEEING THE FLASHBACK STUFF FOR THE FIRST TIME, IT WAS ONE OF THOSE MOMENTS WHEN I STARTED BREATHING EASY, BECAUSE I COULD TELL THAT YOU KNEW EXACTLY WHAT THE FLASHBACKS SHOULD LOOK LIKE.

HARKER...
SIXTY-SIX.
YOU LITTLE DEVIL!
I TOLD THEM YOU WERE TROUBLE.
>COUGH<
OH, WELL. I NEVER LIKED CAPTAIN HARKER MUCH ANYWAY...
HE DESERVES TO DIE IF HE CAN'T HANDLE A LITTLE GIRL LIKE YOU...
BUT THADUS...THADUS KNOWS JUST HOW TO HANDLE YOU...
DON'T DIE YET, SWEETNESS. NOT YET...

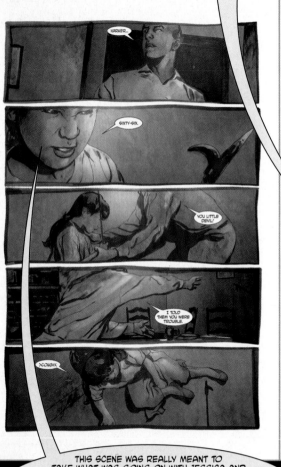

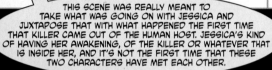

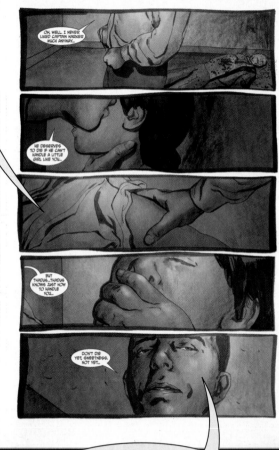

THIS SCENE WAS REALLY MEANT TO TAKE WHAT WAS GOING ON WITH JESSICA AND JUXTAPOSE THAT WITH WHAT HAPPENED THE FIRST TIME THAT KILLER CAME OUT OF THE HUMAN HOST. JESSICA'S KIND OF HAVING HER AWAKENING, OF THE KILLER OR WHATEVER THAT IS INSIDE HER, AND IT'S NOT THE FIRST TIME THAT THESE TWO CHARACTERS HAVE MET EACH OTHER.

WE MENTIONED BEFORE HOW HARKER'S APPEARANCE STAYED THE SAME FROM TIME PERIOD TO TIME PERIOD, BUT I DON'T THINK THAT I EVER SAID ANYTHING ABOUT THIS FLASHBACK CHARACTER'S APPEARANCE. I DON'T KNOW WHAT YOU THINK ABOUT IT, MICHAEL, BUT THADUS' LOOK IN THE PAST MIGHT HAVE JUST BEEN A MANIFESTATION OF HOW I WAS DESCRIBING HIS OLD INCARNATION VS. HOW I WAS DESCRIBING HIS CURRENT ONE.

FOR ME, COMING UP WITH THE CHARACTERS, THE LOOK OF THEM, IT'S KIND OF HARD TO GET INTO WHAT THE WRITER IS ACTUALLY THINKING. YOU KINDA DO SOMETHING AND SEE IF THERE'S ANY FEEDBACK FROM THE WRITER OR THE EDITOR, WHO'LL EITHER TELL YOU THIS IS GOOD, OR THIS IS NOT GOOD.

WE DIDN'T WANT TO HAVE ANY HARD RULES THAT EVERYONE THROUGH THE AGES LOOKED LIKE THEIR FORMER SELF, BECAUSE WE WANTED TO PLAY AROUND WITH HOW PEOPLE WERE BEING REINCARNATED AND BORN.

WHAT I WANTED WAS, AFTER WE'VE SEEN THE OUTRAGE COMMITTED AGAINST JANAHARA, FOR JESSICA'S ATTACK TO BE VERY SNAKE-LIKE. THERE'S NOT A LOT OF THINKING, SHE JUST STRIKES, KILLS HIM AS QUICKLY AS POSSIBLE. ONCE SHE DECIDES TO DO IT, I DIDN'T WANT THERE TO BE ANY WORDS, THOUGH I DO BREAK THAT RULE A COUPLE OF TIMES.

WITH THESE CLOSE-UPS, I WAS CONTINUING WITH THE INTIMACY THAT WE WERE EXPLORING IN THE LAST COUPLE OF PAGES. A DIFFERENT TIME PERIOD, A DIFFERENT SITUATION, BUT JUST AS IMMEDIATE.

WHENEVER ANYBODY PICKS UP SOMETHING THAT I'VE WRITTEN, THE ONE QUESTION THEY ALWAYS ASK ME IS IF I ACTUALLY GOT PAID FOR WRITING ONE OF THOSE SOUND EFFECTS...THEY'RE USUALLY NOT TOO IMPRESSED.

I WANTED TO GET A LOT OF BLOOD AND MAKE IT MESSY, SINCE SHE WENT FOR THE JUGULAR. ESPECIALLY THIS PANEL, THAT BLOOD WAS WRITTEN INTO THE SCRIPT, THAT ROBINSON SMEARS BLOOD ON HARKER'S NICE SUIT AS HE'S REACHING FOR HIM. THIS WAS A PANEL I REALLY ENJOYED DOING, GIVING HARKER THAT LOOK. HE'S MORE WORRIED ABOUT HIS SUIT THAN HE IS ABOUT ROBINSON.

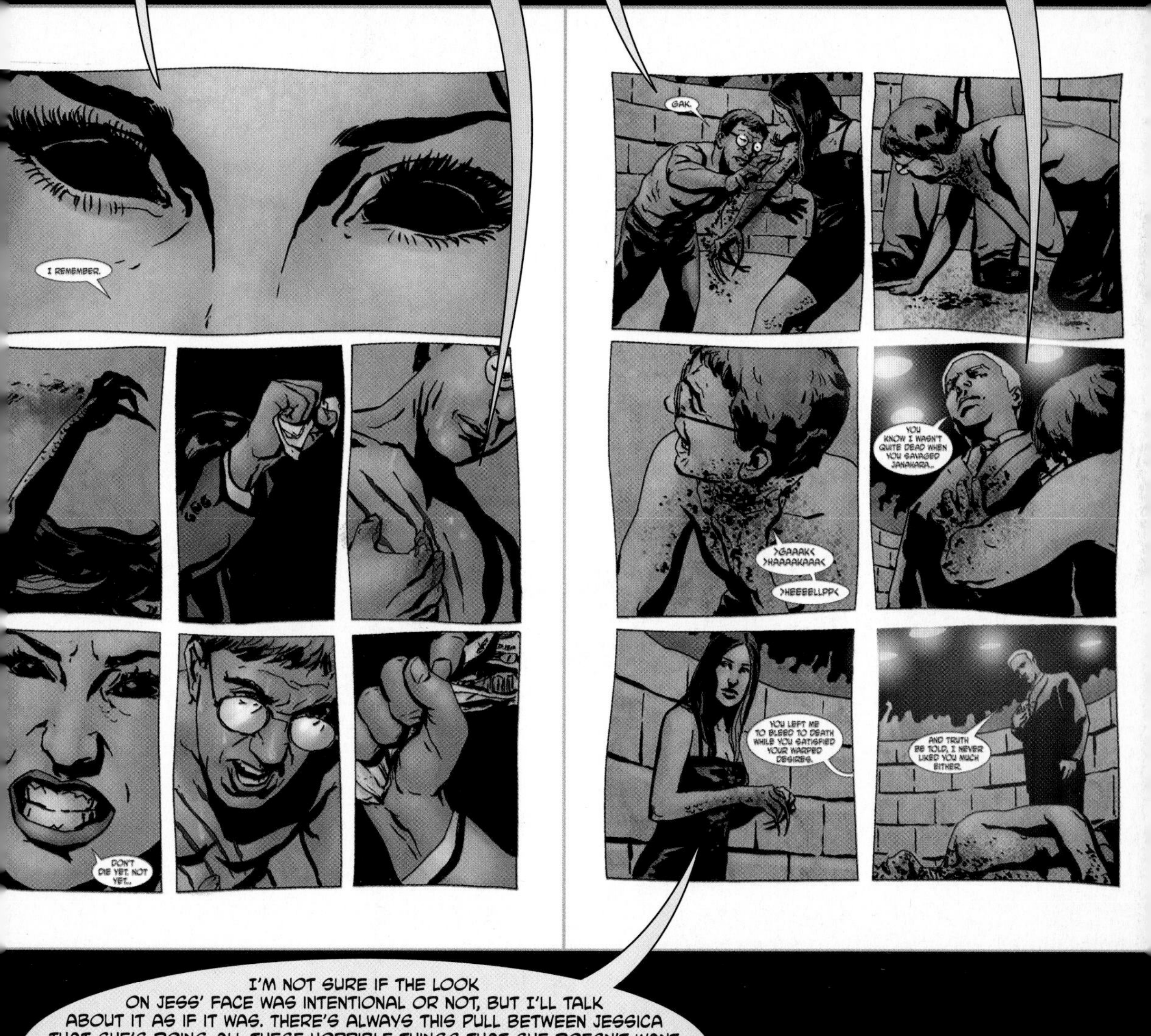
I REMEMBER.
DON'T DIE YET. NOT YET...
GAK.
>GAAAK< >HAAAAKAAA<
>HEEEELLPP<
YOU KNOW I WASN'T QUITE DEAD WHEN YOU SAVAGED JANAHARA...
YOU LEFT ME TO BLEED TO DEATH WHILE YOU SATISFIED YOUR WARPED DESIRES.
AND TRUTH BE TOLD, I NEVER LIKED YOU MUCH EITHER.

I'M NOT SURE IF THE LOOK ON JESS' FACE WAS INTENTIONAL OR NOT, BUT I'LL TALK ABOUT IT AS IF IT WAS. THERE'S ALWAYS THIS PULL BETWEEN JESSICA THAT SHE'S DOING ALL THESE HORRIBLE THINGS THAT SHE DOESN'T WANT TO DO. THERE'S THAT SHAME THAT SHE'S ENJOYING IT, THAT EXERCISING HER POWER OVER SOMEONE ELSE IS ENJOYABLE, NO MATTER HOW MUCH SHE TELLS HERSELF THAT SHE DOESN'T WANT TO DO IT, IT'S ALWAYS GOING TO BE A WARPED DESIRE FOR HER.

AND ALSO, THERE'S A KIND OF CALMNESS I WANTED TO EVOKE. SHE'S NOT REALLY FREAKING OUT AFTER WHAT SHE'S DONE.

WELL, THAT'S IT...THANKS FOR, UH...READING. AND THANK YOU, MICHAEL.

THANK YOU, ZEB. BYE, GUYS.

The Diary of a Snake Woman:
April Manning (1945-1980)

June 6, 1980

It's gotten worse—the headaches, that heavy feeling that greets me each morning. My dreams are becoming more intense, more real, and I wake afterwards, drenched in sweat. It's like I've been chasing something all night. Something I desperately need. I just can't remember what. Michael says they're merely nightmares, but he should understand. He's a part of this somehow. I can feel it. It's almost instinct.

June 27, 1980

Something has gone terribly wrong. I know it now. Because I see his face every time I close my eyes. I hear his screams. He's in trouble. And I think he's Michael. When I wake up I try to warn him, but he dismisses my fears as paranoia. He says, he's getting worried, especially since my last "episode" when he found me in the backyard, my clothes ripped. He thinks I should "see" someone. I want to tell him what's happening, that I'm changing. I think he knows it too, because he doesn't look at me the same way anymore. Actually—he doesn't look at me at all anymore.

July 9, 1980

I thought it was getting better. But I saw him again last night. His face wasn't like Michael's, not as rough, and his eyes were deep black, not Michael's blue, yet so familiar... He was calling me, but it wasn't my name he was saying. His voice was in pain, but so low...like a whisper, a low hissing gasp. I need to help him. It's drawing me from within, the urge to protect him, to fight if I have to...

August 9, 1980

Michael is getting more "concerned" and says he wants to take me on vacation. Somewhere I can relax. But I think he's just afraid. I've become more...feisty, less acquiescent than he's used to and I don't think he likes it. But I think I might. I am remembering my "episodes" bit my bit, and it seems like I'm finally taking charge... for his sake, at least, for the dark-eyed victim in my dreams...

September 3, 1980

I'm on vacation now. Except doors lock at 10 pm and an irritating woman comes in each morning to give me some "goodies," as they call it. Ha! I should have known Michael wouldn't let me live life the way I chose. He says I've done horrible things, that I should be ashamed. He says he doesn't know who I am anymore. I guess he never knew me. Otherwise he'd understand I did what I had to do. The truth is, Michael wasn't my first choice. There was someone else, someone who left me a long time ago, because I was too weak to fight for him. It's him in my dreams, in my memories. How could I forget those eyes? He's reaching out to me again and I refuse to be weak this time. I'm fighting for him now. I'm doing what I need to do, to save him. And I will see him again. Even if it's in another life...

ABOVE EXCERPTS FOUND IN THE ROOM OF
APRIL MANNING, MAIDEN NAME: APRIL SHUSTER
COMMITTED TO HILLSIDE PSYCHIATRIC FACILITIES, AUGUST 31, 1980
DIED: SEPTEMBER 27, 1980.
CAUSE OF DEATH: SUICIDE

From the desk of
Dr. Stanley Braskowitz

THESE NOTES WERE FOUND IN A FILE CONCERNING F. GALVERSON, A POSSIBLE MEMBER OF THE HARKER ORGANIZATION. THE FILES ARE QUITE DETAILED, INCLUDING BIRTH CERTIFICATES, COPIES OF HIS MORTGAGE, A COMPLETE PSYCHOLOGICAL WORKUP AND A DNA SAMPLE. THE FOLLOWING NOTES ARE FROM GALVERSON'S SESSIONS WITH A PSYCHIATRIST, DR. STANLEY BRASKOWITZ, WITH WHOM HE MET IN THE MONTHS LEADING UP TO HIS DEATH.

SESSION REPORT
PATIENT: F.G., DATE: February 12,

First meeting with patient F. G. today. He was referred to me by a colleague; apparently my specialization in dream phenomena makes me better suited for this gentleman's more unique problem. I am doubtful; over 99% of the cases of abnormal phenomena reported from dreams end up being either fabricated or symptoms of a deeper psychological disorder. I've garnered a certain skepticism when it comes to these referrals. F.G. is a successful investment banker, has a (rather beautiful) wife and two children. He lives in an upper-class suburban town and works Downtown. A self-described "regular guy," he enjoys spending time with his family, spicy food and football. Says about six months ago, he began having increasingly vivid nightmares about snakes. A common theme in dreams; in certain cultures, a bad omen, portending business or money troubles, or even death. Here, more likely, it seems like patient has seen too many Indiana Jones films. I've advised him to keep a dream journal, and prescribed a mild sedative.

SESSION REPORT
PATIENT: F.G., DATE: March 5,

Fourth meeting with patient F.G. Nightmares have not abated, will up the strength of his sedatives. Lack of sleep, content of nightmares starting to impair day-to-day life. Patient reports having fights with wife, children. Reports that he's become deathly afraid of snakes, and that thoughts of them now plague his waking hours. He finds it difficult to concentrate at work, and that he's receiving criticisms and ultimatums from his boss regarding productivity. Even more upsetting is hearing him read selections from his dream journal, I've reproduced one such section below:

"And then I'm in a long, dark tunnel. Walls made of stone. Dim torches line the walls. It's stiflingly hot and humid, breathing is difficult. I hear a bunch of men shouting at the end of the hall. As I make my way towards the noise, I see that the walls are not merely stone blocks, but they have intricate carvings on them, of people praying to giant statues of vipers, huge pythons engulfing cities, and long serpents eating their own tails.

"I emerge into the room, and find that I'm in some sort of treasure chamber.

(cont'd)

(cont'd 3/5)

Red firelight shows the faces of men mad with greed, but before I know it, I'm one of them, plunging my hand into chests filled with gold, grabbing rubies and diamonds and stuffing them in my pockets. And then, suddenly, one man screams, a horrible bloody scream: everyone looks over and sees that instead of holding jewel-encrusted necklaces, he's covered in snakes. Another man screams, he too is surrounded by the creatures. I look down into my own hands and find that a constrictor has coiled itself around my arm. I yell, and the next thing I know, I'm in my bed, awake, my wife's grip on my arm replacing the grip of the boa. I'm unable to sleep for the rest of the night."

The vividness of his account causes me to believe that, perhaps, there is more to this case than I am aware.

℞ PATIENT: F. Galverson
DATE: 3/5

Iusonbien
3 MILIIGRAMS DAILY

take before bed

30 doses

DR. STANLEY BRASKOWITZ, MD

SESSION REPORT
PATIENT: F.G., DATE: March 19,

Tenth meeting with patient F.G. I have increased the frequency of our sessions to three times a week. He has been given an indefinite leave of absence from his work, following an episode in the office involving his boss' secretary (according to a report sent to me by the HR officer at his company, he ripped her earrings off her ears... I was surprised to find out that they were replicas of a medallion originally found in an Indian temple to a Snake God). Patient is visibly more agitated. I fear that he is close to a nervous breakdown. Will have to watch him closely over the next few weeks.

SESSION REPORT
PATIENT: F.G., DATE: April 3,

Patient F.G., after missing his last three appointments, returned today to cancel his therapy. Apparently he has found new employment in Los Angeles. When I enquired as to whether his family would be moving with him, he answered with a quick "no", and resisted all further questions about his family—I worry that there was some falling out with his wife, but what is more alarming is his cool exterior and (assuming that he's not telling me the whole truth) his able fibbing. He left after only twenty minutes, paid me in cash for the session, and told me he wouldn't be coming back. I gave him a card of a colleague of mine in LA, and implored him to seek help if the nightmares returned.

SESSION REPORT
PATIENT: F.G., DATE:May 22,

A sad day; I received word regarding the murder of F.G. The circumstances are rather mysterious, and inquiries to the LAPD regarding the investigation have been rebuffed. Attempts to reach his wife or any other family have been unsuccessful, and I am beginning to believe that perhaps F.G. fell in with some sort of organized crime outfit (or, perhaps, espionage? No, that's foolish...). I'm unable to recount the horrific details of his death here, so I've attached the newspaper clipping. I close this file with the single observation that, having never been able to establish anything to the contrary, perhaps F.G. was part of that scarce 1% of dream phenomena cases that have some merit, though what it was, I will never know.

Police Deny "Snake Woman" Connection for Koreatown Evisceration

THE LOS ANGELES TIMES

LOS ANGELES, Yesterday A wealthy investment banker was found dead last night in Koreatown, in a similar manner to the reported "Snake Woman" killings, though police officers on the scene denied that this was the case.

Franklin Galverson, an investment banker for the prestigious Los Angeles firm Harker and Harker, was found around 3 a.m. in an alley off of North Hobart Street. According to a preliminary coroner's report, Galverson died of wounds sustained during some sort of animal attack, or possibly an attack by someone on a hallucinogenic drug. Medical Examiner Maria Reyes commented that "there's no way anyone could have done this, at least, no one with any humanity."

Mark Nguyen, a dishwasher at the Pho Boa Restaurant which backs onto the alley, found the body when he was taking out the trash. "I just opened the lid of the dumpster, and I saw this arm sticking out from under a trash bag," Nguyen said "At first I wasn't going to report it since there's a lot of mob activity in this neighborhood, but then, I thought I'd better do it anyway."

Suzuki Ichiro, reknowned art collector in Japan. He has amassed the most impressive collection of Indian art in the world, with a particular interest paid to pieces originating from the Kabini region of the sub-continent. If he's a member of the 68, he's possibly the reincarnation of Henry Rector, one of the infantrymen, who had aspired to be a painter.

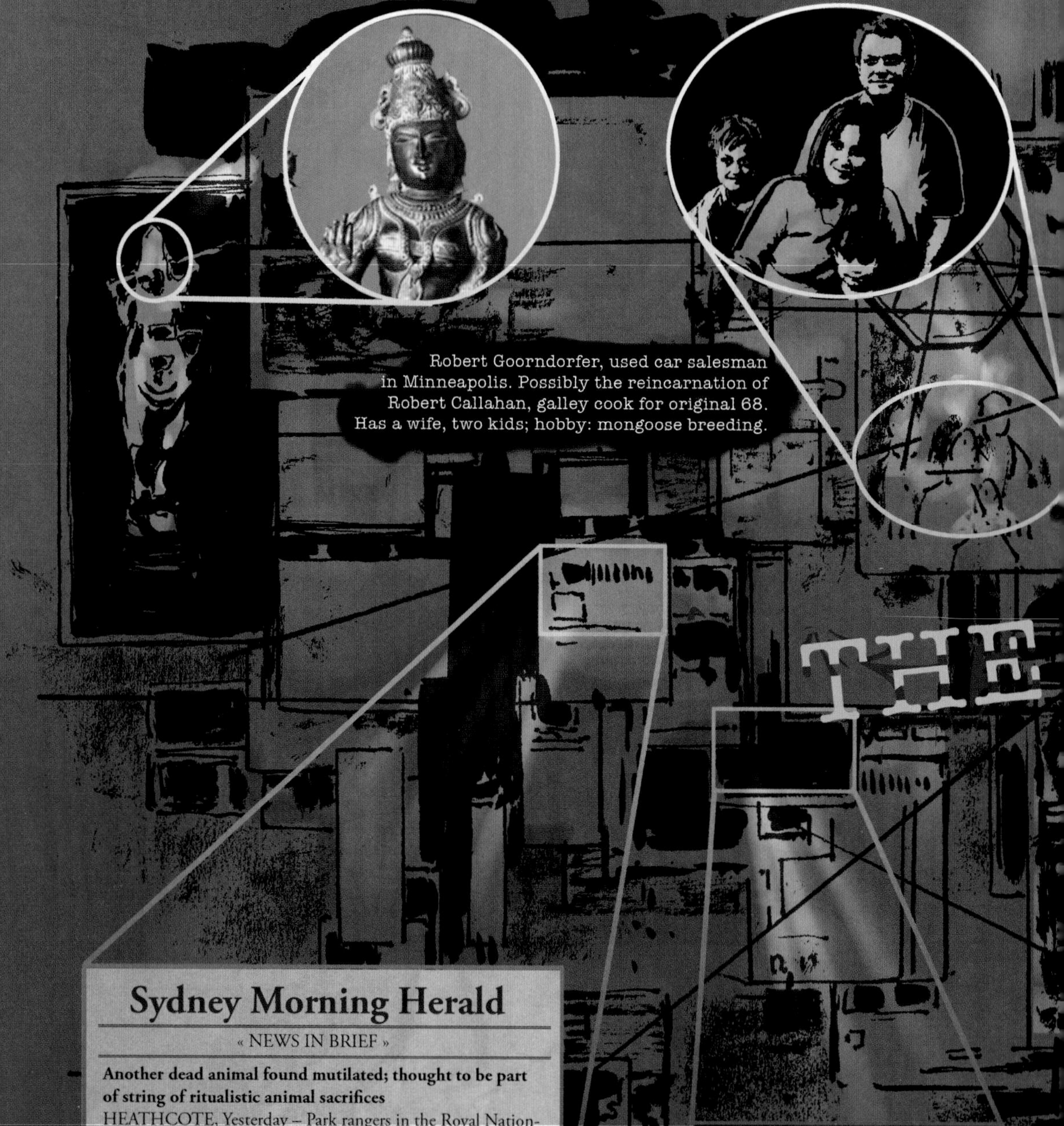
THE

Robert Goorndorfer, used car salesman in Minneapolis. Possibly the reincarnation of Robert Callahan, galley cook for original 68. Has a wife, two kids; hobby: mongoose breeding.

Sydney Morning Herald

« NEWS IN BRIEF »

Another dead animal found mutilated; thought to be part of string of ritualistic animal sacrifices

HEATHCOTE, Yesterday – Park rangers in the Royal National Park reported finding what is being described as the latest in a series of ceremonial animal sacrifices being performed in various parks around Sydney. Involving mainly snakes, this is the fourth such "sacrifice" that park rangers have found in as many months.

Article from the Sydney Morning Herald about a series of ritualistic animal killings, specifically, of snakes. Suggests reincarnation of Joseph Williams, chaplain traveling with the 68. A team has been sent to investigate.

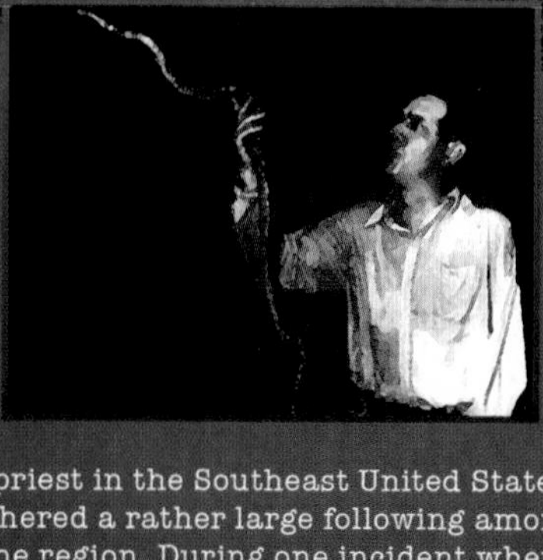

Bill Grubb, evangelical priest in the Southeast United States. Specializes in snake handling, has gathered a rather large following among poorer, rural communities in the region. During one incident where he was arrested on a DUI, his followers stormed the local police station to set him free; it has been proposed that his disciples would make an effective impromptu militia.

Laurence Deerfield created an internet start-up company when he was 19, which he sold for $1.2 billion on his 23rd birthday. Once he was reacquainted with his past life as Zachariah Bloom, engineer-turned-68 treasure-seeker, he felt it necessary to make a generous donation to our cause.

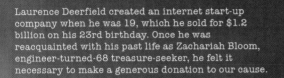

Josef Giordenko, Russian business giant, owns a third of the country through his Mongoose Corp. His predilection for young prep-school boys has not waned in the cycle of reincarnation; fortunately, contacts in London through the Faithful have been able to accommodate him.

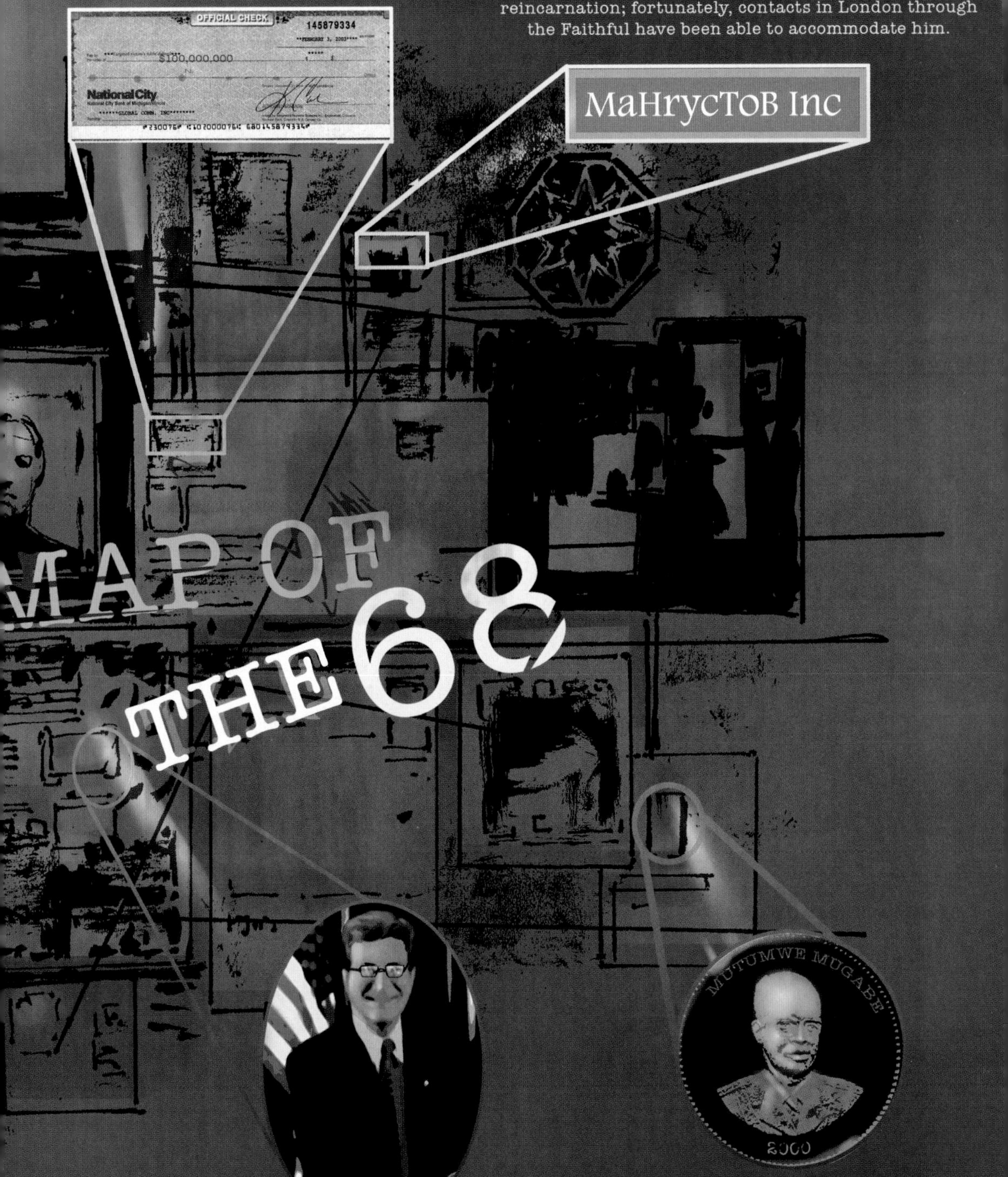
OFFICIAL CHECK
145879334
$100,000,000
National City
MaHrycToB Inc
MAP OF THE 68
MUTUMWE MUGABE
2000

Roy Clemens, two-term senator, eight-term congressman, loyal member of the 68. The reincarnation of Jack Sprawl, a lowly bastard born of an English lord and his Indian scullery maid. Currently, Senator Clemens pushes the most conservative, traditionalist agenda on Capitol Hill.

Mutumwe Mugabe, Supreme General of the Republic of Equatorial Kundu in Central Africa. Most likely the reincarnation of Lord Falcrain, an emissary from Parliament who accompanied the 68 through India. His hunger for power is still intact, matched only by his thirst for blood—as Mugabe, he slaughtered 7,000 of his own citizens, extinguishing entirely a tribe who prayed to an Igbo snake god.

SNAKE WOMAN PROFILES:
CANDIDATE 37, JESSICA PETERSON

Jessica Peterson, pictured here,
age 4. Seems to have an odd
inclination for swallowing things
whole. Pictured here after she
ingested 4 poached eggs in one
go. Parents believe she's very
"advanced" for her age. Clearly
her parents are not.

*Note: Food was swallowed rather
than chewed. She apparently
prefers it that way.

Jessica, age 10, at the
Los Angeles Zoo. She stayed in
the reptile section the longest,
particularly at this tank. She
seems to be developing an unusual
fascination with them.

Jessica volunteers after the
Entertainer dares the crowd to
attempt to lure the snake from
his slumber. Jessica was the only
one who could.

*Note: The flute did not work
for her. The snake responded to
her voice.

Jessica, age 17 pictured here with best (and only) friend, Jin. Jessica is a loner, prefers sitting with her sketchbook to "hanging out." She does not display the same frivolity as her friend Jin. She has no boyfriend. Nor has she ever had one.

SKETCHES FOUND IN JESS'S SKETCH PAD, EXTREMELY SIMILAR TO EAST INDIA COMPANY TATTOO.

Jessica and Jin move to Los Angeles

Concluding thoughts: All research points to Jessica Peterson as the Snake Woman, though she has not come to realize it yet. Must deploy "Cobra" ASAP.

SHEKHAR KAPUR'S
SNAKE WOMAN™

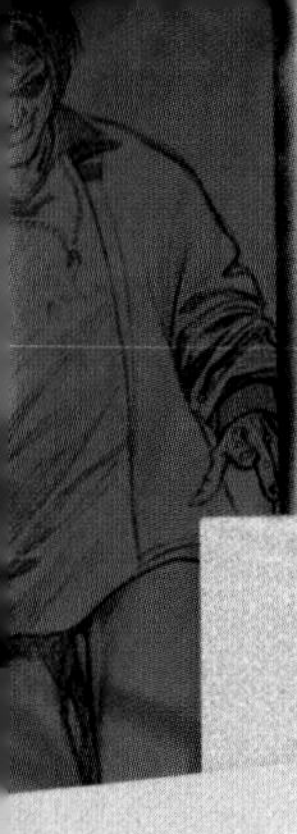

JESSICA (THE SNAKE WOMAN

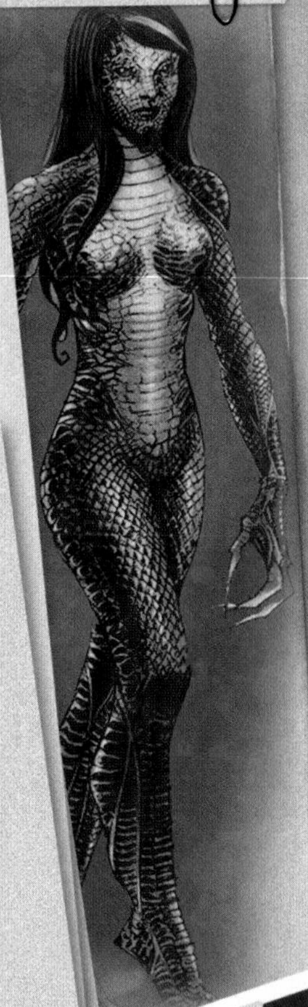

Though we can thank Zeb Wells for writing the series and Michael Gaydos for bringing it to life on the page, the earliest incarnation of Snake Woman came from the mind of Academy Award™ nominated director Shekhar Kapur (Elizabeth, The Bandit Queen). While going through our Snake Woman files to prepare this collection, we came across the very first outline of the Snake Woman series. In keeping with our goal to explore the creation of Snake Woman, we wanted to show where it all began. In addition, we've thrown in some early artwork explorations from our very own Mukesh Singh (Devi, Gamekeeper). After that, all there is to say is: "you've come a long way, baby...."

Snake Woman: THE FIRST INCARNATION

SETTING: Alphabet City, New York City

THE TEASER:

Fueled on by the infidelities of her boyfriend, an inebriated NYC art student named Jessica finds herself in an uncharacteristically casual sexual encounter with a menacing stranger named Vincent. In the middle of the encounter, her new lover reveals a giant snake tattoo across his chest that sends Jessica spinning into a state of delirium and falling out of the bed. Enraged, Vincent grabs the back of Jessica's head, telling her she better finish what she started. Jessica turns around to reveal the shocking visage of the female **"Snake Woman,"** with her fangs lunging and ripping through Vincent's soon lifeless corpse. Awakening hours later, Jessica finds herself covered in a pool of blood. Running to the bathroom she sees her face covered in scales with glowing reptilian black eyes. Terrified, Jessica runs out into the streets where she passes out behind a dumpster. Slowly the secrets of the evening unfold and Jessica discovers she is the victim of reincarnation and destiny with a bloody mission that shatters the foundation of her young life.

THE CHARACTERS:

Jessica (Jess): A 19-year-old painting student living in downtown NYC. An urban city kid, Jess is pale with striking green eyes that contrast against her raven black hair (which has a dark green dye streak on the side). She has an athletic build (not overly voluptuous), with a "cute" and innocent face adorned with a small studded nose ring. Though experimental and "artsy," Jessica is a definite loner, uncomfortable when dragged to the latest rave or club. To earn tuition she bartends at a local hotspot bar called the "Underground."

JIN

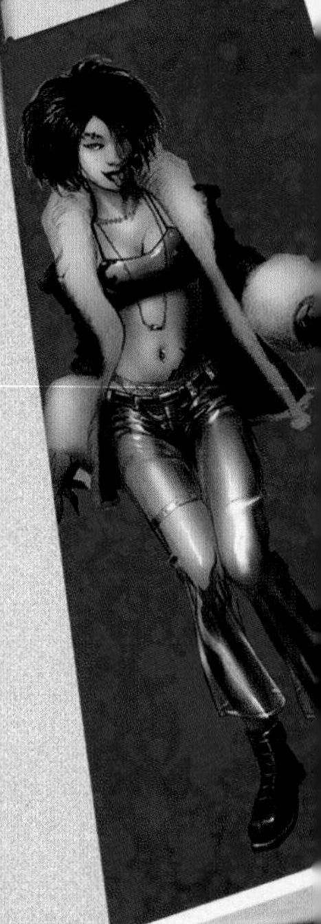

Jin: Jess' roommate and best friend, Jin has also grown up in the city and known Jess all her life. Jin is of Korean background and exudes sexuality, wearing revealing and trendy clothes that accentuate her small, tight frame. The ultimate party & city girl, Jin contrasts Jess' inward nature, spending lavishly on drinks and whatever else promises a good time. Her wild and flirtatious exterior is matched by a biting sharp wit that attacks anyone who rubs her and her friends the wrong way. Sexy, fun, intimidating but loyal at the same time, her one Achilles heel is her secret attraction to the bouncer at the Underground, who unfortunately thinks Jin is an annoying, spoiled NYC rich kid.

Vikram (Vic): Jessica's "on again / off again" Indian boyfriend, Vic is a NYC born "playa," who studies photography at the same college. An aspiring fashion photographer, Vic is trendy, hip and loves to surround himself by the beautiful models of the fashion world. Though he is completely faithless when it comes to Jess, (he insists they have no "formal" commitment) he is incredibly charming and charismatic. Despite his lack of fidelity, Jess always takes him back (much to the anger of Jin). Beneath his playboy exterior, Vic has a great affection for Jess, since she is the only girl who really believes in him. A complicated and confusing personality—if only Vic could get past his constant craving for new women, he would be perfect for Jess.

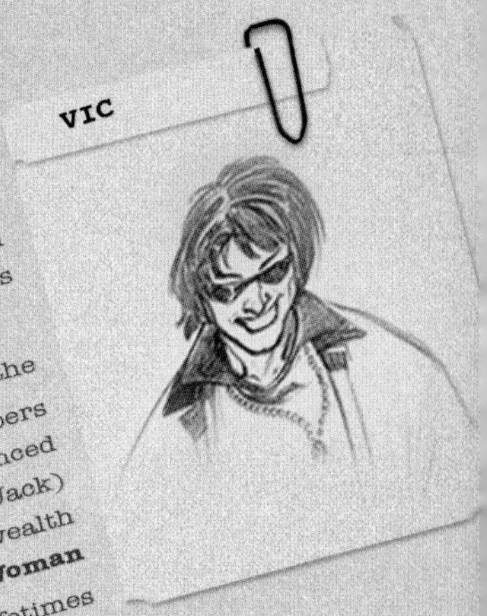
VIC

The 68: After lifetimes of being hunted by the **Snake Woman**, the reincarnated soul of Captain Jonathan Harker remembers. He remembers the dark past of his previous lives and the many murders he has experienced at the hands of the **Snake Woman**. Now, reincarnated as Jonathan (Jack) Rubold, a wealthy aristocrat in NYC, he is determined to use his vast wealth and resources to find this new reincarnation of the **Snake Woman** first—ensuring he can enact his own vengeance for the many past lifetimes she has destroyed and seek a way to end the curse by destroying her soul permanently. Funneling his monies to master dark occultist secrets, he has also been able to find and employ many of the other 68 souls hunted by the **Snake Women**—reawakening the memories of their past lives, each member brandishes a tattoo of snakes in a circular "68" symbol on their arm. Together, Rubold and his men are determined to find and destroy the **Snake Woman** before she inevitably finds them.

The Snake Woman: Fueled by vengeance, powered by rage—cursed with an endless cycle of death and rebirth. The **Snake Woman** has existed for generations, in different countries, wearing different faces and assuming different lives. The reincarnation of an ancient temple guardian snake, she exists to hunt the souls of the men who murdered her family and desecrated her master's temple. In every reincarnation, a moment comes when the **Snake Woman** slowly remembers her origins and past lives. This is usually triggered by a traumatic encounter with one of the reincarnated souls of the 68. Each reincarnation of the **Snake Woman** is unconsciously drawn to these souls like a moth to a flame, guided by the unseen hand of Nagraj to fulfill her destiny and reclaim what was taken. As her memories return, so does control of her abilities and a growing knowledge of what must be done to finally know peace. Some of her reincarnated lives embrace this path, while others, desperate to live a normal life, try and fight their destiny. In the end, all undergo the deadly transformation into a living embodiment of Nagraj's vengeance and struggle to integrate this dark destiny into the current life they desperately struggle to maintain.

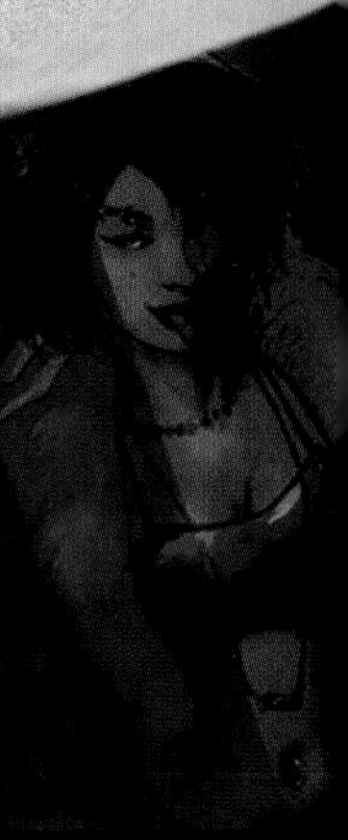

The Myth of the Naga

Snake Woman is a story about many things: revenge, secrecy, the past, reincarnation, and self-discovery, just to name a few. But one thing that **Snake Woman** most definitely is not is a battle between unadulterated good and evil, because none of the characters are one hundred percent good... and, in a way, none of them are a hundred per cent evil, either. Sure, Jessica is clearly the protagonist, and Harker is arguably the main antagonist, but both of them come with a complex set of motives and emotions, and defy such simplistic classification.

Which makes sense, as the inspiration for the **Snake Woman** series also defies simple categories. Sharply contrasting with their Judeo-Christian counterparts (the snakes and serpents from the Bible which represent pure evil), the Naga snake-gods of Hinduism and Buddhism—which provide the background for the struggle in **Snake Woman**—are mysterious and complex, and, like Jessica, often contradictory.

The Nagas of Hinduism continue to be a part of culture and traditions in modern India through to the present. The half-snake, half-men entities are considered nature spirits and are chiefly identified with water.

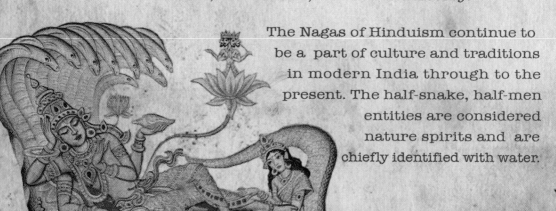

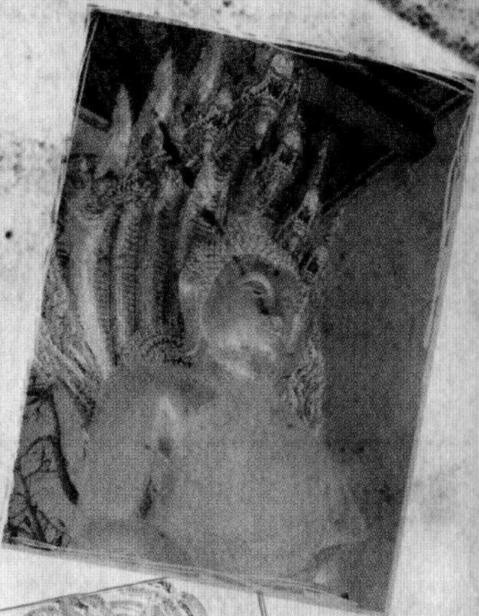

Protecting springs and rivers, the Naga are paradoxically known to bring rain (and are therefore associated with fertility and creation) as well as floods and drought (signifying disaster and destruction). Thought to occupy underground palaces, they're also thought to be the guardians of Mount Sumeru, the sacred mountain considered to be the center of the Universe.

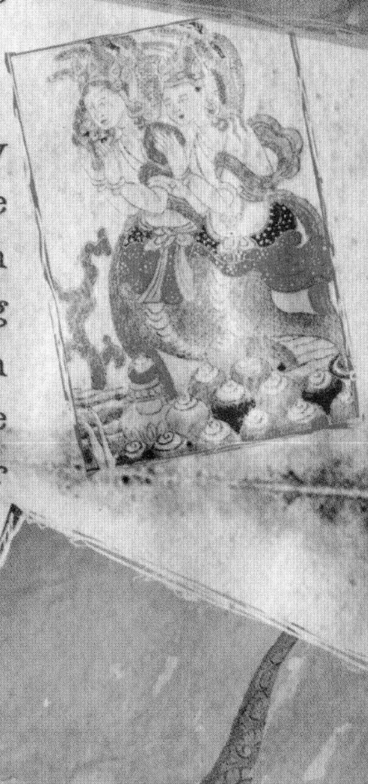

In Buddhism, the Naga occupy a similarly controversial role. While in Tibet the Naga are similar to their Hindu counterparts, living in underground streams and lakes, guarding treasure, the Chinese Naga are equated with the long, snake-like dragons central to Chinese mythology, representing both auspicious power as well as terrible destructive forces, such as floods and tidal waves.

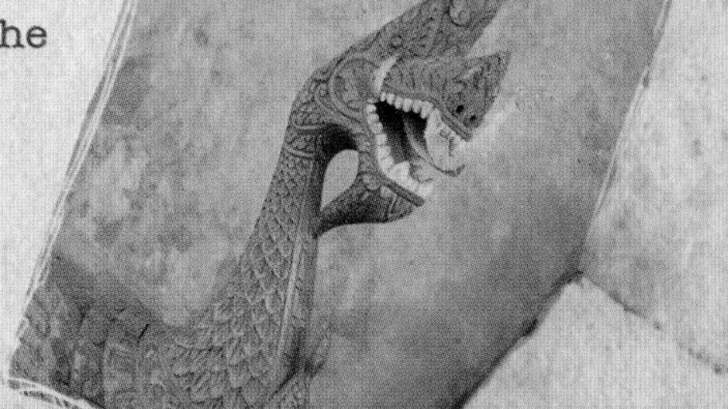

When all is said and done, battles between pure virtue and pure evil are less challenging than a complex set of internal conflicts that our heroine must reconcile. Like the ancient Naga, Jessica is made up of two distinct forces: the shy, quiet girl who she was and the bloodthirsty, revenge-starved goddess that now inhabits her. She is a protector and a destroyer, prey and predator, and as conflicts swirl all around her, the conflict within her also rages on. Who will win? We won't say, but be assured that the battle will be worth watching.

SHEKHAR KAPUR'S SNAKE WOM

Snake Woman Explorations
by Michael Gaydos

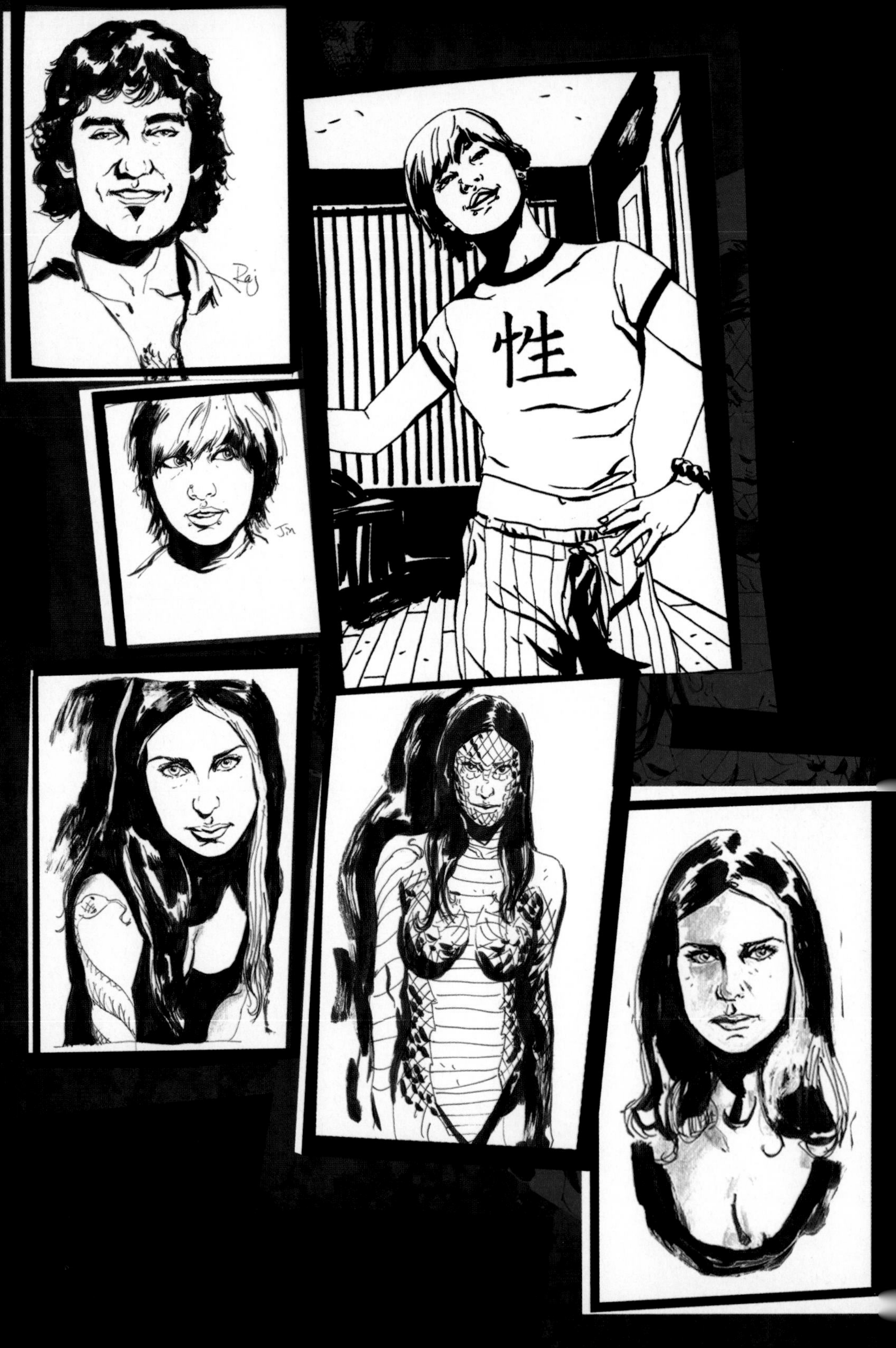
Raj
性

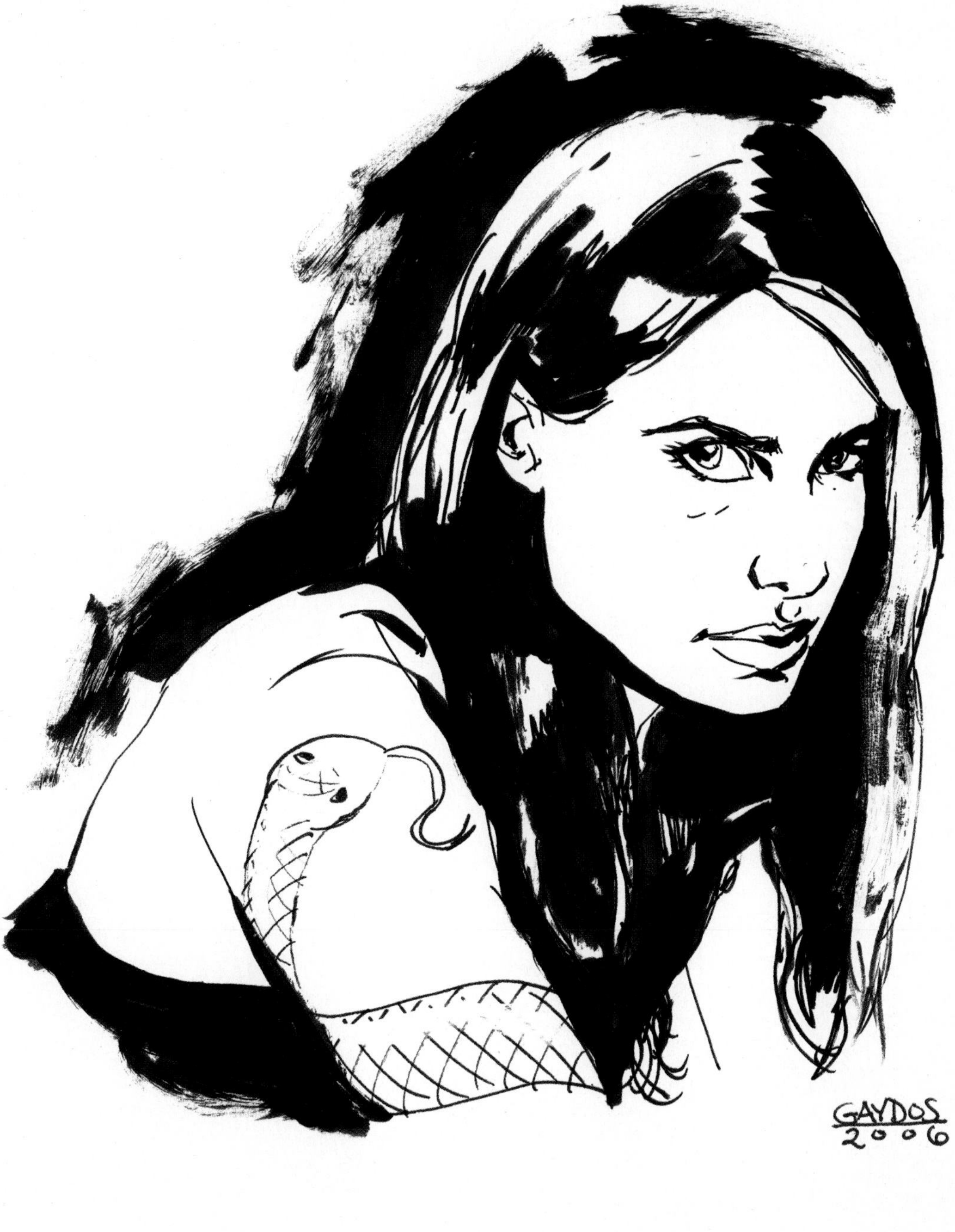
GAYDOS
2006

VIRGIN COMICS
COLLECTED EDITIONS

ON SALE JUNE 2007

ALSO AVAILABLE IN LIMITED EDITION HARDCOVER

DEVI VOL.1

SEVEN BROTHERS VOL.1

SNAKE WOMAN VOL.1

ON SALE JULY 2007

WALK IN

RAMAYAN 3392 A.D. VOL.1

THE SADHU VOL.1